THE BLOSSOM AND THE FRUIT.

PREFACE.

THE great contending forces of good and evil we see battling in the world on every plane. This book is called the story of a black magician, because it shows the struggles and mistakes of one who has been an adept in black magic, and who is endeavoring with great force, but very blindly, to reach toward the White Brotherhood and learn good instead of evil. Fleta, who in her earlier incarnation, took power selfishly into her own hands, became by virtue of that power a black magician: one who has knowledge and uses it for selfish ends. We see her at the masked ball, in the first chapter, endeavoring by her arts to attract the companion of many of her past lives; but her object in doing this is to bring him directly under the influence of Ivan, that one of the White Brotherhood who, in his divine pity, has stretched his hand out toward her. Her aim is to begin the occultist's great work of saving others, especially those whom she has formerly injured. But through what terrible experiences she passes, and those about her, in this endeavor! We see her falling back instinctively on her old rites and using her old powers; we see Hilary deceived by his senses and passions. Fleta forgets that the Lotus flower can only bloom within one's own soul; but oh! reader, do not judge of Fleta, nor of her relation to the White Brotherhood till you have seen her fierce career to its end and read the words in which, at last, Ivan says "Enter."

M. C.

THE BLOSSOM AND THE FRUIT.

INTRODUCTION.

Containing two sad lives on earth,
And two sweet times of sleep in Heaven.

A LIFETIME.

OVERHEAD the boughs of the trees intermingle, hiding the deep blue sky and mellowing the fierce heat of the sun. The boughs are so covered with white blossoms that it is like a canopy of clustered snow-flakes, tinged here and there with a soft pink. It is a natural orchard, a spot favored by the wild apricot. And among the trees, wandering from shine to shade, flitting to and fro, is a solitary figure. It is that of a young woman, a savage, one of a wild and fierce tribe dwelling in the fastnesses of an inaccessible virgin forest. She is dark, but beautiful. Her blue-black hair hangs far down over her naked body; its masses shield the warm, quivering, nervous brown skin from the direct rays of the sun. She wears neither clothing nor any ornament. Her eyes are dark, fierce and tender; her mouth soft and natural as the lips of an opening flower. She is absolutely perfect in her simple savage beauty and in the natural majesty of her womanhood, virgin in herself and virgin in the quality of her race, which is untaught, undegraded. But in her sublimely natural face is the dawn of a great tragedy. Her soul, her *thought, is struggling* to awake. She has done a deed that seemed to her quite simple, quite natural; yet now it is done a dim perplexity is rising within her obscure mind. Wandering to and fro beneath the rich masses of blossom-laden boughs, she for the first time endeavors to question herself. Finding no answer within she goes again to look on that which she has done.

A form lies motionless upon the ground within the thickest shade of the rich fruit trees. A young man, one of her own tribe, beautiful like herself, and with strength and vigor written in every line of his form. But he is dead. He was her lover, and she found his love sweet, yet with one wild treacherous movement of her strong supple arm she had killed him. The blood flowed from his forehead where the sharp stone had made the death wound. The life blood ebbed away from his strong young form; a moment since his lips still trembled, now they were still. Why had she in this moment of fierce passion taken that beautiful life? She loved him as well as her untaught heart knew how to love; but he, exulting in his greater strength, tried to snatch her love before it was ripe. It was but a blossom, like the white flowers overhead: he would have taken it with strong hands as though it were a fruit ripe and ready. And then in a sudden flame of wondrous new emotion the woman became aware that the man was her enemy, that he desired to be her tyrant. Until now she had thought him as herself, a thing to love as she loved herself, with a blind unthinking trust. And she acted passionately upon the guidance of this thing—feeling—which until now she had never known. He, unaccustomed to any treachery or anger, suspected no strange act from her, and thus, unsuspicious, unwarned, he was at her mercy. And now he lay dead at her feet. And still the fierce sun shone through the green leaves and silvern blossoms and gleamed upon her black hair and tender *brown skin*. She was beautiful as the morning when it rose over the tree tops of that world-old forest. But there is a new wonder in her dark eyes; a question that was not there until this strange and potent hour came to her. What ages must pass over her dull spirit ere it can utter the question; ere it can listen and hear the answer?

The savage woman, nameless, unknown save of her tribe, who regard her as indifferently as any creature of the woods, has none to help her or stay in its commencement the great roll of the wave of energy she has started. Blindly she lives out her own emotions. She is dissatisfied, uneasy, conscious of some error. When she leaves the orchard of wild fruit trees and wanders back to the clearer part of the forest beneath the great trees, where her tribe dwells, when she returns among them her lips are dumb, her voice is silent. None ever heard that he, the one she loved, had died by her hand, for she knew not how to frame or tell this story. It was a mystery to her, this thing which had happened. Yet it made her sad, and her great eyes wore a dumb look of longing. But she was very beautiful, and soon another young and sturdy lover was always at her side. He did not please her; there was not the glow in her eyes that had gladdened her in those of the dead one whom she had loved. And yet she shrank not from him, nor did she raise her arm in anger, but held it fast at her side lest her passion should break loose unawares. For she felt that she had brought a want, a despair upon herself by her former deed; and now she determined that she would act differently. Blindly she tried to learn the lesson that had come upon her. Blindly she let herself be the agent of her own will. For now she became the willing slave and serf of one she did not love, and whose passion for her was full of tyranny. Yet she did not, she dared not, resist this tyranny; not because she feared him, but because she feared herself. She had the *feeling that one might have who had come in contact* with a new and hitherto unknown natural force. She feared lest resistance or independence should bring upon her a greater wonder, a greater sadness and loss than that which she had already brought upon herself.

And so she submitted to that which in her first youth would no more have been endured by her than the bit by the wild horse.

The apricot blossom has fallen and fruit has followed it; the leaves have fallen and the trees are bare. The sky is gray and wild above, the ground dank and soft with fallen leaves below. The aspect of the place has changed, but it is the same; the face and form of the woman have changed, but she is the same. She is alone again in the wild orchard, finding her way by instinct to the spot where her first lover died. She has found it. What is there? Some white bones that lie together; a skeleton. The woman's eyes fasten and feed on the sight and grow large and terrible. Horror at last is struck into her soul. This is all that is left of her young love, who died by her hand—white bones that lie in ghastly order! And the long hot days and sultry nights of her life have been given to a tyrant who has reaped no gladness and no satisfaction from her submission; for he has not learned yet even the difference between woman and woman. All alike are mere creatures like the wild things; creatures to hunt and to conquer. Dumbly in her dark heart strange questionings arise. She turns from this graveyard of her unquestioning time and goes back to her slavery. Through the years of her life she waits and wonders, looking blankly at the life around her. Will no answer come to her soul?

AFTER SLEEP, AWAKENING.

SPLENDID was the veil that shielded her from that other *soul, the soul she knew* and of which she showed her recognition by swift and sudden love. But the veil separated them; a veil heavy with gold and shining with stars of silver. And as she gazed upon these stars, with delighted admiration of their brilliance, they grew larger and larger, till at length they blended together, and the veil became one shining sheen gorgeous with golden broideries. Then it became easier to see through the veil, or rather it seemed easier to these lovers. For before the veil had made the shape appear dim; now it appeared glorious and ideally beautiful and strong. Then the woman put out her hand, hoping to obtain the pressure of another hand through the shining gossamer. And at the same instant he too put out his hand, for in this moment their souls communicated, and they understood each other. Their hands touched; the veil was broken; the moment of joy was ended and again the struggle began.

A LIFETIME.

SITTING, singing, on the steps of an old palace, her feet paddling in the water of a broad canal, was a child who was becoming more than a child; a creature on the threshold of life, of awakening sensation. A girl, with ruddy gold hair, and innocent blue eyes, that had in their vivid depths the strange startled look of a wild creature. She was as simple and isolated in her happiness as any animal of the woods or hills—the sunshine, the sweet air with the faint savor of salt in it, her own pure clear girlish voice, and the gay songs of the people that she sang—these were pleasure enough and to spare for her.

But the space of unconscious happiness or unhappiness which heralds the real events of a life was already at an end. The great wave which she had set in motion was *increasing in volume* ceaselessly; how long before it shall reach the shore and break upon that far-off coast? None can know, save those whose eyesight is more than man's. None can tell; and she is ignorant, unknowing. But though she knows nothing of it, she is within the sweep of the wave, and is powerless to arrest it until her soul shall awake.

"My blossom, my beautiful wild flower," said a voice close beside her. A young boatman had brought his small vessel so gently to the steps she had not noticed his approach. He leaned over his boat toward her, and touched her bare white feet with his hand.

"Come away with me, Wild Blossom," he said. "Leave that wretched home you cling to. What is there to keep you there now your mother is dead? Your father is like a savage and makes you live like a savage too. Come away with me, and we will live among people who will love you and find you beautiful as I do. Will you come? How often have I asked you, Wild Blossom, and you have never answered. Will you answer now?"

"Yes," said the girl, looking up with grave, serious eyes, that had beneath their beauty a melancholy meaning, a sad question.

The man saw this strange look and interpreted it as clearly as he could.

"Trust me," he said, "I am not a savage like your father. When you are my little wife I will care for you far more dearly than myself. You will be my soul, my guide, my star. And I will shield you as my soul is shielded within my body, follow you as my guide, look up to you as to a star in the blue heavens. Surely you can trust my love, Wild Blossom?"

He had not answered the doubt in her heart, for he had not guessed what it was, nor could she have told him. For she had not yet learned to know what it was, nor to know *of it more than that it* troubled her. But she put it aside

and silenced it now, for the moment had come to do so.
Not till she had learned her lesson much more fully could
the question ever be expressed even to her own soul, and
before this could be, the question must be silenced many
times.

"Yes," she said, "I will come."

She held out her hand to him as if to seal the compact.
He interpreted the gesture by his own desire, and taking
her hand in his drew her toward him. She yielded and
stepped into the boat. And then he quickly pushed away
from the steps, and, dipping his oars in the water, soon
had gone far away down the canal. Blossom, looking
earnestly back, watched the old palace disappear. In some
of its old rooms and on its sunny steps her child-life had
been spent. Now she knew that was at an end. She understood that all was changed henceforth, though she could
not guess into what she was going, and she waited for her
future with a strange confidence in the companion she had
accepted. This puzzled her dimly. Yet how should she
lack confidence having known him long ago and thrown
away his love and his life beneath the wild apricot trees,
having seen afterward the steadfastness of his love when
her soul stood beside his in soul life?

A long way they went in the little boat. They left the
canals and went out upon the open sea, and still the boatman rowed unwearingly, his eyes all the while upon the
beautiful wild blossom he had plucked and carried away
with him to be his own, his dear and adored possession.
Far away along the coast lay a small village of fishermen's
cots. It was to this that the young man guided his boat,
for it was here he dwelled.

At the door of his cot stood his old mother, a quaint old
woman with wrinkled, rosy face, wearing a rough fishwife's
dress and coarse shawl; her brown hand shaded her eyes
as she watched her son's boat approaching. Presently a

smile came on her mouth. "He's gotten the blossom he's talked of so often in his sleep. Will he be happy now, the good lad?"

He was truly a good lad; for his mother knew him well, and the more she knew him the deeper grew her love. She would do anything for his happiness. And now she took to her arms the child, the Blossom, and cherished her for his sake. Before many days had passed, the fishing village made a *fête* day for the wedding of its strongest boatman. And the women's eyes filled with tears when they looked at the sad, tender, questioning face of the beautiful Wild Blossom.

She had given her love without hesitation, in complete confidence. She had given more; herself, her life, her very soul. The surrender was now complete.

And now, when all seemed done and all accomplished, her question began to be answered. Dimly she knew that, spite of the husband at whose feet she bowed, spite of the babes she carried in her arms, till their tiny feet were strong enough to carry them down over the shore to the marge of the blue waters, spite of the cottage home she garnished and cleansed and loved so dearly, spite of all, her heart was hungry and empty. What could it mean, that though she had all, she had none? Blossom was grown a woman now, and there were some lines of care and of pain on her forehead. Yet still she was beautiful, and still she bore her child-name of Blossom; but the beauty of her face grew sadder and more strange as the years went by, the years that bring ease and satisfaction to the stagnant soul. Wild Blossom's soul was eager and anxious; she could not still the mysterious voices of her heart, and these told her (though perhaps she did not always understand their speech) that her husband was not in reality her king; that he heard no sound from that *inner region in which* she chiefly existed. For him there was contentment in the outward life that he lived, in sheer physical pleasure, in the excitement of hard work, and the dangers of the sea, in the beauty of his wife, the mirth of his happy children. He asked no more. But Wild Blossom's eyes had the prophetic light in them. She saw that all this peace must pass, this pleasure end; she recognized that these things did not, could not, absolutely satisfy the spirit; her soul seemed to tremble within her as she began to feel the first dawn of the terrible answer to her sad questioning.

A deeper dream of rest,
A stronger waking.

MANY a long year later, a solitary woman dwelled in that fisherman's cottage on the shore of the blue sea. She was old and bowed with age and trouble. But still her eyes were brighter than any girl's in the village, and held in them the mysterious beauty of the soul; still her hair, once golden, now gray, waved about her forehead. The people loved her and were kind to her, for she was always gentle and full of generous thought. But they never understood her, for they were long ages behind her in her growth. She was ready now for the great central test of personal existence; the experience of life in civilization. When the old fishwife lay dead within her cottage, and the people came to grieve beside her body, they little guessed that she was going on to a great and glorious future; a future full of daring and of danger. When her eyes closed in death, her inner eyes opened on a sight that filled her with absolute joy. She was in a garden of fruit trees, and the blossom of the trees was at its full. When her eyes fell on this white maze of flowers and drank in its beauty, she *remembered the* name she had borne on earth and dimly understood its meaning. The blossoms hid from her the sky and all else until a soft pressure on her hand drew her eyes downward; and then she saw beside her that one whom she had loved through the ages, and who, side by side with her, was experiencing the profound mystery, and learning the strange lesson of incarnation in the world where sex is the first great teacher. And with each phase of existence that they passed through, these two forged stronger and stronger links that held them together and compelled them again and again to meet, so that together they were destined to pass through the vital hour; the hour when the life is shaped for great ends or for vain deeds.

Here within this sheltered place, where blossoms filled the air with sweetness and beauty, it seemed to them that they had attained to the full of pleasure. They rested in perfect satisfaction, drinking deep draughts of the joy of living. To them existence was a final and splendid fact in itself; existence as they then had it. The moment in which they lived was sufficient, they desired none other, nor any other place, nor any other beauty, than those they had. None knows, and none can tell what time or age was passed in this deep contentment and fulfilment of pleasure. At last Wild Blossom's soul woke from its sleep, satiated; the hunger returned to gnaw at her heart; the longing to know reasserted itself. Holding tight the hand she held in hers, she sprang from the soft couch on which she lay. Then, for the first time, she noticed that the ground was so soft and pleasant, because there, where she had lain, had drifted great heaps of the fallen fruit blossoms. The ground was all white with them, though some had begun to lose their delicate beauty, to curl and wrinkle and turn dark. Then she looked overhead and saw that the trees had, with the loss of the delicate petals, lost their first fairness, the splendor of the spring. Now they were *covered with small*, hard, green fruit, scarce formed, un-

beautiful to the eye, hard to the touch, acid to the taste.
With a shudder of regret for the sweet spring-time that
was gone, Wild Blossom hurried away from the trees, still
holding fast that other hand in hers. She was going to
face new, strange experiences, perhaps terrible dangers:
her task seemed the easier for that tried companionship,
for the nearness of that other who was climbing the same
steep ladder of life.

CHAPTER I.

IN a masked ball there is an element of adventure that appeals to the daring of both sexes, to the bright and witty spirits. Hilary Estanol was just such an one as the hero of a bright revel should be. A beautiful boy, with a lovely face, and eyes that had in them a deep sadness. In repose his face was almost womanish in its softness; but a chill brilliance was in his smile, a certain slight cynicism colored all his speech. Yet Hilary had no reason to be a cynic, and he was not one who adopted anything from fashion or affectation. The spring of this uncalled-for coldness and indifference lay in himself.

To-night he was the centre of attraction in Madame Estanol's drawing-rooms. This *bal masqué* was to celebrate his coming of age and Hilary had never looked so womanish as when he stood among his friends, receiving their congratulations and admiring their gifts. He wore the dress of a troubadour, and it was one which became him well, not only in its picturesqueness as a costume, but in the requirements of the character. He had the faculty of the improvisatóre, his voice was rich and soft, his musical and poetic gifts swift and versatile. Hilary was adored by his friends, but disliked, indeed almost hated, by his one near relation, his mother. She was standing near him now, talking to a group who had gathered round her. She was one of the cleverest women of the day, and, still beautiful and full of a charming pride, held a court of her own. Her dislike for Hilary was founded on her estimate of his character. To one of her intimate friends she had said, not long before this night, "Hilary will disgrace his name and family before there is one gray thread in his dark hair. He has the qualities that bring despair and insure remorse. God will surely forgive me that I say this of my son; but I see it before me, an abyss into which he will drag me with him; and I wait for it every day."

A guest, just arrived, approached Madame Estanol with a smile, and after greeting her affectionately, said, in a whisper, "I have brought a friend with me. Welcome her in her character as a fortune-teller. She is very witty, and will amuse us presently, if you like."

She moved aside a little, and Madame Estanol saw standing behind her a stooping figure, an old haggard crone, with palsied head, and hand that trembled as it grasped her stick.

"Ah, Countess! it is not possible to recognize your friend under this disguise," said Madame Estanol. "Will you not tell me who she is?"

"I am pledged to say nothing but that she is a fortune-teller," said the Countess Bairoun. "Her name she herself will reveal only to one person; and that person must be born under the star that favored her own birth."

The fortune-teller turned her bent head toward Madame Estanol, and fixed a pair of brilliant and fascinating eyes on hers. Immediately Madame Estanol became aware of a strong charm that drew her toward this mysterious person. She advanced and held out her hand to assist the old woman in moving across the room.

"Come with me," she said, "I should like to introduce you to my son. He is the hero of this scene to-night, for the ball is held in honor of his coming of age."

They went through the maskers that were now beginning to throng the large drawing-rooms, and every one turned to look at the strange figure of the tottering old crone. *Hilary Estanol* was leaning against the high carved oak mantel frame of the inner drawing-room, surrounded by a laughing group of his intimate friends. He held his mask in his hand, and as he stood there smiling, his dark curls falling on his forehead, his mother thought, as she approached him, "My boy grows handsomer every hour of his gay young life." When Hilary saw his mother's strange companion he advanced a step, as if to welcome her. But Madame Estanol checked him with a smile. "I cannot introduce our visitor to you," she said, "for I do not know her name. She will tell it to but one person, who must have been born under the same star as herself. Meantime, we are to greet her in her character as the fortune-teller."

This announcement was welcomed by a murmur of amusement and interest.

"Then will our kind visitor perhaps exercise her craft for us?" asked Hilary, gazing with curiosity at the trembling head and gray locks before him. The old woman turned her head sideways, and gave him a look from those strange brilliant eyes. He, too, like his mother, felt the charm from them. But he felt more. Something suddenly wakened within him; a rush of inexplicable emotion roused him into amazement; he put his hand to his forehead: he was bewildered, almost faint.

There was a small drawing-room which opened out of the room they were in. It was so tiny that it held but a table covered with flowers, a low couch and an easy-chair. The laughing group that surrounded Hilary went eagerly to convert this room into the sanctum of the prophetess. They lowered and softened the shaded light; drew close the blinds and shut the doors, locking all but one. Here was placed a guardian who was to admit grudgingly and one by one those who were fortunate enough to speak alone with the sybil, for she would only see certain of the guests whom she selected herself from the throng, describing *their appearance and dress* to the guardian of her improvised temple. These were all ladies of great position. They entered laughing and half defiant. They came out, some pale, some red, some trembling, some in tears,—" Who can she be?" they whispered in terrified tones to one another, and in that terror showed how she had penetrated their hearts and touched on their secret thoughts.

At last the guardian of the door said that Hilary himself was to enter.

When Hilary went in, the young man, as he closed the door on the fortune-teller and her new guest, turned with a laugh to the group behind him.

"Already she has startled him," he said; "I heard him utter almost a cry as he entered."

"Could you see in?" asked one; "perhaps she has taken off her disguise for her host!"

"No, I saw nothing," he answered. "Can none of you who have been in guess who she is?"

"No," answered a girl who had come out from the ordeal with white trembling lips. "It is impossible to guess. She knows everything."

It was as they had supposed. She had taken off her disguise for her host. The staff, the large cloak, the wig and cap lay on the ground. With the swift use of a cosmetiqued kerchief she had removed from her fair skin the dark complexion of the ancient sybil. When Hilary entered she had completed this rapid toilette and sat leaning back in a low chair. She was dressed in a rich evening costume; she held a mask in her hand ready for use. But now her face was uncovered; her strange and brilliant eyes were fixed on Hilary; her beautiful mouth wore a half smile of amusement at his surprise. It was more than surprise that he experienced. Again that rush of inexplicable emotion overpowered him. He felt like one intoxicated. He regarded her very earnestly for a few moments. "Surely," he said, "we have met before!"

"We were born under the same star," she answered, in a voice that thrilled him. Until now he had not heard her speak. The sense of some strong link or association that united them, was made doubly strong by the sound of that voice, rich, strong and soft. Suddenly he recognized the meaning of his emotion. He no longer struggled against it, he no longer was bewildered by it.

He approached her and sat down upon the couch at her side. He regarded her with wonder and adoration, but no longer with awe or surprise. For he understood that the event which he had imagined would never come was already here—he was in love.

"You said you would disclose your name to the one who was born under the same star as yourself."

"Do you not know me?" she said, with a slight look of surprise. She fancied every one knew her at least by sight.

"I do not," he answered, "though indeed I am perplexed to think I can ever have lived without knowing you."

Flattery produced no effect upon her, she lived in an atmosphere of it.

"I am the Princess Fleta," she answered. Hilary started and colored a little at the words, and could ill control his emotion. The Princess Fleta held a position in the society of the country which can only belong to one who stands next to a throne that rules an important nation. She was a personage among crowned heads, one to whom an emperor might, without stooping, offer his love; and Hilary, the child of an officer of the Austrian army, and of a poor daughter of a decayed aristocratic family, Hilary had in the swift stirring of love at first sight, told his own heart that he loved her! It could never be unsaid, and he knew it. He had whispered the words within himself, the whisper would find a hundred echoes. He must *always love her.*

The Princess turned her wonderful eyes on him and smiled.

"I have done my work for to-night," she said. "I have amused some of the people, now I should like to dance."

Hilary was sufficient of a courtier not to be deaf to this command, though his whole soul was in his eyes and all his thoughts fixed on her beauty. He rose and offered her his arm, she put on her mask and they left the room. When Hilary appeared among the crowd that hung round the door of the fortune-teller's sanctum, accompanied by a slender, graceful woman, whose face was hidden save for the great dark eyes, there was an irrepressible murmur of excitement and wonder. "Who can she be?" was repeated again a hundred times. But no one guessed. None dreamed this could be the Princess Fleta herself; for there were but few houses she would visit at, and no one imagined that there could be any inducement to bring her to Madame Estanol's. The mystery of her presence she explained to Hilary while they danced together.

"I am a student of magic," she said, "and I have already learned some useful secrets. I can read the hearts of the courtiers who surround me, and I know where to look for true friends. Last night I dreamed of the friend I should find here. Do you care for these mystic occupations?"

"I know nothing of them," said Hilary.

"Let me teach you, then," said the Princess, with a light laugh. "You will be a good pupil, that I know. Perhaps I may make a disciple of you! and there are not many with whom that is possible."

"And why?" asked Hilary. "Surely it is a fascinating study to those who can believe in the secrets."

"Scepticism is not the great difficulty," answered the Princess, "but fear. Terror turns the crowd back from the threshold. Only a few dare cross it."

"And you are one of the few," said Hilary, gazing on her with eyes of burning admiration.

"I have never felt fear," she answered.

"And would it be impossible to make you feel it, I wonder?" said Hilary.

"Do you desire to try?" she answered, with a smile at his daring speech. It did not sound so full of impertinence as it looks, for Hilary's eyes and face were all alight with love and admiration, and his voice trembled with passion.

"You can make the attempt if you choose," she said, glancing at him with those strange eyes of hers. "Terrify me if you can."

"Not here, in my own house, it would not be hospitable."

"Come and see me, then, some day when you think it will amuse you. Try and frighten me. I will show you my laboratory, where I produce essences and incenses to please the gnomes and ghouls."

Hilary accepted this invitation with a flush of pleasure.

"Take me to the Countess," she said at last. "I am going home. But I want her first to introduce me to your mother." The Countess was delighted that the Princess had made up her mind to this. She hardly thought Madame Estanol would be pleased to discover that the great lady had been masquerading in her drawing-room, and had not cared to throw off her disguise even for her hostess. And the Countess valued the friendship of Madame Estanol; so she was glad the wilful Princess had decided to treat her with politeness.

Madame Estanol could scarcely conceal her surprise at learning what the dignity was which had been hidden under the disguise of the old fortune-teller. The Princess did not remove her mask, and, with a laugh, she warned Madame Estanol that some of her guests would not be pleased to discover who the sybil was who had read their hearts so shrewdly.

When she had gone, Hilary's heart and spirits had gone with her. It seemed as if he hardly cared to speak; his laughter had died away altogether. His thoughts, his very self, followed the fascinating personality that had bewitched him.

Madame Estanol saw his abstraction, his flushed eager look, and the new softness of his eyes. But she said no word. She feared the Princess, who was well known to be full of caprice and wilfulness. She feared lest Hilary should be mad enough to yield to the charm of the girl's beauty and confident manner; the charm of power, peculiar, or rather, possible only to one in a royal place. But she would say no word; knowing Hilary well, she knew that any attempt to influence him against it would only intensify his new passion.

CHAPTER II.

TWO days later Hilary nerved himself to pay the visit to the Princess. He thought she could not consider it to be too soon, for it seemed to him two months since he had seen her.

She lived in a garden-house some two or three miles away in the country. Her father's palace in the city never pleased her; she only came there when festivities or ceremonials made her presence necessary. In the country, with her chaperone and her maids, she was free to do as she chose. For they were one and all afraid of her, and held her "laboratory" in the profoundest respect. None of them would have entered that room except to avoid some dreadful doom.

Hilary was taken to the Princess in the garden, where she was walking to and fro in an avenue of trees which were covered with sweet-scented blossoms. She welcomed Hilary with a charming manner, and the hour he spent with her here in the sunshine was one of the wildest intoxication. They began openly to play the pretty game of love. Now that no eyes were on them the Princess let him forget that she belonged to a different rank from his own. When she was tired of walking, "Come," she said, "and I will show you my laboratory. No one in this house ever enters it. If you should say in the city that you have been in that room you will be besieged with questions. *Be careful to say* nothing."

"*I would die sooner*," exclaimed Hilary, to whom the

idea of talking about the Princess and her secrets seemed like sacrilege.

The room was without windows, perfectly dark but for a softened light shed by a lamp in the centre of the high ceiling. The walls were painted black, and on them were drawn strange figures and shapes in red. These had evidently not been painted by an artisan hand; though bold in touch, they were irregular in workmanship. Beside a great vessel which stood upon the ground, was a chair, and in this chair a figure upon which Hilary's attention immediately became fastened.

He saw at once that it was not human, that it was not a lay figure, that it was not a statue. It resembled most a lay figure, but there was something strange about it which does not exist in the mere form on which draperies are hung. And its detail was elaborated; the skin was tinted, the eyes darkened correctly, the hair appeared to be human. Hilary remained at the doorway unable to advance because of the fascination this form exercised upon him.

The Princess looked back from where she stood in the centre of the room beneath the light; she saw the direction of his gaze and laughed.

"You need not fear it," she said.

"Is it a lay figure?" asked Hilary, trying to speak easily, for he remembered that she despised those who knew fear.

"Yes," she answered, "it is my lay figure."

There was something that puzzled Hilary in her tone.

"Are you an artist?" he asked.

"Yes," she answered, "in life—in human nature. I do not work with pencil or a brush; I use an agent that cannot be seen yet can be felt."

"What do you mean?" asked Hilary.

She turned on him a strange look, that was at first distrustful, and then grew soft and tender.

"I will not tell you yet," she said.

Hilary roused himself to answer her lightly.

"Have I to pass through some ordeal before you tell me?" he asked.

"Yes," she answered gayly, "and already an ordeal faces you. Dare you advance into the room or no?"

Hilary made a great effort to break the spell that was on him. He went hastily across the room to where she stood. Then he realized that he had actually passed through an ordeal. He had resisted some force, the nature of which he knew not, and he had come out the victor. Realizing this brought to him another conviction.

"Princess," he said, "there is some one else in this room besides you and me. We are not alone."

He spoke so suddenly, and from so great a sense of startled surprise, that he did not pause to think whether his question were a wise one or not. The Princess laughed as she looked at him.

"You are very sensitive," she said. "Certainly we were born under the same star, for we are susceptible to the same influences. No, we are not alone. I have servants here whom no eyes have seen but mine. Would you like to see them? Do not say yes hastily. It means a long and tedious apprenticeship, obtaining mastery over these servants. But unless you conquer them you cannot often see me; for if you are much near to me they will hate you, and their hate is greater than your power to resist it."

She spoke seriously now, and Hilary felt a strange sensation as he looked at this beautiful girl standing beneath the lamp light. He experienced a sudden dread of her as of some one stronger than himself; and also an impassioned desire to serve her, to be her slave, to give his life to her utterly. Perhaps she read the love in his eyes, for she *turned away* and moved toward the figure in the chair.

"*I know this distresses* you," she said. "You shall see

it no longer." She opened a large screen which was formed
of some gold-colored material covered with shapes outlined
in black. She arranged this so that the figure was altogether hidden from view and also the great vessel which
stood beside it.

"Now," she said, "you will breathe more freely. And
I am going to show you something. We did not come out
of the sunshine for no purpose. And we must be quick,
for my good aunt will be terrified when she finds I have
brought you in here. I believe she will hardly expect to
see you alive again."

She opened a gold vessel, which stood upon a cabinet,
while she spoke, and the air immediately became full of a
strong sweet perfume. Hilary put his hand to his forehead. Was it possible that he could be so immediately
affected, or was it his imagination that the red shapes and
figures which were on the black wall moved and ordered
and arranged themselves? Yet, so it was; to his eyes the
forms mingled and again broke up and re-mingled. A
word was formed and then another. It was unconsciously
imprinted on Hilary's memory before it changed and vanished; he noticed only the mysterious occurrence which
was happening before his eyes. Suddenly he became aware
that a sentence had been completed; that words had been
written there which he would never have dared to utter;
that on the wall before him had appeared in letters as of
fire the secret of his heart. He staggered back and drew
his eyes with difficulty from the wall to fix them in amazement and fear upon the Princess. Her face was flushed,
her eyes were bright and tender.

"Did you see it?" he asked in a trembling voice.

For a moment she hesitated; then she answered, "Yes,
I saw it."

There was a brief silence. Hilary looked again at the
wall, expecting to see the thought in his mind written

there. But the shapes were returning to their original appearance, and the perfume was dying out of the air.

"Come," said the Princess, suddenly, "we have been here long enough. My aunt will be distressed. Let us go to her."

She led the way from the room, and Hilary followed her. In another moment they were in a large drawing-room, flooded with sunshine and fragrant flowers; the Princess' aunt was busied with silks which she had entangled while at her embroidery; the Princess was on her knees beside her, holding a skein of yellow silk upon her hands. Hilary stood a moment utterly bewildered. Had he been dreaming? Was that black room and its terrible atmosphere a phantasy?

He had stayed long enough, and he now took his leave reluctantly. The Princess, who would have no ceremony at the garden house, rose from her knees and said she would open the gate for him. Hilary flushed with pleasure at this mark of kindness.

The gate she took him to was a narrow one that stood in a thick-set hedge of flowering shrubs. When he had passed through he looked back, and saw the Princess leaning on the gate, framed in gorgeous blossoms. She smiled and held out her hand to him. The richness of her presence intoxicated him, and he lost all sense of the apparently impassable gulf between them.

"You read the words," he said, "and you give me your hand in mine?"

"I read the words," she answered, in a soft voice that thrilled him, "and I give you my hand in yours. Good-by!"

She had touched his hand for an instant, and now she was gone. Hilary turned to walk through the flowering *hedges to* the city. But his heart, his thought, his soul *remained behind.* She had read the words, and she was not angry. She knew of his love for her and she was not angry. She had read his heart and had not taken offence. What might he not hope for?

Then came another thought. She had read the words. Then that black room was no phantasy, but a fact as actual as the sunshine. What were the powers of this strange creature that he loved? He knew not; but he knew that he loved her.

* * * * * *

An overpowering desire carried him daily on that road between the flowery hedges to the Garden House. Only sometimes had he the courage to enter. Most often he lingered at that narrow gate embosomed in flowers and looked longingly over it. The first time that he entered after the visit in which his secret was written before his eyes, he found the Princess standing within the gate. She held out her hand to him, saying simply, "I knew you were coming. I have prepared something, and I have persuaded my aunt that no terrible thing will happen if you are in my laboratory for a little while. So come with me."

It was brilliantly lit, this black-walled room she called her laboratory. The great vessel stood in the midst of the floor beneath the lamp, and from it rose flame and smoke. A strong and vivid perfume filled the air, and the upper part of the high room was clouded with gray blue smoke, that shone in the light like silver.

In the chair beside it sat a figure: it was that of a beautiful woman. A strange mixture of emotions overpowered Hilary. At the first glance he felt that this figure was the same he had seen the other day; at the second he recognized his mother. He rushed forward to her and became aware that she was lifeless, then he turned passionately upon the Princess with anger and horror in his face.

"What have you done? What have you done?" he cried.

"Nothing," she said, with a smile. "I have done no harm. Do you not see that is only an image? My lay figure, as I told you."

He gave a long look at the inanimate shape that was so perfect a representation of his mother, and then he turned upon the Princess a look of more intense horror than before.

"What are you doing?" he asked, in a low voice.

"No harm!" she answered, lightly. "Your mother hates and fears me. I cannot endure that. I am making her love me. I am making her desire your presence here with me."

For awhile they stood in silence by the side of the vessel and its flaming contents; then suddenly Hilary cried out— "I cannot bear it! Put an end to this terrible spell."

"Yes," said the Princess, "I will, but not to its results."

She drew the screen before the seated figure, and threw something into the vessel that instantly quenched the flame.

Then she led Hilary from the room, and they walked up and down beneath the trees, talking of things as lovers talk—things that interested themselves but none other.

When Hilary returned home his mother rose from her couch and held out her hand to him. She drew him to sit beside her.

"Hilary," she says, "something tells me you have been with the Princess Fleta. It is well, and I am glad. She is a good friend for you; ask her if I shall come to see her."

Hilary rose without replying. The dew stood on his brow. For the first time he was conscious of actual fear, and the fear he felt was of the woman he loved.

CHAPTER III.

IN a chapel of the great cathedral in the city there was at certain hours always a monk who gave advice to all who consulted him.

To him went Hilary some days later. In the interim he had not seen the Princess. His soul had been torn hither and thither, to and fro. His passion for the beautiful girl held him fast, while his horror of the magician repelled him from her. He went to the cathedral in the afternoon determined that he would reveal all his distress to the monk. Father Amyot was in the vestry, but some one was with him, for the door was closed. Hilary knelt down at the small altar of the chapel there to wait. Presently there was a slight sound; he turned his head to see if the superior was now free. The Princess Fleta stood beside him, her eyes fixed on him; it was she who at this instant only had been in consultation with the superior. Hilary, amazed and dumb with wonder, could only gaze upon her. She kept her strange and fascinating eyes fixed on his for a moment and then turned and with swift, soft steps left the chapel. Hilary remained kneeling motionless before the altar, his mind absorbed in what was hardly so much thought as amazement. Fleta was not then what he thought her. If she were sensitive to religious impressions she could not be the cold magician which she had appeared to him to be when he recollected the last scene in the laboratory. Perhaps after all she used her power generously and for good. He began to see her in another light. He began to worship her for her goodness as well as for her strong attractions. His heart leaped with joy at the thought that her soul was as beautiful as her body. He rose from his knees and turned instinctively and without thought to follow her. As he did so he passed Father Amyot, who came slowly down the long aisle, and, without paying the slightest heed to any one, flung himself at full length upon the ground. He wore a long robe of coarse black cloth, tied at the waist with a black cord; a hood of the same cloth covered his long hair. He was like a skeleton, perfectly fleshless and emaciated. His face lay sideways on the stone; he seemed unconscious, so profound was his abstraction. The eyes were open, but had no sight in them. They were large gray-blue eyes, full of a profound melancholy, which gave them an appearance as if tears stood in them. This melancholy affected Hilary strangely; it touched his heart, made thrill and vibrate some deeply sensitive chord in his nature. He stood gazing a moment at the prostrate figure, and then with a profound obeisance left the chapel.

The Princess Fleta had her horse waiting for her. She was a constant and daring rider, and seldom entered the city except on horseback, to the amazement of the Court ladies, who in the city rode in carriages, that they might dress beautifully. But Fleta had no vanity of this kind. Probably no other girl of her age would have willingly adopted the hideous dress of the witch and worn it before so many curious eyes. Her own beauty and her own appearance were subjects of but the slightest thought to her. She would walk down the fashionable promenade in her riding-habit among the magnificent toilets of the Court ladies. This she was doing now while a servant led her horse up and down. Hilary watched her from a distance, unable to summon courage to approach her in the midst of such a throng of personages. But presently Fleta saw him *and came with her* swift light step toward him. "Will you walk with me?" she asked. "There is no one here to be my companion but you."

"And why is that?" asked Hilary, as with flushed face and eager steps he accompanied her.

"Because there are none that sympathize with me. You alone have entered my laboratory."

"But would not any of these be glad to come if you would admit them?"

"Not one would have the courage, except perhaps some few wild spirits who would dare anything for mere excitement. And they would not please me."

Hilary was silent. Her words showed him very plainly that he pleased her. But there was a chill in his nature which now asserted itself. Here in the midst of so many people her hold on him was lessened, and he doubted her more than ever. Was she merely playing with him for her own amusement? Her high position gave her this power, and he could not resent it, for even to be her favorite for a day would be accounted by any man an honor and a thing to boast of. And Hilary was being signalled out for public honor. He felt the envious glances of the men whom he met, and immediately a cold veil fell on his heart. He desired no such envy. To his mind love was a thing sacred. His scorn of life and doubt of human nature awakened at this moment of triumph. He did not speak, but the Princess answered his thought.

"We will go away from here," she said. "In the country you are a creature of passion. Here you become a cynic."

"How do you know my heart?" he asked.

"We were born under the same star," she answered, quietly.

"That is no sufficient answer," he replied. "It conveys no meaning to me, for I know nothing of the mysterious sciences you study."

"Come, then, with me," she answered, "and I will teach you."

She signed to her servant, who brought her horse; she mounted and rode away with merely a smile to Hilary. She knew that, in spite of the chill that was on him, he would hunger for her in her absence and soon follow. And so he did. The pavements appeared empty, though crowds moved over them; the city seemed lifeless and dull, though it was one of the gayest in the world. He turned from the streets, and walking into the country, found himself very soon at the narrow wicket-gate of the Princess Fleta's Garden House.

She was wandering up and down the avenue between the trees. Her dress was white now, and very long and soft, falling in great folds from her shoulders. As she moved slowly to and fro, the dancing sunlight playing on her splendid form, it seemed to Hilary that he saw before him not a mere woman, but a priestess. Her late visit to the Cathedral recurred to him; if the religious soul was in her, might she not, indeed, spite of her strange acts, be no magician, but a priestess? He returned to his former humor, and was ready to worship at her feet. She greeted him with a smile that thrilled him; her eyes read his very soul, and her smile brought to it an unutterable joy. She turned and led the way to the house, and Hilary followed her.

She opened her laboratory door, and immediately Hilary became aware of the strong odor of some powerful incense. The dim smoke was still in the room, but the flame had all died away in the vessel. By the side of the vessel lay a prostrate figure. Hilary uttered a cry of amazement and of horror as he recognized Father Amyot. He turned such a look of dismay upon the Princess that she answered his thought in a haughty tone which she had never before used in addressing him.

"It is not time yet to ask me the meaning of what you may see here. Some day, perhaps, when you know more, you may have the right to question me; but not now. See, I can change this appearance that distresses you in a moment."

She raised the prostrate figure, and flung off from it the white robe that resembled Father Amyot's. Beneath, it was clothed in a dull red garment such as Hilary had first seen it in. With a few swift touches of her hand the Princess changed the expression of the face. Father Amyot was gone, and Hilary saw sitting in the chair before him that unindividualized form and face which, at his visit to the laboratory, had affected him with so much horror. The Princess saw the repugnance still in his face, and, with a laugh, opened the screen with which she had hidden the figure before.

"Now," she said, "come and sit beside me on this couch."

But before she left the great vessel she threw in more incense and lit it. Already Hilary was aware that the fumes of that which had been already burned had affected his brain. The red figures moved upon the black wall, and he watched them with fascinated eyes.

They shaped themselves together not, this time, into words, but into forms. And the wall, instead of black, became bright and luminous. It was as though Hilary and Fleta sat alone before an immense stage. They heard the spoken words and saw the gestures and the movements of these phantasmal actors as clearly and with as much reality as though they were creatures of flesh and blood before them. It was a drama of the passions; the chief actors were Hilary and Fleta themselves. Hilary almost forgot that the real Fleta was at his side, so absorbed was he in the action of the phantasmal Fleta.

He was bewildered, and he could not understand the

meaning of what he saw clearly, though the drama was enacted in front of him. He saw the orchard full of blossoming trees; he saw the splendid savage woman. He knew that he himself and this Fleta at his side, were in some strange way playing a part in this savage guise; but how or what it was he could not tell., Fleta laughed as she watched his face. "You do not know who you are," she cried. "That is a great loss, and makes life much more difficult. But you will know by-and-by if you are willing to learn. Come, let us look at another and a very different page of life."

The stage grew darker, and moving shadows passed to and fro upon it,—great shadows that filled Hilary's soul with dread. At last they drew back and left a luminous space where Fleta herself was visible. Fleta, in this same human shape that she wore now, yet strangely changed. She was much older and yet more beautiful; there was a wonderful fire in her brilliant eyes. On her head was a crown, and Hilary saw that she had great powers to use or abuse—it was written on her face. Then something drew his eyes down and he saw a figure lying helpless at her feet —why was it so still? It was alive!—yes, but it was bound and fettered; bound hand and foot.

"Are you afraid?" broke out Fleta's voice, with a ring of mocking laughter in it. "Surely you are not afraid — why should I not reign? why should you not suffer? You are a cynic; is there anything good to be expected?"

"Perhaps not," said Hilary. "It may be that you are heartless and false. And yet, as I stand here now, I feel that though you may betray me by-and-by, and take my life and liberty from me, yet I love your very treachery."

Fleta laughed aloud, and Hilary stood silent, confused by the words he had spoken hastily without pausing to *think whether they* were fit to speak or not. Well, it was done now. He had spoken of his love. She could refuse ever to see him again, and he would go into the outer darkness.

"No," she said, "I shall not send you away. Do you not know, Hilary Estanol, that you are my chosen companion? Otherwise, would you be here with me now? The word love does not alarm me; I have heard it too often. Only I think it very meaningless. Let us put it aside for the present. If you let yourself love me you must suffer; and I do not want you to suffer yet. When pain comes to you the youth will go from your face; you do not know how to preserve it, and I like your youth."

Hilary made no answer. It was not easy to answer such a speech, and Hilary was not in the humor for accomplishing anything difficult. His brain was confused by the fumes of the incense and by the strange scenes so mysteriously enacted before his eyes. He scarcely knew what Fleta this was that stood beside him. And yet he knew he loved her though he distrusted her! With each moment that he passed by her side he worshipped her more completely, and the disbelief interfered less and less with his proud joy in being admitted to her intimacy.

"Now," said Fleta, "I want you to do a new thing. I want you to exercise your will and compel my servants who have been pleasing us with phantasies, to show us a phantasy of your own creation. You can do this very well, if you will. It only needs that you shall not doubt you can do it. Ah! how quickly does the act follow the thought!" She uttered the last words with a little cry of amused pleasure. For the dim shadows had rapidly masked the stage and then again withdrawn, leaving the figure of Fleta very clearly visible, beautiful and passionate, her face alight with love, held clasped in Hilary's arms, her lips pressed close to his.

The real Fleta who sat beside him rose now with a shake of her head, and a laugh which was not all gay. The shadows closed instantly over the stage, and a moment later the illusion was destroyed and the solid wall was there before Hilary's eyes. He had become so accustomed to witness the marvellous inside of this room that he did not pause to wonder; he followed Fleta as she crossed to the door, and tried to attract her attention.

"Forgive me, my Princess," he murmured over and over again.

"Oh, you are forgiven," she said at last, lightly. "You have not offended, so it is easy for me to forgive. I do not think a man can help what is in his heart; at all events, no ordinary man can. And you, Hilary, have consented to be like the rest. Are you content?"

"No!" he answered, instantly. And as he spoke he understood for the first time the fever that had stirred him all through his short bright life. "Content! How should I be? Moreover, is not our star the star of restlessness and action?"

For the first time, Fleta turned on him a glance of real tenderness and emotion. When he said the words "our star," it seemed as if he had touched her heart.

"Ah!" she said, "how sorely I long for a companion!"

Then she turned from him very abruptly, and almost before he knew she had moved she had opened the door, and was standing outside waiting for him. "Come!" she said, impatiently. He followed her immediately, for he had no choice but to do so; yet he was disappointed. He was more deeply disappointed when he found that she led the way with swift steps into the room where her aunt sat. Arrived there, Fleta threw herself into a chair, took up a great golden fan and began to fan herself, while she talked about the gossip of the Court. The change was so sudden that for some moments Hilary could not follow her. He stood bewildered, till the aunt pushed a low chair toward him; and he felt then that the old lady was not surprised at his manner, but only sorry for him. And then suddenly the cynic re-asserted itself in his heart. A thought that bit like flame suddenly started into life. Had the bewildered emotion that had been, as he knew, visible on his face, been seen on others before? was Fleta not only playing with him, but playing with him as she had played with many another lover? The thought was more hateful than any he had ever suffered from; it wounded his vanity, which was more tender and delicate than his heart.

Fleta gave him no opportunity of anything but talk such as seemed in her stately presence too trivial to be endured, and so at last he rose and went his way. Fleta did not accompany him to the gate this time. She left him to go alone, and he felt as if she had withdrawn her favor in some degree; and yet, perhaps, that was foolish, he told himself, for after all, both he and she had said too much to-day.

Fleta was betrothed. She has been betrothed at her christening. Before long her marriage would take place; and then that crown seen in the vision would be placed on her head. Had it needed the vision to bring that fact to his mind? asked Hilary of himself. If so, 'twas time, he bitterly added, for Fleta was not a woman who was likely to give up a crown for the sake of love. His heart rose fiercely within him as he thought of all this. Why had she tempted him to speak of love? For surely he never would have dared to so address her had she not tempted him; so he thought.

If he could have seen Fleta now! As soon as he left the room she had risen and slowly moved back to her laboratory. Entered there, she drew away a curtain which concealed a large mirror let deep into the wall. She did this resolutely, yet as if reluctantly. Immediately her gaze became fixed on the glass. She saw Hilary's figure within it moving on his way toward the city. She read his thoughts and his heart. At last she dropped the curtain with a heavy sigh, and let her arms fall at her side with a gesture that seemed to mean despair; certainly it meant deep dejection. And presently some great tears dropped upon the floor at her feet.

None, since Fleta was born, had seen her shed tears.

CHAPTER IV.

FATHER AMYOT on the next morning sent a message to Hilary praying him to come and see him. This Hilary did at once, and in much perplexity as to what the reason of such a summons could be. He went straight to the Cathedral, for there he knew the ascetic monk passed all his time. He found him, as he expected, prostrate on the ground, and almost in the same attitude he had seen him in yesterday. Horribly too it reminded him of the attitude of that figure lying on the floor of Fleta's laboratory when he had entered it. He had to touch Father Amyot to attract his attention; then at once the monk rose and led the way out of the Cathedral into the cloisters, which joined it to the monastery close at hand. He went on, without speaking, his head drooped. Hilary could but follow. At last they reached a bare cell in which was no furniture but a crucifix and a perpetual lamp burning before it, and against the wall a bench.

Here Father Amyot sat down, and he motioned with his hand to Hilary to sit beside him.

Then he fell into a profound reverie; and Hilary, watching him, wondered much what was in his mind. Was Fleta even now working her spells upon him and moulding his thoughts according to her will?

It almost seemed like it, for her name was the first word he uttered. "The Princess Fleta," he commenced, "is about to go upon a long and dangerous journey."

Hilary started and turned his face away, for he knew that he had turned pale. Was she really going to leave the city? How unexpected! How terrible!

"In a very short time," went on Father Amyot, "the Princess will be married, and she has a mission which she desires to accomplish before her wedding, and she says that you can assist her in this. It is for the fulfilment of this mission that she is undertaking the journey I speak of; supposing you should agree to help her you would have to accompany her."

Hilary made no answer. He had no answer ready. His breath was taken away, and he could not recover it all in an instant. The whole thing seemed incredible; he felt it to be impossible; and yet a conviction was already falling on him that it would take place.

"Of course," resumed Father Amyot, seeing that Hilary was not disposed to speak, "you will want to know your errand, you will want to know why you are going on this journey. This it will be impossible for you to know. The Princess does not choose to inform any one of what her errand is."

"Not even the person whom she says can help her?" exclaimed Hilary, in amazement.

"Not even you."

"Well," said Hilary, rising with a gesture of indignation, "let her find some one else to go blindly in her wake. I am not the man."

So saying he walked across the cell to the doorway, forgetting even to say good-by to Father Amyot.

But the priest's voice arrested him.

"You would travel alone, save for one attendant."

Hilary turned and faced the priest in amazement.

"Oh, impossible!" he exclaimed, "——yet it is true."

To Hilary the cynic, the thing suddenly assumed an intelligible form. Fleta wanted to take a journey in which she would prefer a companion because of its danger; yet *she could not give her* confidence to any one. She *proposed to herself to* use his love for her; she offered him her society as a bribe to take care of her, to ask no questions and tell no tales. The idea did not please him.

"I have heard of princesses risking anything, relying on the power of their position; I have heard that the royal caprice is not to be measured by the reason of other men and women. Perhaps it is so. But Fleta! I thought her different even from her own family."

These were the first thoughts that came into his mind. His ready conclusion was that Fleta was willing that he should be her lover if he would be her servant also. But immediately afterward came the fair vision of Fleta herself in her white robes, and with the face of a priestess. Her purpose was inscrutable, like herself. He confessed this as he stood there, surging doubts in his mind. And then suddenly a fragrance came across his sense—a strong perfume, that he associated with Fleta's dress—the next a breath of incense. His brain grew dizzy; he staggered back and leaned against the wall. He no longer appeared to himself to be in Father Amyot's cell—he was in Fleta's laboratory, and her hand touched his face, her breath was on his brow. Ah, what madness of joy to be with her! To travel with her, to be her associate and companion, to pass all the hours of the day by her side. Suddenly he roused himself, and, starting forward, approached Father Amyot.

"I will go," he said.

"It will cost you dear," said the monk. "Think again before you decide."

"It is useless to think," cried Hilary. "Why should I think? I feel—and to feel is to live."

Father Amyot seemed not to hear his words. He was apparently already buried in prayer. Evidently he had said all that he intended to say; and Hilary, after a glance at him, turned and left the cell. He knew the monk's moods too well to speak again, when once that deep cloud of profound abstraction had descended on his face.

He went away, passing back, as he had come, through the cathedral. At the high altar he paused an instant, and then knelt and murmured a prayer. It was one he had learned, and he scarce attached any meaning to the familiar words. But it comforted him to feel that he had prayed, be it never so meaningless a prayer. For Hilary had been reared in all the habits of the devout Greek Catholic.

Then he went out and took his way toward the Garden House, walking with long strides. He was determined to know the truth, and that at once. Amid all the brilliant men who crowded her father's Court was he indeed the only one who could touch her heart? An hour ago he would have laughed at any one who had told him he had touched it; yet now he believed he had. And what intoxication that belief was! For the first time he began to feel the absolute infatuation of love. And looking back it seemed to him that an hour ago he had not loved Fleta —that he had never loved her till this minute.

He found her standing at the gate, among the flowers. She was dressed in white, and some crimson roses were fastened at her neck. Her face was like a child's, full of gayety and gladness. Hilary's heart bounded with the delight it gave him to see her like this. She opened the gate for him, and together they walked toward the house.

"I have been to see Father Amyot," said Hilary. "He sent for me this morning."

"Yes," answered Fleta, quietly. "He had a message to you from me. Are you willing to undertake a tiresome task for one you know so little?"

"My Princess," murmured Hilary, bending his head as he spoke.

"*But not your* Queen," said Fleta, with a laugh full of

the glorious insolence only possible to one who had the royal blood in her veins, and knew that a crown was waiting for her.

"Yes, my Queen," said Hilary.

"If you call me that," said Fleta, quickly, and in a different tone, "you recognize a royalty not recognized by courtiers."

"Yes," replied Hilary, simply.

"The royalty of real power," added Fleta, significantly, and with a penetrating look into his eyes.

"Call it what you will," answered Hilary, "you are my Queen. From this hour I give allegiance."

"Be it so," said Fleta, with a light girlish laugh, "be ready, then, to-morrow at noon. I will tell you where to meet me. I will send a message in the morning."

Suddenly a recollection crossed Hilary's mind which had hitherto been blotted out of it. "My mother," he said.

"Oh," said Fleta, "I have been to see Madame Estanol. My father goes into the country to-day, and she believes you go with him. She is glad you should join the court."

"Strange," said Hilary, unthinkingly, "for she has always set her face against it." Then the smile on Fleta's face made him think his words foolish.

"It is as my Queen orders. Seemingly, men and women obey her even in their inmost hearts."

"No," said Fleta, with a sigh, "that is just what they do not! It is that power which I have yet to obtain. They obey me, yes, but against the dictates of their inmost hearts. If you really loved me, we could obtain that power; but you are like the others. You do not love me with your inmost heart."

"I do not!" exclaimed Hilary, in amazement, stunned by her words.

"No," she answered, mournfully, "you do not. If you really loved me you would not calculate chances and risks, you would not consider whether I am profligate or virtuous, whether I am my father's daughter or a child of the stars! I tell you, Hilary Estanol, if you were capable of loving me truly, you might find your way to the gods with me and even sit among them. But it is not so with you. You vacillate even in your love. You cannot give yourself utterly. That means grief to you, for you cannot find perfect pleasure in a thing which you take doubtingly and give but by halves. Still you shall travel with me; and you shall be my companion and friend. There is none other to whom I would give this chance. How do you think you will reward me? Oh, I know too well. Go now, but be ready when I send for you."

So saying, she turned and went into the house, leaving him in the garden. For a few moments he stood there embarrassed, not knowing which way to turn or what to do. But he was not annoyed or disturbed, as his vanity might have led him to be at another time, by such cavalier treatment. He was aghast, horrified. Was this the girl he loved? this tyrant, this proud spirit, this strange woman, who before he had wooed her reproached him with not loving her enough? Within him lurked a conventional spirit, strong under all circumstances, even those of the most profound emotion, and Fleta's whole conduct shocked and distressed that spirit so that it groaned, and more, upbraided him for his mad love. But the fierce growth of that love could not be checked. He might suffer because it lived, but he was not strong enough to kill it.

He turned and walked away from the house and slowly returned to the city. He was ashamed and disheartened. His love seemed to disgrace him. He had entertained lofty ideas which now were discarded forever. For he knew that to-morrow he would start upon a long journey, *the end of which* was to him unknown, by the side of a *girl whom he could* never marry, yet of whom he was the avowed lover. Well, be it so. Hilary began to look at these things from a fatalistic point of view; his weakness led him to shrug his shoulders and say that his fate was stronger than himself. So he went home gloomily, yet with a burning and feverish heart. He immediately set to work making ready for his departure for an indefinite period. His mother he found was prepared for this, as Fleta had told him; and more—seemed to regard Fleta as a kind of gentle goddess who had brought good fortune into his path.

"I have always resisted the idea of your hanging about the Court," she said, "but it is different if indeed the King wishes to have you with him. That must lead to your obtaining some honorable post. What I dreaded was your becoming a mere useless idler. And I am glad you are going into the country, dear, for you are looking very pale and quite ill."

Hilary assented tacitly, and without comment, to the deceit with which Fleta had paved the way for him.

CHAPTER V.

ADVENTURE is said to be sweet to the young; if it was so to Hilary, he must soon have found abundant pleasure in the possession of enough sweets. For the next few days scarcely an hour passed without an event large enough in his eyes to be an adventure.

He was ready at the hour Fleta had named; and had provided against all possible contingencies by taking with him the smallest amount of luggage. For aught he knew they might have to climb mountains in the course of this journey. And moreover, he knew Fleta's unprincess-like distaste for superfluities; he would not have been surprised to see her start in her riding habit and take no luggage at all. The difficulty he dreaded was his mother's surprise at this scant provision of his. But good luck—or was it something else?—took her away. She was summoned to visit a sick friend at a little distance out of the city, and said good-by to Hilary before her departure. So Hilary made his preparations without being troubled by criticism.

At noon a lad presented himself at the door of the Estanols' house, with a note which he said he was to give into Hilary's own hand. Hilary immediately went to him and took it; as he guessed, it was from Fleta. A single line!—and no signature!

"I am waiting for you outside the north gate."

Hilary took his valise in his hand, afraid to hire a carriage lest it should not please her that he brought any eyes *to note their meeting*. He walked out of the city by the *quietest side streets* he could select, hoping not to encounter any of his friends. He met no one he knew, and with a sigh of relief passed out through the gate and walked on to the broad country road beyond it. Drawn up under some trees was a handsome travelling carriage, with four horses and postilions. Hilary was surprised. He had not expected so much luxury. When he reached the carriage he was even more surprised. Fleta was hardly dressed as for a journey; she wore a much richer robe than usual, and her head and shoulders were covered with beautiful black lace. She leaned back in a corner of the roomy carriage, with a voluptuous dreamy expression on her face which was new to Hilary. Opposite her sat Father Amyot. Hilary could not but regard the monk with amazement. Was the town to lose its favorite preacher? How then could all the gossips in it be prevented from hearing of the Princess Fleta's journey? But Hilary resolved not to harass himself with conjecture. He entered the carriage, and Fleta motioned to him to seat himself at her side.

At her side! Yes, that was his place. And Father Amyot, the popular preacher, beloved and almost worshipped by the people, whose inspired words touched upon the secrets and the sorrows of the city: Amyot, who was the model of piety to all who knew him, sat opposite in the carriage. Did he watch the lovers? Seemingly not. His eyes were lowered and his gaze was apparently fixed on his clasped hands. He sat there like a statue. Once or twice when Hilary glanced at his face, he fancied he must be there unwillingly. Was it so? Was he Fleta's tool and servant, held by her domineering temper to do her bidding? Surely not. Father Amyot was too well known as a man of power for the idea to be credible. Hilary checked himself for the hundredth time in these hopeless speculations, and determined to enjoy the moment he was in possession of, and not trouble about the next one till it came; nor yet endeavor to read others' hearts. And so this young philosopher went open-eyed, as he believed, to his destruction.

The carriage rolled away at a great speed; it was drawn by four beautiful Russian horses, and the postilions were Fleta's own, and accustomed to her likings. She was a most daring and intrepid rider, and nothing pleased her in the way of motion except great speed. She was a lover of animals, and her horses were the finest kept in the city. It was strange to Hilary to try and realize her singular independence of position, as to-day he felt compelled to. For himself he was still to a great extent in leading-strings; he had made no position for himself, nor even planned any career; he was dependent on his mother's fortune, and consequently, to a certain extent, could act only according to her approval. He was still so young that all this seemed natural enough. But Fleta was younger than himself, though it was difficult always to remember it, so dominant was her temper. A glance at her fresh face, still so soft in its outlines as to have something childish about it when her expression permitted; at her figure, so slender in spite of its stateliness, recalled the fact that the Princess was indeed only a girl. Did the man who was about to marry her suppose that this young Queen was a creature unformed, fresh from the schoolroom, altogether malleable to his hand?

During the whole of the afternoon they drove on with scarcely a pause, and with very little conversation to pass the time. Yet for Hilary, it flew with swift wings. The mere sensation of his novel position was enough for him as yet. To be beside Fleta and to watch her mysterious face for so long together satisfied for the moment his longing soul. Fleta herself seemed buried in profound thought. She sat silent, her eyes on the country they *passed through,* but her mind, as far as Hilary could judge, *wandering in some* remote region. As for Father Amyot, his regard remained fixed upon a small crucifix which he held hidden within his clasped hands, and now and then his lips moved in prayer, while on that austere face no expression seemed to have room but that of adoration or contemplation of the divine.

At sundown they stopped at a very small way-side inn. Hilary could not believe they were going to stay here, for it looked little more than a place where men drink and horses are fed. Yet so it was. The carriage was driven round to the side of the small house, the horses taken out of it, and Fleta led the way in at a side door, followed by her two companions.

Within they found a motherly, plain, and kindly woman, who evidently knew Fleta well; Hilary learned afterward that this landlady had been a kitchenmaid in the royal household. And now he saw strange things indeed. For this inn was in reality nothing but a drinking shop for the drivers who passed along the road. It had no parlor, nor any accommodation for travellers of a better sort. And Fleta knew this, as was evident at once. She drew a hard chair forward, close to the great fire which flamed up the wide open chimney, and sat down seemingly quite at her ease.

"We must have some supper," she said to the landlady. "Get us what you can. Can you find room for these gentlemen to-night?"

The landlady came near to Fleta and spoke in a low voice; the Princess laughed.

"There are no bedrooms in this house, it seems," she said, aloud; "in fact, it is not a hotel. Shall we drive on or shall we sit here through the night?"

"The horses are tired," said Father Amyot, speaking for the first time since they left the city.

"True," said Fleta, absently—for already she appeared

to be thinking of something else. "I suppose, then, we must stay here."

Hilary had never passed, nor ever contemplated passing, a night in such rough fashion. He was fond of comfort, or rather of luxury. But what could he do when his Princess, the greatest lady in the land, set him the example? Any protest would have appeared effeminate, and his pride held him silent. Still, when, after a very indifferent supper, they all returned to the hard wooden chairs beside the fire, Hilary for the moment very sincerely wished himself at home in his own comfortable rooms. As he wished this, suddenly he became aware that Fleta's dark eyes had turned upon him, and he would not look up, for he believed she had read his thought. He wished he could have hidden it from her, for he had no mind to be held as more effeminate than herself.

There was a sort of second kitchen, even rougher and more cheerless than the one in which they sat, and there the postilions and other men, the ordinary customers of the house, were crowded together, drinking and talking, and singing. Their presence was horrid to Hilary, who was conscious of refined susceptibilities, but Fleta seemed quite indifferent to the noise they made and the odor of their coarse tobacco; or rather it might be that she was unaware of anything outside her own thoughts. She sat, her chin on her hand, looking into the fire; and so graceful and perfect was her attitude that she had the air of being a masterpiece of art placed amid the commonest surroundings. She looked more lovely than ever from the contrast, but yet the incongruity was painful to Hilary.

The silence in the room in which they sat became the more marked from contrast with the increasing noise in the crowded room without. At last, however, the hour *came for the* house to be closed, and the landlady politely *showed her customers* the door; all except those who were travellers on the road. These, including the postilions, gathered into the chimney corner and became quiet, at last falling sound asleep. To Hilary it seemed now that he was living through a painful dream, and he longed for the awakening—willing to awake, even if that meant that he would be at home and away from Fleta.

At last sleep came to him and his head drooped forward; he sat there, upright in the wooden chair, fast asleep. When he awoke, it was with a sense of pain in every limb, from the posture which he had maintained; and he could scarcely refrain from crying out when he attempted to move. But he instantly remembered that if the others were sleeping he must not wake them. Then he quickly looked round. Father Amyot sat near, looking just as he had looked since they entered the house; he might have been a statue. Fleta's chair was empty.

Hilary roused himself, sat up and stared at her empty place; then looked all round the kitchen. It occurred to him that possibly the landlady had found some resting-place for the young Princess. A sense of oppression came over him; the kitchen seemed stifling. He rose with difficulty and stretched himself, then found his way out into the air. It was a glorious morning; the sun had just risen, the world seemed like a beautiful woman seen in her sleep. How sharp the sweet fresh air was! Hilary drew a deep breath of it. The country in which this lonely little inn stood was exceedingly lovely, and at this moment it wore its most fascinating appearance. A sense of great delight came upon Hilary; the uneasiness of the past night was at an end, and he was glad now and full of youth and strength. He turned and walked away from the house, soon leaving the road and plunging into the dewy grass. There was a stream in the valley, and here he determined to bathe. He quickly reached it, and in another moment had hastily undressed, and was plunged in the ice-cold water. An intoxicating sense of vigor came over him as he experienced the keen contact. Never had he felt so full of life as now! It was not possible to remain long in the water, it was so intensely cold; he sprang out again and stood for a moment on the bank in the brilliant morning sunshine, looking like a magnificent figure carved by the god of the day, his flesh gleaming in the light. Slowly he began at last to put on his dress, feeling as if in some way this meant a partial return and submission to civilization. Something of the savage which lay deep hidden in him had been roused and touched. A fire burned that hitherto he had never felt, and which made him long for pure freedom and uncriticised life. And this was Hilary Estanol! It seemed incredible that a draught of fresh morning air, a plunge into ice-cold water beneath the open sky, should have been enough to unloose the savage in him, which was held fast beneath his conventional and languid self, as it is in all of us, and all those whom we meet in ordinary life. He moved hastily, striding on as though he were hurrying to some end, but this haste was only due to a new pleasure in motion. There was a grove of old yew trees near the stream; a grove which with the superstitious was held to be sacred. That it should be revered was no wonder, so stately were the ancient trees, so deep the shadow they cast. Hilary went toward this grove, attracted by its splendid appearance; as he approached its margin a dim sense of familiarity came over him. Never had he left the city by this road, yet it seemed to him that he had entered the grove of yews by the early morning light already many a time. We are all accustomed to meet with this curious sensation; Hilary laughed at it and put it away. What if he had visited this spot in a dream? Now it was broad daylight, and he felt himself young and a giant. He plunged into the deep shadow, pleased by the contrast it made to the brilliant light without.

Suddenly his heart leaped within him and his brain reeled. For there, before him, stood Fleta; and the brilliant Princess looked like a spirit of the night, so pale and grave and proud was her face and so much a part did she seem of the deep shadow of the wood.

"Is it you?" she said with a smile, a smile of mystery and deep, unfathomable knowledge.

"Yes, it is!" he answered, and felt, as he spoke, that he said something in those words which he did not himself understand. They stood side by side for a moment in silence; and then Hilary remembered himself to be alone with this woman, alone with her in the midst of the world. They were separated by the hour from other men and women, for the world still lay asleep; they were separated by the deep shadow of the wood from all moving life that answered to the sun. They were alone—and overwhelmed by this sudden sense of solitude Hilary spoke out his soul.

"Princess," he said, "I am ready to be your blind servant, your dumb slave, speaking and seeing only when you tell me. You know well why I am willing to be the tool in your hands. It is because I love you. But you must pay a price for your tool if you would have it! I cannot only worship at your feet. Fleta, you must give yourself to me, absolutely, utterly. Marry that man to whom you are betrothed if you desire to be a queen, but to me you must give your love, yourself. Ah! Fleta, you cannot refuse me!"

Fleta stood still a long moment, her eyes upon his face.

"No," she said, "I cannot refuse you."

And to Hilary, for an instant of horror, it seemed to him that in her eyes was a glance of ineffable scorn. And there *was* ice in the smile on her lips and in the touch of her hand as she laid it in his.

"The bond is made," she said, "all that you can take *of me is yours.* And I will pay you for your love with my love. Only do not forget that you and I are different—that we are, after all, two persons—that we cannot love in exactly the same way. Do not forget this!"

Hilary knew not what to answer. As she spoke the last words he recognized his princess, he saw the queen before him. What did she mean? Well, he was so unhappy that his love had gone from him to a lady of royal birth. It could not be undone, this folly. He must be content to take that part which a subject may take in the life of a queen, even though he be her lover.

The thought brought a pang, a swift stab to his heart, and a sigh burst from his lips. Fleta put her hand on his arm.

"Do not be sad so soon," she said, "let us wait for trouble. Come, let us go out into the sunshine."

They went out, hand in hand; they wandered down beside the stream and looked into the gleaming waters.

CHAPTER VI.

THAT day the journey began early, and was very protracted. Twice during it they halted at little inns to rest the horess and to obtain what food they could. By the evening they had entered upon the most deserted region of the great forest which was one of the prides of the country. The King's hunting seat, where he now was, stood in a part of this forest, but in quite another region, a long distance from the wild place where Hilary and his companions now were. Hilary had never been within the forest, as few from the city ever penetrated it except as part of the King's retinue, and then they only saw such tracts of it as were preserved and in order. Of this wilder region practically little was known, and the spirit of adventure within Hilary made him rejoice to find that their joruney led them through this unpopulated district. His curiosity as to their destination was not now very acute, for the experiences of the passing moments were all-sufficient. It is true that he was conscious of the great gulf fixed between himself and Fleta. He knew her to be his superior in every respect. He knew not only that he must always be separated from her by their difference in station, but that he was more vitally separated from her by their difference in thought—and that even now. But he was made happy by a look of love that plunged deep from her eyes into his own now and again, and he was thrilled to the heart when her hand touched his with a light and delicate pressure that he alone could understand. Ah! that secret understanding which separates lovers from all the rest of the world. How sweet it is! How strange it is, too, for they are overpowered by a mutual sense of sympathy which appears to be a supreme intelligence, giving each the power to look into the other's heart. Dear moments are they when this is realized, when all life outside the sacred circle in which the two dwell is obscure and dim, while that within is rich, and strong, and sweet. Hilary lived supremely content only in the consiousness of being near this woman whom he loved; for now that he had actually asked her love, and been granted it, nothing else existed for him save that sweet fact. He was indifferent to the hardships, and, indeed, probable dangers, of the journey they were upon, which might have made a more intrepid spirit uneasy; for now he was content to suffer, or even to die, if all conditions were shared with Fleta. All her life could not be shared with him, but all his could be shared with her. When a man reaches this point, and is content to face such a state of things between himself and the woman he loves, he may be reckoned as being in love indeed.

Quite late at night it was when this day's journey ended, and the splendid horses were really tired out. But a certain point evidently had to be reached, and the postilions pushed on. Fleta at last seemed to grow a little anxious, and several times rose in the carriage to look on ahead; once or twice she inquired of the postilions if they were certain of their way. They answered yes; though how that could be was to Hilary a mystery, for they had been for a long while travelling over mere grass tracts, of which there were many, to his eyes undistinguishable one from the other. But the postilions either had landmarks which he could not detect, or else knew their way very well. At last they stopped; and in the dim light Hilary saw that there was a gate at the side of the track, a gate wide enough *to drive* through, but of the very simplest construction. *It might have defended* merely a spot where young trees

were planted, or some kind of preserving done; and it was
set in a fence of the same character, almost entirely hidden
by a thick growth of wild shrubs. The Princess Fleta
produced from her dress a whistle on which she sounded
a clear ringing note, and then everybody sat still and
waited. It seemed to Hilary that it was quite a long while
that they waited; perhaps it was not really long, but the
night was so still, the silence so profound, the feeling of
expectancy so strong. He was, for the first time since they
started, really very curious as to what would happen next.
What did happen at last was this: There was a sound of
laughter and footsteps, and presently two figures appeared
at the gate; one that of a tall man, the other that of a
young slight girl. The gate was unlocked and thrown
wide open, and a moment later the young girl was in the
carriage, embracing Fleta with the greatest enthusiasm
and delight. Hilary hardly knew how everything happened, but presently the whole party was standing together
inside the gate, the carriage had driven in and was out of
sight. Then the tall man shut and locked the gate, after
which he turned back, and walked on ahead with the young
girl at his side, while Hilary followed with Fleta. The
moon had risen now, and Hilary could see her beautiful
face plainly, wearing on it an unusually gay and happy expression; her lips seemed to smile at her own thoughts.
The sweet gladness in her face made Hilary's heart spring
with joy. It could not be rejoining her friends that made
her so glad, for they had gone on and left her alone with
him.

"Fleta—my princess—no, my Fleta," he said, "are you
happy to be with me? I think you are!"

"Yes, I am happy to be with you—but I am not Fleta."

"Not Fleta!" echoed Hilary, in utter incredulity.

He stopped, and catching his companion's hand, looked

into her face. She glanced up, and her eyes were full of shy coquetry and ready gayety.

"I might be her twin sister, might I not, if I am not Fleta herself? Ah! no, Fleta's fate is to live in a court, mine to live in a forest. Live!—no, it is not life!"

What was it in that voice that made his heart grow hot with passion? Fiercely he exclaimed to himself that it *was*, it *must*, be Fleta's voice. No other woman could speak in such tones—no other woman's words give him such a sense of maddening joy.

"Oh! yes," he said, "it is life—when one loves, one lives anywhere."

"Yes, perhaps, when one loves!" was the answer.

"You told me this morning that you loved me, Fleta," cried Hilary, in despair.

"Ah! but I am not Fleta," was the mocking answer. It sounded like mockery indeed as she spoke. And yet the voice was Fleta's. There was no doubt of that. He looked, he listened, he watched. The voice, the face, the glorious eyes, were Fleta's. It was Fleta who was beside him, say she what she might.

They had been following the others all this while, and had now reached a clearing in the wood where was a garden full of sweet flowers, as Hilary could tell at once by the rich scents that came to him on the night air.

"I am glad we have reached the house," said his companion, "for I am very tired and hungry. Are not you? I wonder what we shall have for supper. You know this is an enchanted place, which we call the palace of surprises. We never know what will happen next. That is why one can enjoy a holiday here as one can enjoy it nowhere else. At home there is a frightful monotony about the eating and drinking. Everything is perfect, of course, *but it is* always the same. Now here one is fed like a *Russian one day*, and a Hungarian the next. There is a perpetual novelty about the *menus*, and yet they are always good. Is not that extraordinary? And oh! the wines, great heavens! what a cellar our sainted father keeps. I can only bless, with all my heart, the long dead founders of his order, who instituted such a system."

Hilary had regarded his companion with increasing amazement during this speech. Certainly it was unlike Fleta. Was she acting for his benefit? But at the words "sainted father" another idea thrust that one out of his head. What had become of Father Amyot? He had not seen him leave the carriage, or approach the house.

"Oh, your holy companion has gone to his brethren," said the girl, with a laugh. "They have a place of their own where they torture themselves and mortify the flesh. But they entertain us well, and that is what I care for. We will have a dance to-night. Oh! Hilary, the music here! It is better than that of any band in the world!"

"If you are not Fleta, how do you know my name?"

"Simple creature! What a question! Why, Fleta has told me all about you. Did you never hear that the princess had a foster-sister, and that none could ever tell which was which, so like were we—and are we! Did you never hear that Fleta's mother was blonde, and dull, and plain, and that Fleta is like none of her own family? Oh, Hilary, you, fresh from the city, you know nothing!"

A sudden remembrance crossed Hilary's mind.

"I *have* heard," he said, "that no one could tell where Fleta had drawn her beauty from. But I believe you draw it from your own beautiful soul!"

"Ah, you still think me Fleta? I have had some happy hours in the city before now when Fleta has let me play at being a princess. Ah, but the men all thought the princess in a strange, charming, delightful humor on these days. And when next they saw her, that humor was gone, and they were afraid to speak to her. Come in. I am starving!"

They had entered a wide, low doorway, and stood now within the great hall. What a strange hall it was! The floor was covered with the skins of animals, many of them very handsome skins; and great jars held flowering plants, the scent from which made the air rich and heavy. A wood fire burned on the wide hearth, and before it, still in the dress she had travelled in, stood—Fleta.

Yes, Fleta.

The girl who stood at Hilary's side laughed and clapped her hands as he uttered a cry of amazement, even of horror.

"This is some of your magic, Fleta!" he exclaimed, involuntarily.

The Princess turned at his words. She was looking singularly grave and stern; her glance gave Hilary a sense almost of fear.

"No," she answered in a low, quiet voice that had a tone, as Hilary fancied, of pain, "it is not magic. It is all very natural. This is Adine, my little sister; so like me that I do not know her from myself."

She drew Adine to her with a gesture which had a protecting tenderness in it. This was the Princess who spoke, queen-like in her kindness. Hilary stood, unable to speak, unable to think, unable to understand. Before him stood two girls—each Fleta. Only by the difference of expression could he detect any difference between them. One threw him back the most coquettish and charming glance, as she went toward her grave sister. He could feel keenly how vitally different the two were. Yet they stood side by side, and though Fleta said "my little sister" there was no outward difference between them. Adine was as tall, as beautiful—and the same in everything!

"*Do not be startled*," said Fleta, quietly; "you will soon *grow used to the likeness*."

"Though I doubt," added Adine, with a wicked glance from her brilliant eyes, "whether you will ever tell us apart except when we are not together."

"Come," said Fleta, "let us go and wash the travel stains off. It is just supper time."

Fleta talked of travel stains, but as Hilary looked at her queenly beauty, he thought she seemed as fresh as though she had but this moment come from the hands of her maid. However, the two went away arm in arm, Adine turning at the door to have one last glance of amusement at Hilary's utterly perplexed face. He was left alone, and he remained standing where he was, without power of thought or motion.

Presently some one came and touched him on the shoulder; this was necessary in order to attract his attention. It was the tall man who had come to the gate to meet them. He was very handsome, and with the most cheerful and good-natured expression; his blue eyes were full of laughter.

"Come," he said, "come and see your room. I am master of the ceremonies here; apply to me for anything you want—even information! I may, or may not give it, according to the decision of the powers that be. Call me Mark. I have a much longer name, in fact, half a dozen much longer ones and a few titles to boot; but they would not interest you, and in the midst of a forest where nobody has any dignity, a name of one syllable is by far the best." While he talked on like this, apparently indifferent as to whether Hilary listened or no, he led the way out of the hall and down a wide, carpeted corridor. He opened the last door in this, and ushered Hilary in.

Hilary found himself in a room which no longer permitted him to regret his own rooms at home, for it was more luxurious. A great bath stood ready filled with perfumed *water, and he hastened* to bathe himself therein, with a sort of idea that he was perhaps suffering from hallucinations, some of which he might wash away. His scanty luggage had been brought into the room, and when the bath was over Hilary got out a velvet suit which he thought would do well for evening-dress in this palace of surprises. He was but just ready when a knock came at his door, and, without further ceremony, Mark opened it and looked in.

"Come," he said, "we don't wait for anybody here. The cook won't stand it. He is a very holy father indeed, and nobody dare say him nay, unless it were the Princess herself. She always does as she likes. Are you ready?"

"Quite," replied Hilary.

Opening out of the entrance-hall was a great oak door, double, and very richly carved. This had been shut when Hilary passed by it before; now it stood open, and Mark led the way through it. They entered an immense room, of which the floor was polished so that it shone like a mirror. Two figures were standing in the midst of this room, dressed alike in clouds of white lace; they were the two Fletas, as to Hilary's eyes they still seemed.

His heart was torn as he gazed on them, waiting for a glance of love, a gleam of love-light, to tell him which was his own, his Fleta, his princess, the Fleta whom he served. There was none; they had been talking together very earnestly and both looked sad and a little weary.

As Hilary's eyes wandered from one face to the other his mind grew confused. And then suddenly a flash of bewitchingly beautiful laughter came on one of the faces; and immediately he decided that must be Adine. And yet, had he not seen just such laughter flash across Fleta's face? But all this passed in a moment, and no more time was given him for thought. A table stood at one end of the hall, set as a king's table might be; covered with the *finest linen*, *edged* with deep lace, and with gold dishes of *fruit upon it; it was* decorated with lovely flowers. Hilary opened his eyes a little even in the midst of his other much greater perplexities, to see this luxury here in the midst of the forest. And was it prepared in honor of Fleta, who ate a crust of dry bread in an alehouse with perfect cheerfulness, or rather, indifference? Fleta took her place at the end of the table; at least, one sister did so, and the other took her place beside Hilary—he could not yet determine which was which, and his whole soul was absorbed in the attempted solution of that problem. Mark sat at the other end of the table, evidently prepared to do such labors of carving as might be necessary. Two places more were set at the side of the table, but no one came to fill them. A very elaborate dinner was served, and a very good one; and Hilary thought he was satisfied now that it was Adine who sat next him, for she showed herself an unmistakable little gourmand. He had just come to this conclusion when his attention was distracted by the great doors being thrown open again for two persons to enter. Every one rose, even Fleta, who advanced with a smile to meet these new-comers. Hilary rose also and turned from the table. Two men stood there; one a man but little older than himself, and of extremely fine appearance. Little more than a boy, yet he had a dignity which made him something much more, and Hilary felt immediately a kind of jealousy, undefined, vague, but still jealousy. For Fleta had put both her hands into those of this handsome young man and greeted him with great warmth. At his side stood a small shrivelled old man, in the same dress that Father Amyot always wore. This circumstance again made Hilary wonder what had become of Father Amyot, but he concluded Adine's account had been the correct one.

There was something familiar in the face of the young man, so Hilary thought; while he was thinking this, Fleta turned and introduced them to each other.

He was the young king to whom Fleta was betrothed.

This is a history of those things which lie behind the scenes, not a history of that which is known to all the world. We will give this young King the name of Otto. Let those who like fix upon his kingdom and assign to him his true name.

He sat down opposite Hilary; and the old priest took his place beside him. Hilary returned to his chair, feeling that all strength, and hope, and power, and life had gone from him. By a fierce and terrible revulsion of his whole nature and all his recent feelings, he returned to his cynical estimate of mankind and most of all of Fleta. She had brought him to this place simply to taunt and harass him, and show him his madness and folly in aspiring to her love in the face of such a rival. It cut Hilary's heart like a knife to find the young King so magnificent a creature. And Fleta, why had she come here to meet him? Why had she brought her unhappy lover with her? Hilary tore himself with doubts, and fears, and questions; and sat silent, not even noticing the plates that were placed before him and taken away untouched. The others talked and laughed gayly, Otto being apparently possessed of a hundred things to say. Hilary did not hear what they were, but it annoyed him to find his rival speaking so much in that rich, musical voice of his, while he himself sat dumb, silenced by a bitter pain that tore his heart.

"You are sad," said a soft voice at his side, "it is hard, if you love Fleta, to see her monopolized by some one else. How often have I had to suffer it? Well, it must be so, I suppose. Why am I sorry for you, I wonder? For if Otto were not here you would monopolize Fleta, and have no eyes for any one else. Ah me!"

The sigh was very tender, the voice very low and soft; *and that voice* was Fleta's voice, those lovely eyes uplifted *to his* were Fleta's eyes. Yes, it was so! he thought as he looked back. Did he not know Fleta well enough by now?

"Ah, you are playing with me," he exclaimed eagerly, "it is Fleta now, not Adine! Is it not so? Oh, my love, my love, be honest and tell me!"

He spoke like this under cover of the others' voices, but Fleta looked round alarmed.

"Hush!" she said, "take care. Your life would be lost if you revealed our secret here. After dinner is over, come with me."

This appointment made Hilary happy again; his heart leaped up, his pulses throbbed; all the world changed. He found some fruit was before him, he began to eat it, and to drink the wine in his glass. Fleta was watching him.

"You have just begun to dine!" said Fleta with a soft laugh. "Well, never mind; you are young and strong. Do you think you could live through a great many hardships?"

Hilary made the lover's answer, which is so evident that it need not be recorded. He did not know how he said it, but he desired to tell her that for her he would endure anything. She laughed again.

"It may be so!" she said, thoughtfully; and then he caught her eyes fixed upon him with a searching glance that for an instant seemed to turn the blood cold in his veins. His terrible thoughts and doubts of her returned again the more fiercely for their momentary repulsion. He emptied his glass, but ate nothing more, and was very glad when they all rose from the table together, a few moments later. He followed the figure of the girl who had sat next him since Otto's entrance, believing that Fleta had then changed her place. She went across the great room and led the way into a greenhouse which opened out of it. A *very wonderful* greenhouse it was, full of *the strangest plants*. They were extremely beautiful, and yet in some way they inspired in him a great repugnance. They were of many colors, and the blossoms were variously shaped, but evidently they were all of one species.

"These are very precious," said Fleta, looking at the flowers near her tenderly. "I obtain a rare and valuable substance from them. You have seen me use it," she added, after a moment's pause. Hilary longed to leave the greenhouse and sit elsewhere; but that was so evidently not Fleta's wish that he could not suggest it. There were seats here and there among the flowers, and she placed herself upon one of them, motioning Hilary to sit beside her.

"Now," she said, "I am going to tell you a great many things which you have earned the right to know. To begin with, you are now in a monastery, belonging to the most rigid of all religious orders."

"Are you a Catholic?" asked Hilary, suddenly. And then laughed at himself for such a question. How could Fleta be catalogued like this? He knew her to be a creature whose thought could not be limited.

"No," she answered, simply. "I am not a Catholic. But I belong to this order. I fear such an answer will be so unintelligible as to be like an impertinence. Forgive me, Hilary."

Ah, what a tone she spoke in, gentle, sweet—the voice of the woman he loved. Hilary lost all control over himself. He sprang to his feet and stood before her.

"I do not want to know your religion," he exclaimed, passionately, "I do not want to know where we are, or why we are here. I ask you only this—Are you indeed my love, given to me, as you said this morning?—or is your love given to the king, and are you only laughing at me? It is enough to make me think so, to bring me here to *meet him!* Oh, it is a cruel insult, a cruel mockery! For, *Fleta, you have* made me love you with all my heart and soul. My whole life is yours. Be honest and tell me the truth."

"You have a powerful rival," said Fleta, deliberately. "Is he not handsome, courtly, all that a king should be? And I am pledged to him. Yes, Hilary, I am pledged to him. Would you have the woman you love live a lie for your sake, and hourly betray the man she marries?"

"I would have her give me her love," said Hilary, despairingly, "at all costs, at all hazards. O Fleta, do not keep me in agony. You said this morning that you loved me, that you would give yourself to me. Are you going to take those words back?"

"No," said Fleta, "I am not. For I do love you, Hilary. Did I not see you first in my sleep? Did I not dream of you? Did I not come to your house in search of you? Unwomanly, was it not? No one but Fleta would have done it. And Fleta would only have done it for love. You do not know what she risked—what she risks now—for you! O Hilary, if you could guess what I have at stake. Never mind. None can know my own danger but myself."

"Escape from it!" said Hilary in a sort of madness. A passionate desire to help her came over him and swept all reasonable thoughts away. "You are so powerful, so free, there is no need for you to encounter danger. Does it lie in these people, in this strange place? Come back, then, to the city, to your home. What is there to induce you to run risks, you that have all that the world can offer? Is there anything you need that you cannot have?"

"Yes," said Fleta, "there is. I need something which no power of royalty can give me. I need something which I may have to sacrifice my life to obtain. Yet I am ready to sacrifice it—oh, how ready! What is my life to me? What is my life to me? Nothing!"

She had risen and was impatiently walking to and fro,

moving her hands with a strange eager gesture as she did
so; and her eyes were all aflame. This was the woman he
loved. This, who said her life was nothing to her. Hilary
forgot all else that was strange in her words and manner
in the bitter thought. Could she then return his love—
no, it was impossible, if she meant these strange and terrible words that she uttered!

"Ah, this it is that keeps me back," she said, before he
had time to speak. Her voice had altered, and her face
had grown pale, so pale that he forgot everything else in
watching her.

"This it is that keeps me from my strength, this longing
for it!" And with a heavy sigh she moved back to her
seat and fell into it with a weariness he had never seen in
her before. Her head drooped on her breast, she fell into
profound thought. Presently she spoke again, disjointedly, and in such words as seemed unintelligible.

"I have always been too impatient, too eager," she said
sadly, "I have always tried to take what I longed for without waiting to earn it. So it was long ago, Hilary, when
you and I stood beneath those blossoming trees, long ages
ago. I broke the peace that kept us strong and simple.
I caused the torment and pain and peril to arise in our
lives. We have to live it out—alas, Hilary, we have to
live it out!—and live beyond it. How long will it take us
—how long will it take!"

There was a despair, an agony in her voice and manner,
that were so new, he was bewildered, he hardly recognized
her. Her moods changed so strangely that he could not
follow them, for he had not the key; he could not read her
thought. He sat dumb, looking in her sad drawn face.

"My love, my love," he murmured at last, hardly knowing that he spoke, hardly knowing what his thought was
that he spoke, only full of longing. "Would that I could
help you! Would that I understood you!"

"Do you indeed wish to?" asked Fleta, her voice melting into a tone of tender eagerness.

"Do you not know it?" exclaimed Hilary.. "My soul is burning to meet yours and to recognize it, to stand with you and help you. Why are you so far off, so like a star, so removed and unintelligible to me, who love you so! Oh, help me to change this, to come nearer to you!"

Fleta rose slowly, her eyes fixed upon his face.

"Come," she said. And she held out her hand to him. He put his into it, and together, hand in hand, they left the conservatory. They did not enter the great dining hall, where now there was music and dancing, as Hilary could see and hear. They left the house of the strange flowers by a different doorway, which admitted them to a long dim corridor. Fleta opened the door by a key that was attached to a chain hanging from her waist; and she closed it behind her. Hilary asked no questions, for she seemed buried in thought so profound that he did not care to rouse her.

At the end of the corridor was a small and very low doorway. Fleta stooped and knocked, and without waiting for any answer pushed the door open.

"May I come in, Master?" she said.

"Come, child," was the answer, in a very gentle voice.

"I am bringing some one with me."

"Come," was repeated.

They entered. The room was small, and was dimly lit by a shaded lamp. Beside the table, on which this stood, sat a man, reading. He put a large book which he had been holding, on to the table, and turned toward his visitors.

Hilary saw before him the handsomest man he had ever seen in his life. He was still young, though Hilary felt himself to be a boy beside him; he rose from his chair and stood before them very tall and very slight, and yet there was that in his build which suggested great strength. He looked attentively at Hilary for a moment, and then turned to Fleta.

"Leave him here." Fleta bowed and immediately went out of the room without another word. Hilary gazed upon her in amazement. Was this the proud, imperious princess who yielded such instant and ready obedience? It seemed incredible. But he forgot the extraordinary sight immediately afterward in the interest excited by his new companion, who at once addressed him:

"The Princess has often spoken to me of you," he said, "and I know she has much wished that this moment should arrive. She will be satisfied if she thinks you appreciate with your inner senses the step you are about to take if you accord with her wishes. But I think it right you should know it in every aspect as far as that is possible. If you really desire to know Fleta, to approach her, to understand her, you must give up all that men ordinarily value in the world."

"I have it not to surrender," said Hilary, rather bitterly, "my life is nothing splendid."

"No, but you are only at the beginning of it. To you the future is full of promise. If you desire to be the Princess Fleta's companion, your life is no longer your own."

"No—it is hers—and it is hers now!"

"Not so. It is not hers now, nor will it be hers then. Not even your love does she claim for her own. She has nothing."

"I don't understand," said Hilary, simply. "She is the Princess of this country; she will soon be the Queen of another. She has all that the world has to give a woman."

"Do you not know the woman you love better than to suppose that she cares for her position in the world?" demanded this man whom Fleta called her master. "At *a word from me*, at any hour, at any time, she will leave her throne and never return to it. That she will do this certainly some day I know very well; and her sister will take her place, the world being no wiser than it now is. Fleta looks forward to this change eagerly."

"Well, perhaps," admitted Hilary.

"Neither has she your love nor your life as her own. In loving her you love the great order to which she belongs, and she will gladly give your love to its right owner. She has done this already in bringing you to me."

Hilary started to his feet, stung beyond endurance.

"This is mere nonsense, mere insult," he said, angrily, "Fleta has accepted my love with her own lips."

"That is so," was the answer, "and she is betrothed to King Otto."

"I know that," said Hilary, in a low voice.

"And what did you hold Fleta to be then? A mere pleasure seeker, playing with life like the rest, devoid of honor and principle? Was this your estimate of the woman you loved? What else indeed could it be, when you said, let her give her hand to King Otto while you know her love is yours! And you could love such a woman! Hilary Estanol, you have been reared in a different school than this. Does not your own conscience shame you?"

Hilary stood silent. Every word struck home. He knew not what to say. He had been wilfully blinding himself; the bandages were rudely drawn aside. After a long pause he spoke, hesitatingly:

"The Princess cannot be judged as other women would be; she is unlike all others."

"Not so, if she is what you seem to think her, then she is just like the rest, one of the common herd."

"How can you speak of her in that way?"

"How can you think of her as you do, dishonoring her by your thoughts?"

The two stood opposite each other now, and their eyes

met. A strange light seemed to struggle into Hilary's soul as these bitter words rang sharply on his ear. Dishonoring her? Was it possible? He staggered back and leaned against the wall, still gazing on the magnificent face before him.

"Who are you?" he said at last.

"I am Father Ivan, the superior of the order to which the Princess Fleta belongs," was the reply. But another voice spoke when his ceased, and Hilary saw that Fleta had entered, and was standing behind him.

"And he is the master of knowledge, the master in life, the master in thought, of whom the Princess Fleta is but a poor and impatient disciple. Master, forgive me! I cannot endure to hear you speak as if you were a monk, the mere tool of a religion, the mere professor of a miserable creed."

She sank on her knees before Father Ivan, in an attitude strangely full of humility. The priest bent down and lifted her to her feet. They stood a moment in silence, side by side, Fleta's eyes upon his face devouring his expression with a passionate and adoring eagerness. How splendid they looked! Suddenly Hilary saw it, and a wild, fierce, all-devouring flame of jealousy awoke in his heart —a jealousy such as King Otto, no, nor a hundred King Ottos could not have roused in him.

For he saw that this Ivan, who wore a priest's dress, yet was evidently no priest, who spoke as if this world had no longer any meaning for him, yet who was magnificent in his personal presence and power—he saw that this man was Fleta's equal. And more, he saw that Fleta's whole face melted and softened, and grew strangely sweet, as she looked on him. Never had Hilary seen it like that. Never had Hilary dreamed it could look like that. Stumbling *like a blind* man he felt for the door, which he knew *was near,* and escaped from the room—how, he knew not. Hurriedly he went on, through places he did not see, and at last found himself in the open air. He went with great strides away through the tall ferns and undergrowth until he found himself in so quiet a spot that it seemed as if he were alone in the great forest. Then he flung himself upon the ground and yielded to an agony of despair which blotted out sky and trees, and everything from his gaze, like a great cloud covering the earth.

CHAPTER VII.

THE cloud lifted to reveal Fleta's face. She was bending over him; she was at his side; she was almost leaning on his face.

"My dear, my dear," she said, in a soft whispering voice, "has the blow been too great? Tell me, Hilary, speak to me? Have you still your senses?"

"And you love that man?" was Hilary's sole answer, fixing his eyes in a cold strange gaze on her.

"Oh! Hilary, you talk of what is unknown to you! I love him, yes, and with a love so profound it is unimaginable to you."

"And you tell me this! You tell this to the man who loves you, and who has already devoted his whole life to you! Do you want a madman for your service?"

"A life!" exclaimed Fleta, with a strange tone that had a ring as of scorn in it. "What is a life? I count it nothing. Our great aims lie beyond such considerations."

Hilary raised himself and looked into her face.

"Then you are mad," he said, "and if so, a madman in your service is but fit. Nevertheless, my Princess, do not forget with what forces you have to contend. I am but a man; you have accepted my love. Only just now you have made me a murderer at heart—in desire. How soon shall I be one in reality? That depends on you, Fleta. The next time I see your gaze fixed on that man's face as I saw it but now I will kill him."

Fleta rose to her full height and lifted her face to the sky; as she stood there a sort of shiver passed through her, a shiver as of pain. Instantly Hilary's humor changed.

"You are ill," he exclaimed. She turned her eyes on him.

"When that murderous mood is on you, it will not be Father Ivan that you kill, but me, whom you profess to love. Do you understand that?"

"Ah!" cried Hilary, uttering a sound as if his heart was bursting under the torture, "that is because you love him so! Well, I can only long and serve. I have no power to protest. Yet I ask you, oh! Princess, is it fit to use a man's heart to play at your queenly coquetries with? A king, your betrothed—a mysterious priest, the man you love—are not these enough but that you must take a boy, obscure and untaught in such misfortunes, and trample on his love? It is unlike the nobility I have seen in you. Good-by, for this, Princess! I am never your lover again as I was before. I can never believe in your pure sweet heart—only this morning it seemed to me as a pearl, as a drop of limpid water. Good-by, my idol! Yet I am your servant to obey always, for I gave you my life to do with as you would. Call me, and I come, like your dog; but I will not stay by you, for no longer is it anything but pain to do so."

With these wild, fierce reproaches, which seemed to stir the quiet air of the woodland, and make it seethe and burn with passion and despair, he turned and went from her. Fleta stood motionless, and her eyes drooped heavily; only she murmured, "We were born under the same star!"

Her voice was very low, yet it reached Hilary's ear. The words seemed to lash his heart.

"Under the same star!" he repeated, in a voice of agony, standing suddenly still. "No, Fleta. You are the queen, I the subject. Not only so, but you know it, and use your power to the full. Did you not promise yourself utterly to me to be mine?"

"I promised to give you my love for yours; I promised to give you all that you can take of me. My love is greater than you can even imagine, else I would not have listened to one word of your reproaches. They have humbled me, but I have borne it."

"Ah, Fleta! you talk enigmas," exclaimed Hilary, moving rapidly back to her side; "you are enough to madden a man; yet I cannot but love you. Why is this? Every act of yours proves you heartless, faithless, and yet I love you! Why is this? Oh, that I could read the riddle of your existence! Who are you?—what is this mysterious place?—Who is that priest whose rule you acknowledge? I *will* know!"

Fleta turned on him a sudden sweet smile, that seemed to light up his inner being as the flame of a lamp illumines a dusky room.

"Yes," she said, "find out. I cannot tell you, yet I desire you—oh! indeed, I desire you to know. Compel the secret—force it. Yes, yes, Hilary!"

She spoke eagerly, with a bright ring in her voice that thrilled his soul. He forgot the Princess, the conspirator, the religieuse—he only remembered the girl he loved— young, fresh, flower-like, with the fair sweet face close to his own. With an unutterable cry of love he held out his arms to her.

"Oh, my dear, my love, come!" he said, in trembling tones that vibrated with his passion. But Fleta turned away without a word and walked through the tall ferns, her robe trailing on the ground. No backward glance, no turn of the head, not even a movement of those white statuesque hands which hung at her sides. In one was a long grass which she had plucked before she came to him. Even that, though it fluttered in the wind, had a strangely stiff air, as if it had become a part of that statue which *but a moment* since was a woman. Hilary stood gazing after this retreating figure, powerless to move, powerless to rouse in his mind any thought but one; and that was not a thought. It was knowledge—consciousness. He knew, he felt, that he dared not follow Fleta and address her as men address the women they love; he dared not woo her with the fever on his lips that burned there. And why? Not because of her royal birth, or her beauty, or her power. He knew not why—he could not understand himself. It was as though a spell were cast on him that held him silent and motionless.

When at last she was out of sight a sudden reaction took place. The whole burning force of the strong young man's nature broke loose and raged wildly through his whole system; he no longer was capable of thought, he only felt the blood that rushed to his head and made his brain reel as though he had drunk strong wine. He suddenly became aware that he had aged, grown, become a new creature in these last moments of experience. He had called himself a man five minutes ago; but now he knew that when he had uttered those words, he was only a boy. Across a great gulf of feeling he looked back at the love that was in him when he had spoken. Now his passion burned like a fire on the altar of life; every instant the flames grew stronger and mounted more fiercely to his inflamed brain.

The savage had burst forth. The savage, untamed man, which smoulders within, and hides behind the cultivated faces of a gentle age. One strong touch on the chord of passion, and Hilary Estanol, a chivalric and courteous product of a refined time, knew himself to be a man, and knew that man to be a savage. A savage full of desire, of personal longing, thinking of nothing but his own needs. And to Hilary this sudden starting forth of the nature within him seemed like a splendid unfolding. He remained *standing erect,* strong, resolute. His seething mind hastily went over his whole position and Fleta's. Everything suddenly bore a new, vivid, stirring aspect.

"This is a nest of conspirators!" he exclaimed to himself. "That man, Ivan, is a conspirator or worse, else he would not hide here. What crowned head is it that he threatens? He is a criminal. I will discover his secret; I will rescue Fleta from him; by the strength of my love I will win her love from him; I will make her my own. Come, I must calm myself—I must be sober, for I have to find out the meaning of this mysterious place."

He walked slowly through the wood, trying to still the throbbing in his brain, to check the fierce pulsations of his heart and blood. He knew that now he needed all his instincts, all his natural intelligence, all his power of defence; for, in his present humor, he walked as an enemy to all men; by his new tide of feeling he had made every man his enemy. The young King Otto had a prior right to the Fleta whom he desired to make his own; King Otto was indeed his enemy. Ivan had her love; how bitterly did Hilary hate that priest! And Adine, the false Fleta— what was she but a mere tool of the priest's, a creature used to baffle and blind him? She was the one most likely to trip his steps, for she defied even the knowledge which his love gave him of Fleta's face!

He was full of energy and activity, and his blood desired to be stilled by action. He had quickly decided that he must immediately do two things: inspect the whole exterior of the house, so as to get some notion of what rooms were in it, and what their uses; and explore the outer circle of the grounds, to see if there was any difficulty about leaving them. As the latter task involved most exercise,— he chose to undertake it first, and swiftly, with long strides, made his way through the woodlands in the direction *where the boundaries must lie.* It did not take him long *to traverse a consider*able distance; for he felt stronger than ever in his life before. He had been a delicate lad, now he knew himself to be a strong man, as if new blood ran in his veins. The moon was high in the heavens, it was nearly full and its light was strong. By it he soon discovered that the strange place in which he was had a more cunning and effective defence than any high wall or high barrier. It was surrounded by tangled virgin woodland growth, where, as it seemed, no man's foot could have ever trodden

Hilary found it hard to believe that such wild land existed within a drive of the city. But it was there, and there was no passing through it, unless he worked his way with a wood-axe, inch by inch, as men do when they made a clearing. Such a task was hopeless, even if he had the tools, for it was impossible to tell in what direction to move.

He returned at last, after many fruitless efforts; there seemed to be no vestige of a path. He had discovered the gate by which their entrance had been made; and discovered also that it was guarded. A figure moved slowly to and fro in the shadow of the trees; not with the air of one strolling for pleasure, but with the regular movements of a sentry. It was an unfamiliar figure, but dressed in the garb of the order.

Hilary went quietly along by the side of the path that led to the house. It was useless to waste more time on this investigation; quite clearly he was a prisoner. And it seemed to him equally clear that unless he could escape, no information would be of any use to him. He must be able to carry it to the city, where he would be free to take it to Fleta's father, or even to other crowned heads in other countries, according to its nature. As he walked quietly on, revolving his position, he saw that the task he had set himself was no light one, even for a strong man possessed by love. These monks belonged to an extraordinarily *powerful order*, and were men of great ability.

Here he was, in the very heart of one of their secret centres, which was, presumably, political. Fleta and King Otto were under their influence. And they were magicians; very certain he felt that they knew some of Nature's secrets, and had trained Fleta in her mysterious powers. And from this hidden and carefully-guarded place he was determined to escape, taking with him its secret—and Fleta! Fleta, his love, his own, yet whom he had to win by his strength.

CHAPTER VIII.

IN the long corridor through which Fleta had led Hilary to Father Ivan's room there was another door, which was fastened in a very different manner. It was held in its place by iron clamps which would puzzle the beholder, for they fastened on the outside as though they secured the door of a prison instead of being any protection for the inhabitant of the room beyond. It was inside this door that Fleta was now lying down to rest for the night. Had Hilary known this what agony would have torn him! He would have felt that he must break those bars and release the prisoner within them, however supernatural the strength might be which would be needed. He was spared the sharp pain of knowing this, however, and he was not likely to learn it, for a strange sentinel patrolled the long corridor with even step—Father Ivan himself. Without any pause he went steadily to and fro.

It was about midnight that Father Ivan went into his room and glanced at a clock on the chimney-piece; not quite midnight, but very nearly. Hilary was lying awake in his room, tossing to and fro on a very luxurious and tempting bed, which gave him, however, no hope of rest. He had wandered round and round the house a dozen times, only to find himself bewildered by its strange shape, and the shrubberies which grew up close to the walls, and disheartened by the solid barricading of those windows which it was easy to approach. And yet at last he found a window wide open, and a room brightly lit; a lamp stood on the table and showed the pleasant room, well-furnished,

and with a bed in it, dressed in fine linen and soft laces
such as perhaps only members of an ascetic order know
how to offer to their guests. Hilary stood a moment on
the threshold, and then suddenly recognized it as his own
room. It gave him an odd feeling, this, as if he had been
watched and arranged for; treated like a prisoner. Well,
it was useless to evade that dark fact—a prisoner he was.
Recognizing defeat for the moment, Hilary determined to
accept it as gracefully as might be. He entered, closed
his window and the strong shutters which folded over it,
and then quickly laid himself down with intent to sleep.
But sleep would not come, and he found all his thoughts
and all his interest centred on Father Ivan. He tried to
prevent this but could not; he chased Fleta's image in
vain—he could scarcely remember her beautiful face!
What was its shape and color? He tortured himself in
trying to recall the face he loved so dearly. But always
Father Ivan's figure was before his eyes; and suddenly it
struck him that this vision was almost real, for he saw
Ivan raise his hand in a commanding gesture which seemed
to be directed toward himself. A moment later and he
fell fast asleep, like a tired child. At this moment Ivan
was standing in his own room, looking for an instant at
the clock. He stood, perhaps, a little longer than was
needed in order to see the time, and a frown came on his
fine, clear forehead which drew the arched eyebrows together. Then he turned quickly, left his room, and closed
its door behind him. He went to the door which was so
strongly barred, and noiselessly loosened its fastenings,
which swung heavily yet quite softly away from it. He
opened the door and went in.

In a sort of curtained recess was a low divan, which
quite filled it, rising hardly a foot from the ground. This
was covered with great rugs made of bear and wolf skin.
Fleta lay stretched upon them, wrapped in a long cloak of

some thick white material, which was bordered all round with white fur, and, indeed, lined with it, too. And yet when Ivan stooped and touched her hand it was cold as ice.

"Come," he said; and turning, went slowly away from her. Fleta rose and followed him. Her eyes were half-closed, and had something of the appearance of a sleep-walker's, and yet not altogether, for though they appeared dim and unseeing yet there was purpose, and consciousness, and resolution in them. No one who had not seen Fleta before in this state could have recognized those eyes, so set and strange were they. Ivan approached a large curtained archway, and drawing the curtain aside he motioned to Fleta to pass through. As she did so he touched one of her hands, as it hung at her side. Immediately she raised it, and throwing the cloak aside showed that she held a white silk mask. Her dress beneath the cloak was of white silk. Slowly she raised the mask to her face and was about to put it on when a change of state came so suddenly upon her that it was like a tropical tornado. She opened her starry eyes wide and vivid light flashed from them; she flung the mask away upon the floor and clasped her hands violently together, while her whole frame shook with emotion.

"Why must I mask myself?" she exclaimed. "You have not told me why."

"I have," said Ivan, very quietly. "No woman has ever entered there till now."

"What then?" cried Fleta, fiercely. "There is no shame in being a woman! Have I not assailed that door in vain in a different character? Now, a woman, I demand entrance. Master, I will not disguise myself."

"Be it so," said Ivan, "yet take the mask with you lest your mood should change again. You were willing, you remember, but a while since."

Fleta stood *motionless*, regarding the mask as it lay on

the floor. Then she lifted her head suddenly and looked Ivan straight in the eyes.

"I will cast my sex from me: and mask my womanhood without any such help as that."

Immediately that she had spoken Ivan walked on. They were in a long corridor, lit, and with the walls faintly colored in pale pink on which shone some silver stars. Yet, bright though it was, this corridor seemed strangely solemn. Why was it so? Fleta looked from side to side, and could not discover. There was something new to her which she did not understand. Though she had been instructed in so many of the mysteries, and so much of the knowledge of the order, she had never entered this corridor, nor indeed had she before known of its existence. They slowly neared the end of it where was a high door made of oak, and seemingly very solidly fastened; but Father Ivan opened it easily enough.

"My God!" cried Fleta instantly, in a low voice of deep amazement. "Where am I? What country am I in? Father, was that corridor a magic place? This is no longer my own country! How far have you carried me in this short time?"

"A long way, my daughter; come, do not delay."

A vast plain, prairie-like, stretched before them, encircled on the right by the narrowing end of a huge arm of mountains which disappeared upon the far horizon. Upon the plain was one spot, was one place, where a livid flame-like light burned, and could be seen, though the whole scene was bathed in strong moonlight. Ivan commenced to rapidly take his way down a steep path which lay before them. And then Fleta became aware that they were themselves upon a height and had to descend into the plain. She did not look back; all her thoughts were *centred on* that vivid light which she now saw came from *the windows of* a great building. Then she suddenly saw that a number of persons were in the plain; although it was so large yet there were enough people to look like a crowd, which was gathering together from different directions. All were approaching the building.

"Father," she said to Ivan, who was leading the way rapidly. "Will they go in?"

"Into the temple? Those on the plain? Indeed no. They are outside worshippers; that crowd is in the world and of it, and yet has courage to come here often when there is no light, and the icy winds blow keen across the plain."

"And they never enter. Why, my master, they can have no strength."

Ivan glanced back for an instant, a curious look in his eyes.

"It is not always strength that is needed," he said in a low voice. Fleta did not seem to hear him: her eyes were fixed on the temple windows. Suddenly she stopped and cried out:

"Is this a dream?"

"You are not asleep," said Ivan with a smile.

"Asleep! no," she answered, and went on her way with increased rapidity.

Very soon they stood on the plain and advanced with great speed toward the temple. Fleta was naturally hardy; but now it seemed to her that the very idea of fatigue was absurd. She could scale mountains in order to reach that light. And yet what was it in it that drew her so? None but herself could have told. But Fleta's heart beat passionately with longing at the sight of it. Ivan turned on her a glance of compassion.

"Keep quiet," he said.

He was answered with a look and tone of fervor.

"Yes; if it is in human power," she replied.

The *great crowds* were slowly gathering toward the

temple and formed themselves into masses of silent and scarcely moving figures. Fleta was now among them, and though so absorbed by the idea of the goal before her, she was attracted by the strange appearance of these people. They were of all ages and nationalities, but more than two-thirds of them were men; they one and all had the appearance of sleep-walkers, seeming perfectly unconscious of the scene in which they moved and of their object in reaching it. Their whole nature was turned inward; so it appeared to Fleta. Why, then, had they come to this strange place, so difficult of access, if when come they could neither see nor hear? Fleta considered these things rapidly in her mind, and would again have asked an explanation of Father Ivan but that while her steps slackened a little, his had hastened. He had already reached the door of the temple—when Fleta reached it he was not there. Of course he had entered, and Fleta, without fear or hesitation, put her hand on the great bar which held the door and lifted it. It was not difficult to lift; it seemed to yield to her touch, and swung back smoothly. With a slight push the great door opened a little before her—not wide; only as far as she had pushed it. Ah! there was the light! There, in her eyes! It was like life and joy to Fleta. She turned her eyes up to gaze on it, and stood an instant with her hands clasped, in ecstasy.

Some one brushed lightly by, and, passing her, went straight in. That reminded her that she, too, desired to go straight in. She nerved herself for the supreme effort. For she was learned enough to know that only the initiate in her faith could enter that door; and she had not, in any outward form, passed the initiation. But she believed she had passed it in her soul; she had tested her emotions on every side and found the world was nothing to her; she *had flung* her mask away, believing her woman's shape and *face to be the* merest outward appearance, which would be unseen at the great moment. And now it hardly seemed as if she were a woman—she stood transfigured by the nobility of her aspirations—and some who stood on the step outside remained there awestruck by her majestic beauty. By a supreme effort she resolved to face all—and to conquer all. She boldly entered the door and went up the white marble steps within it. A great hall was before her, flooded with the clear, soft light she loved; an innumerable number of objects presented themselves to her amazed eyes, but she did not pause to look at them—she guessed that the walls were jewelled from their sparkling—she guessed that the floor was covered with flowers, which lay on a polished silver service, from the gleaming and the color—and who were these, the figures in silver dresses with a jewel like an eye that saw, clasped at the neck? A number came toward her. She would not allow herself to feel too exultant—she tried to steady herself—and yet joy came wildly into her heart, for she felt that she was already one of this august company. But their faces, as they gathered nearer, were all strange and unfamiliar. She looked from one to another.

"Where is Ivan?" she murmured.

Suddenly all was changed. The white figures grew in numbers till there seemed thousands—with outstretched hands they pushed Fleta down the steps—down, down, down, resist how she might. She did more. She fought, she battled, she cried aloud, first for justice, then for pity. But there was no relenting, no softening in these superhuman faces. Fleta fled at last from their overpowering numbers and inexorable cruelty, and then there came a great cry of voices, all uttering the same words:

"You love him! Go!"

Fleta fell, stunned and broken, at the foot of the outer step, and the great door closed behind her. But she was not unconscious for more than a few minutes. She opened her eyes and looked at the starry sky. Then she felt suddenly that she could not endure even that light and that the stars were reading her soul. She rose and hurried away, blindly following in any path that her feet found. It did not take her to any familiar place. She found herself in a dark wood. The moss was soft and fragrant, and violets scented it. She lay down upon it, drawing her white cloak round her and hiding her eyes from the light.

CHAPTER IX.

IT seemed to her that for long ages she was alone. Her mind achieved great strides of thought which at another time would have appeared impossible to her. She saw before her clearly her own folly, her own mistake. Yesterday she would not have credited it—yesterday it would have been unmeaning to her. But now she understood it, and understood too how heavy and terrible was her punishment; for it was already upon her. She lay helpless, her eyes shut, her whole body nerveless. Her punishment was here. She had lost all hope, all faith.

A gentle touch on her hand roused her consciousness, but she was too indifferent to open her eyes. It mattered little to her what or who was near her. The battle of her soul was now the only real thing in life to her.

A voice that seemed strangely familiar fell on her ears; yet last time she had heard it it was loud, fierce, arrogant; now it was tender and soft, and full of an overwhelming wonder and pity.

"You, Princess Fleta, here? My God! what can have happened? Surely she is not dead? No! What is it, then?"

Fleta slowly opened her eyes. It was Hilary who knelt beside her; she was lying on the dewy grass, and Hilary knelt there, the morning sun shining on his head and lighting up his beautiful boy's face. And Fleta, as she lay and looked dully at him, felt herself to be immeasurable *older than he was*; to be possessed of knowledge and experience which seemed immense by his ignorance. And yet she lay here, nerveless, hopeless.

"What is it?" again asked Hilary, growing momently more distressed.

"Do you want to know?" she said gently, and yet with an accent of pity that was almost contempt in her tone. "You would not understand."

"Oh, tell me!" said Hilary. "I love you—let me serve you!"

She hardly seemed to hear his words, but his voice of entreaty made her go on speaking in answer:

"I have tried," she said, "and failed."

"Tried what?" exclaimed Hilary, "and how failed? Oh, my Princess, I believe these devils of priests have given you some fever—you do not know what you are saying!"

"I know very well," replied Fleta; "I am in no fever. I am all but dead—that is no strange thing, for I am stricken." Hilary looked at her as she lay, and saw that her words were true. How strange a figure she looked, lying there so immovably, as if crushed or dead, upon the dewy grass; wrapped in her white robes. And her face was white with a terrible whiteness; the great eyes looked out from the white face with a sad, smileless gaze; and would those pale drawn lips never smile again? Was the radiant, brilliant Fleta changed forever into this paralyzed white creature? Hilary knew that even if it was so he loved her more passionately and devotedly than before. His soul yearned toward her.

"Tell me, explain to me, what has done this?" he cried out, growing almost incoherent in his passionate distress. "I demand to know by my love for you. What have you tried to do in this awful past night?"

Fleta opened her eyes, the lids of which had drooped heavily, and looked straight into his as she answered:

"I have tried for the Mark of the White Brotherhood. I have tried to pass the first initiation of the Great Order. I did not dream I could fail, for I have passed through many initiations which men regard with fear. But I have failed."

"I cannot believe," said Hilary, "that you could fail in anything. You are—dreaming—you are feverish. Let me lift you, let me carry you into the house."

"Yes, I have failed," answered Fleta, dully; "failed, because I had not measured the strength of my humanity. It is in me—in me still! I am the same as any other woman in this land. I, who thought myself supreme—I, who thought myself capable of great deeds! Ah, Hilary, the first simple lesson is yet unlearned. I have failed because I loved—because I love like any other fond and foolish woman! And yet no spark of any part of love but devotion is in my soul. That is too gross. Is it possible to purge even that away? Yes, those of the White Brotherhood have done it. I will do it even if it takes me a thousand years, a dozen lifetimes!"

She had raised herself from the ground as she spoke, for a new fierce passion had taken the place of the dull despair in her manner; she had raised herself to her feet, and then unable to stand had fallen on to her knees. Hilary listened, yet hardly heard; only some of her words hurried into his mind. He bent down till his face touched her white cloak where it lay on the grass, and kissed it a dozen times.

"You have failed because of love? Oh, my Princess, then it is not failure! Men live for love, men die for love! It is the golden power of life. Oh, my Princess, let me take you from this terrible place—come back with me to the world where men and women know love to be the one great joy for which all else is well lost. Fleta, while I doubted that you loved me I was as wax; but now that I know *you* do, and with a love so great that it has power to check the career of your soul, now I am strong, I am able to do all that a strong man can do. Come, let me raise you and take you away from here to a place of peace and delight."

He had risen to his feet and stood before her, looking magnificent in the morning sunshine. He was slight of build, yet that slightness was really indicative of strength; when Hilary Estanol had been effeminate it was because he had not cared to be anything else. He stood grandly now, his hands stretched toward her; a man, lofty, transformed by the power of love. Fleta looking at him saw in his brilliant eyes the gleam of the conquering savage. She rose suddenly and confronted him.

"You are mistaken," she said, abruptly. "It is not you that I love."

Then, as suddenly as Fleta had moved and spoken, the man before her vanished, with his nobility, and left the savage only, unvarnished, unhumanized.

"My God," gasped Hilary, almost breathless from the sudden blow, "then it is that accursed priest?"

"Yes," answered Fleta, her eyes on his, her voice dull, her whole form like that of a statue, so emotionless did she seem, "it is that accursed priest."

She moved away from him and looked about her. The spot was familiar. She was in the woodland about the monastery. She could find her way home now without difficulty. And yet how weak she was, and how hard it was to take each footstep! After moving a few paces she stood still and tried to rouse herself, tried to use her powerful will.

"Where are my servants?" she said in a low voice. "Where are those who do my bidding?"

She closed her eyes, and standing there in the sunlight, *used all her power to call the forces into action which she had learned to control.* For she was a sufficiently learned magician to be the mistress of some of the secrets of Nature. But now it seemed she was helpless—her old powers were gone. A low, bitter cry of anguish escaped from her lips as she realized this awful fact. Hilary, terrified by the strange sound of her voice, hastily approached her and looked into her face. Those dark eyes, once so full of power, were now full of an agony such as one sees in the eyes of a hunted and dying creature. Yet Fleta did not faint or fail, or cling to the strong man who stood by her side. After a moment she spoke, with a faint yet steady voice.

"Do you know the way to the gate?" she asked.

"Yes," replied Hilary; who indeed had but recently explored the whole demesne.

"Take my hand," she said, "and lead me there."

She used her natural power of royal command now; feeble though she was, she was the princess. Hilary did not dream of disobeying her. He took the cold and lifeless hand she extended to him, and led her as quickly as was possible over the grass, through the trees and flowering shrubs, to the gateway. As they neared it she spoke:

"You are to go back to the city," she said. "Do not ask why—you must go; yet I will tell you this—it is for your own safety. I have lost my power—I can no longer protect you, and there are both angels and devils in this place. I have lost all! all! And I have no right to risk your sanity as well as my own. You must go."

"And leave you here?" said Hilary, bewildered.

"I am safe," she answered, proudly. "No power in heaven or earth can hurt me now, for I have cast my all on one stake. Know this, Hilary, before we part: I shall never yield or surrender. I shall cast out that love that kills me from my heart—I shall enter the White Brotherhood. And, Hilary, you too will enter it. But, oh! not yet! Bitter lessons have you yet to learn! Good-by, my brother."

The sentinel who guarded the gate now approached them in his walk; Fleta moved quickly toward him. After a few words had passed between them he blew a shrill, fine whistle. Then he approached Hilary.

"Come," he said, "I will show you the way for some distance and will then obtain you a horse and a guide to the city."

Hilary did not hesitate in obeying Fleta's commands; he knew he must go. But he turned to look once more into her mysterious face. She was no longer there. He bowed his head and silently followed the monk through the gate into the outer freedom of the forest.

Fleta meantime crept back to the house through the shelter of the trees. Her figure looked like that of an aged woman, for she was bowed almost double and her limbs trembled as she moved. She did not go to the centre door of the house, but approached a window which opened to the ground and now stood wide. It was the window of Fleta's own room; she hurried toward it with feeble, uncertain steps. "Rest! Rest! I must rest!" she kept murmuring to herself. But on the very threshold she stumbled and fell. Some one came immediately to her and tried to raise her. It was Father Ivan. Fleta disenaged herself, tremblingly yet resolutely. She rose with difficulty to her feet and gazed very earnestly into his face.

"And you knew why I should fail?" she said.

"Yes," he answered, "I knew. You are not strong enough to stand alone amid the spirit of humanity. I knew you clung to me. Well have you suffered from it. I know that very soon you will stand alone."

"Of what use would that mask have been?" demanded *Fleta,* pursuing her own thoughts.

"*None.* If you had obeyed me and worn it you would

have been of so craven a spirit you could never have reached the temple, never have seen the White Brotherhood. You have done these things, which are more than any other woman has accomplished."

"I will do yet more," said Fleta. "I will be one of them."

"Be it so," answered Ivan. "To do so you must suffer as no woman has yet had strength to suffer. The humanity in you must be crushed out as we crush a viper beneath our feet."

"It shall be. I may die, but I will not pause. Good-by, my master. As I am a queen in the world of men and women, so you are king in the world of soul, and to you I have done homage; that homage they call love. It is so, perhaps. I am blind yet, and know not. But no more may you be my king. I am alone, and all knowledge I gain I must now gain myself."

Ivan bowed his head as if in obedience to an unanswerable decree, and in a moment had walked away among the trees. Fleta watched him stonily till he was out of sight, then dragged herself within the window to fall helplessly upon the ground, shaken by sobs and strong shudders of despair.

CHAPTER X.

IT was late in the day before Fleta again came out of her room. She seemed to have recovered her natural manner and appearance; and yet there was a change in her which any one who knew her well must see. She had not been into the general rooms, or greeted the other guests; nor did she do so now. Her face was full of resolution, but she was calm, at all events externally. Without going near the guest rooms or the great entrance hall, she made her way round the house to where a very small door stood almost hidden in an angle of the wall. It was such a door as might lead to the cellars of a house, and when Hilary had explored the night before he had scarcely noticed it. But it was exceedingly solid and well fastened. Fleta gave a peculiar knock upon it with a fan which she carried in her hand. It was immediately opened, and Father Amyot appeared.

"Do you want me?" he asked.

"Yes; I want you to go on an errand for me."

"Where am I to go?"

"I do not know; probably you will know. I must speak to one of the White Brotherhood."

Amyot's face clouded and he looked doubtfully at her.

"What is there you can ask that Ivan cannot answer?"

"Does it matter to you?" said Fleta imperiously. "You are my messenger, that is all."

"*You* cannot command me as before," said Father *Amyot.*

"What! do you know that I have failed? Does all the world know it?"

"The world?" echoed Amyot, contemptuously. "No; but all the Brotherhood does, and all its servants do. No one has told me, but I know it."

"Of course," said Fleta to herself. "I am foolish." She turned away and walked up and down on the grass, apparently buried in deep thought. Presently she raised her head suddenly, and quickly moved toward Amyot, who still stood motionless in the dim shadow of the little doorway. She fixed her eyes on him; they were blazing with an intense fire. Her whole attitude was one of command.

"Go," she said.

Father Amyot stood but for a moment; and then he came out slowly from the doorway, shutting it behind him.

"You have picked up a lost treasure," he said. "You have found your will again. I obey. Have you told me all your command?"

"Yes. I must speak to one of the White Brothers. What more can I say? I do not know one from another. Only be quick!"

Instantly Amyot strode away over the grass and disappeared. Fleta moved slowly away, thinking so deeply that she did not know any one was near her till a hand was put gently on her arm. She looked up, and saw before her the young king Otto.

"Have you been ill?" he asked, looking closely into her face.

"No," she answered. "I have only been living fast— a century of experience in a single night! Shall I talk to you about it, my friend?"

"I think not," answered Otto, who now was walking quietly by her side. "I may not readily understand you. I am anxious above all to advance slowly and grasp each truth as it comes to me. I have been talking a long time to-day to Father Ivan; and I feel that I cannot yet understand the doctrines of the order except as interpreted through religion."

"Through religion?" said Fleta. "But that is a mere externality."

"True, and intellectually I see that. But I am not strong enough to stand without any external form to cling to. The precepts of religion, the duty of each toward humanity, the principle of sacrifice one for another, these things I can understand. Beyond that I cannot yet go. Are you disappointed with me?"

"No, indeed," answered Fleta. "Why should I be?"

Otto gave a slight sigh as of relief. "I feared you might be," he answered: "but I preferred to be honest. I am ready, Fleta, to be a member of the order, a devout member of the external Brotherhood. How far does that place me from you, who claim to stand among the wise ones of the inner Brotherhood."

Fleta looked at him very seriously and gravely.

"I claim it," she said; "but is it mine? Yet I will win it, Otto; even at the uttermost price, I will make it mine."

"And at what cost?" said Otto. "What is that uttermost price?"

"I think," she said slowly, "I already feel what it is. I must learn to live in the plain as contentedly as on the mountain tops. I have hungered to leave my place in the world, to go to those haunts where only a few great ones of the earth dwell, and from them learn the secret of how to finally escape from the life of earth altogether. That has been my dream, Otto, put into simple words; the old dream of the Rosicrucian and those hungerers after the occult who have always haunted the world like ghosts, unsatisfied, homeless. Because I am a strong-willed creature, *because* I have learned how to use my will, because I have *been taught a few* tricks of magic, I fancied myself fitted to be one of the White Brotherhood. Well, it is not so. I have failed. I shall be your queen, Otto."

The young king turned on her a sudden look full of mingled emotions. "Is that to be, Fleta? Then may I be worthy of your companionship!"

Fleta had spoken bitterly, though not ungently. Otto's reply had been in a strange tone, that had exultation, reverence, gladness in it; but not any of the passion which is called love. A coquette would have been provoked by a manner so entirely that of friendship.

"Otto," said Fleta, after a moment's pause, during which they had walked on side by side. "I am going to test your generosity. Will you leave me now?"

"My generosity?" exclaimed Otto. "How is it possible for you to address me in that way?" Without any further word of explanation he turned on his heel and walked quickly away. Fleta understood his meaning very well; she smiled softly as she looked for a moment after him. Then, as he vanished, her whole face changed, her whole expression of attitude too. For a little while she stood quite still, seemingly wrapt in thought. Then steadily and swiftly she began to move across the grass and afterward to thread her way through the trees. Having once commenced to move she seemed to have no hesitation as to the direction in which she was going. And, indeed, if you had been able to ask her how she knew what path to take, she would have answered that it was very easy to know. For she was guided by a direct call from Amyot, as plainly heard as any human voice, though audible only to her inner hearing. To Fleta, the consciousness of the double life—the spiritual and the natural—was a matter of constant experience, and, therefore, there was no need for the darkness of midnight to enable her to hear a voice from what ordinary men and women call the unseen world. To Fleta that world was no more unseen than unheard.

She saw at once, conquering time and space, the spot where she would find Father Amyot at the end of her rapid walk; and more, the state she would find him in. The sun streamed in its full power and splendor straight on the strange figure of the monk, lying rigidly upon the grass. Fleta stood beside him and looked down on his face, upturned to the sky. For a little while she did nothing, but stood there with a frown upon her forehead and her dark eyes full of fierce and changing feeling. Amyot was in one of his profound trances, when, though not dead, yet he was as one dead.

"Already my difficulties crowd around me," exclaimed Fleta, aloud. "What folly shall I unknowingly commit next? My poor servant—dare I even try to restore you—or will nature be a safer friend?"

Full of doubt and hesitation she turned slowly away, and began to pace up and down the grass beside the figure of the priest. Presently she became aware that she was not alone—some one was near her. She started and turned quickly. Ivan stood but a pace from her, and his eyes were fixed very earnestly upon her.

He was not dressed as a priest, but wore a simple hunting dress, such as an ordinary sportsman or the king incognito might wear. Simple it was, and made of coarse materials; but its easy make showed a magnificent figure which the monkish robes had disguised. His face had on it a deep and almost pathetic seriousness; and yet it was so handsome, so nobly cut, and made so brilliant by the deep blue eyes, which were bluer than their wont now; even in the full blaze of the sun—that in fact as a man merely, here stood one who might make any woman's heart, queen or no queen, beat fiercely with admiration. Fleta had never seen him like this before; to her he had always been the master, the adept in mysterious knowledge, the recluse *who hid his love of* solitude under a monkish veil. This was Ivan! Young, superb, a man who must be loved. Fleta stood still and silent, answering the gaze of those questioning, serious blue eyes, with the purposeful, rebellious look which was just now burning in her own. The two stood facing each other for some moments without speaking—without, as it seemed, desiring to speak. But in these moments of silence a measuring of strength was made. Fleta spoke first.

"Why have you come?" she demanded. "I did not desire your presence."

"You have questions to ask which I alone can answer."

"You are the one person who cannot answer them, for I cannot ask them of you."

"It is of me that you must ask them," was all Ivan's reply. Then he added: "It is of me you have to learn these answers. Learn them by experience if you like, and blindly. If you care to speak, you shall be answered in words. This will spare you some pain, and save you years of wasted time. Are you too proud?"

There was a pause. Then Fleta replied deliberately:

"Yes, I am too proud."

Ivan bowed his head and turned away. He stooped over Father Amyot, and taking a flask from his pocket, rubbed some liquid on the monk's white and rigid lips.

"I forbid you," said Ivan, "to use your power over Amyot again."

"You forbid me?" repeated Fleta, in a tone of profound amazement. Evidently this tone was entirely new to her.

"Yes, and you dare not disobey me. If you do, you will suffer instantly."

Fleta looked the amazement which was evidently beyond her power to express in words. Ivan's manner was cold, almost harsh. Never had he addressed her without gentleness before. Hastily she recovered herself, and, without pausing to address to him any other word, she turned away and went quickly through the trees and back to the house. Otto was standing at one of the windows; she went straight to him.

"I wish to go back to the city at once," she said, "will you order my horses?"

"May I come with you?"

"No, but you may follow me to-morrow if you like."

CHAPTER XI.

IT was the day of the Princess Fleta's wedding, and the whole city was *en fête*.

Hilary Estanol paced the streets wildly, like a creature distracted. He had never seen her face since the day he returned from the secret monastery. He could not trust himself to go near her.* He felt that the savage in him must kill, must destroy, if too much provocation were given him.

He held this savage in check as well as he could. He would not trust himself under the same roof with the woman he loved as he loved nothing else in life, and who had given him her love while she gave herself to another man. Herself! How much that meant Hilary seemed only now to know, now that he heard her marriage bells ringing, now that she was absolutely given. Yes, she had given herself away to another man. Was it possible? Hilary stood still now and again in the midst of the crowded street trying to remember the words she had said to him in that wood in the early morn when she had accepted his love. What had she taken from him then? He had never been the same since. His heart lay cold, and chill, and dull within him save when her smile or its memory woke him to life and joy. Were these gone forever? Impossible. He was still young—a mere boy. She could not have stolen so much from him! No—he had the first right—he would be her lover still and always, to whoever else she gave herself in name. This was the point of thought to which Hilary perpetually returned. Undoubtedly she was his, and he would claim her. But obscured and excited as his mind was, he had sufficient intelligence to know that his must be a secret claim, even though it stood before all others. He could not go and claim her at the altar, for she had not given him any right to. What she had said was, "Take from me what you can." Well, he could not make her his wife. He could not marry a royal Princess. She was not of his class. This being so, what could he hope for? Nothing—and yet he had her love—yes, the last kind touch of her hand, the last sweet smile on her lips, were still with him, and drove his blood rioting through his veins.

At last the procession is coming—the soldiers have already cleared the way and with their horses keep back the crowd. Hilary stands now, still as a carven figure, watching only for one face. He sees it suddenly—ah! so beautiful, so supremely beautiful, so mysterious—and everything in heaven and earth becomes invisible, non-existent, save that one dear face. A voice rang out on the air, clear. shrill, above all other voices:

"Fleta! Fleta! My love! my love!"

What a cry! It penetrated to Fleta's ears; it reached the ears of her bridegroom.

In the church, amid the pomp and ceremony, and the crowd of great people, Otto did a thing which made those near him stare. He went to meet his bride and touched her hand.

"Fleta," he said, "that voice was the voice of one who loves you. What answer do you make to it?"

Fleta put her hand in his.

"This is my answer," she said.

And so they stepped up the broad low steps to the altar. None heard what had been said except the king.

Fleta's father was strangely unlike herself. He was a

rugged, morose, sombre man, ill-disposed toward all humanity, as it would seem, save those few who held the key to his nature. Of these, his daughter was one; some said she was the only one. Others said her power lay in the fact that she was not his daughter, but a child of other parents altogether than those reputed to be hers; and that a State secret was involved in the mystery of her birth.

At all events, it was seldom indeed that the king interfered with Fleta. But he did so now, at this moment, with all the eyes of the Court upon them.

He spoke low into her ear; he stood beside her.

"Fleta," he said, "is this marriage right?"

Fleta turned on him a face so full of torture, of deathly pain, that he uttered an ejaculation of horror.

"Say no word, my father," she said, "it is right."

And then she turned her head again, and fixed her glorious eyes on Otto.

What a strangely beautiful bride she was! She was dressed with extraordinary simplicity; her robe had been arranged by her own hands in long, soft lines that fell from her neck to her feet, and a long train lay on the ground behind her, but it was undecked by any lace or flowers. No flowers were in her hair, no jewels on her neck. Never had a princess been dressed so simply, a princess who was to be a queen. The Court ladies stared in amazement. But they knew well that there was a grace so supreme, a dignity so lofty, in this royal girl, that however simple her dress she outshone them all, and would outshine any woman who stood beside her.

No one heard any of what passed between the three chief actors in this scene; yet every one was aware that there was something unusual in it. There was an atmosphere of mystery, of excitement, of strangeness. And yet what else would be possible where the Princess Fleta was concerned? In her father's Court she was looked upon as a wild, capricious, imperious creature whose will none could resist. None would have wondered had they believed her carriage to have passed over the body of an accepted lover, now thrown aside and discarded. So did these people interpret the character of Fleta. Otto knew this, felt it, understood it; knew that those creatures of intrigue and pleasure would have thought her far less worthy had they judged her character more nearly as he did. To him she was pure, stainless, unattainable; virgin in soul and thought. This he said to her when, on leaving the cathedral, they entered a carriage together and alone. They had together passed through crowds of congratulators, nobles, great ladies, diplomats from different parts of Europe. They had bowed and smiled, and answered courteously the words addressed to them. And yet how far away were their thoughts all the while! They neither of them knew whom they had met, whom they had spoken to. All was lost in one absorbing thought. But it was not the same thought. No, indeed, their minds were separated widely as the poles.

Fleta was filled with the sense of a great purpose. This marriage was but the first step in a giant programme. Her thoughts had flown now from this first step and were dwelling on the end, the fulfilment; as an artist when he draws his first sketch sees in his own mind the completed picture.

Otto had but one overwhelming thought; a very simple one, expressed instantly, in the first words he uttered when they were alone:

"Fleta, you did not fancy that I doubted you? I never meant that! And yet it seemed as if there was reproach in your eyes! No, Fleta, never that. But the cry was so terrible—it cut my heart. You did not fancy I meant any doubt!—assure me, Fleta!"

"No, I did not," replied Fleta, quietly. "You know whose voice it was."

"No—it was unrecognizable—it was nothing but a cry of torture."

"Ah! but I knew it," said Fleta. "It was Hilary Estanol who cried out my name."

"He said 'Fleta, my love, my love,'" added Otto. "Is he that to you?"

"Yes," said Fleta unmoved, indeed strangely calm. "He is. More, Otto; he has loved me long centuries ago when this world wore a different face. When the very surface of the earth was savage and untaught so were we. And then we enacted this same scene. Yes, Alan, we three enacted it before, without this pomp, but with the natural splendor of savage beauty and undimmed skies. Otto, I sinned then; I expiated my sin. Again and again have I expiated it. Again and again has Nature punished me for my offence against her. Now at last I know more, I see more, I understand more. The sin remains. I desired to take, to have for myself, to be a conqueror. I conquered—I have conquered since! How often! That has been my expiation: satiety. But now I will no longer enjoy. I will stand on that error, that folly, and win from it strength which shall lift me from this wretched little theatre where we play the same dramas forever through the fond weariness of recurring lives."

Otto had drawn back from her, and gazed intently upon her as she spoke, passion and vehemence gradually entering her low voice. As she ceased, he passed his hand over his forehead.

"Fleta," he said, "is this some spell of yours upon me? While you spoke I saw your face change and become the face of one familiar to me, but far, far back! I smelled the intense rich scent of innumerable fruit blossoms—— Fleta, tell me, are you dreaming or speaking fables, or is this thing true? Have I lived for you before, loved you, served you, ages back, when the world was young?"

"Yes," said Fleta.

"Ah!" cried Otto, suddenly, "I feel it—there is blood on you—blood on your hand!"

Fleta raised her beautiful hand, and looked at it with an infinite sadness on her face.

"It is so," she answered. "There is blood on it, and there will be, until I have got beyond the reign of blood and of death. You held me down, then, Otto; you triumphed by brute force, not knowing that in me lay a power undreamed of by you—a vital, stirring will. I could have crushed you. But already I had used my will once, and found the bitter, unintelligible suffering it produced. I determined to try and understand Nature before I again used my power. So I submitted to your tyranny; you learned to love it, and through many lives have learned to love it more. It has brought you a crown at last, and a little army of soldiers to defend it for you, and half-a-dozen crafty old diplomats who want you to keep it, and who think they can make you do just as their respective monarchs wish. Move your puppets, Otto. No such kingdom satisfies me. I mean to win my own crown. I will be a queen of souls, not of bodies; a queen in reality, not in name."

She seemed to wrap herself in an impenetrable veil of scorn as she ceased speaking and leaned back in the carriage.

Some great emotion was stirring Otto through and through. At last he spoke; and the man was changed—a different being. From under the gentle manner, the docile, ready air, came struggling up the fierce spirit of *opposition*.

"*You despise the crown you married me for? Is that so? Well, I will teach you to respect it.*"

A smile dawned on Fleta's clouded face and then was gone again in a moment. This was all the answer she vouchsafed to the kingly threat. Otto turned and looked at her steadily.

"A magnificent creature," he said, "beautiful, and with a brain of steel, and perhaps for all I know, a heart like it. You won a great deal from me, Fleta, a little while since. Did I not submit to the masquerading of your mysterious Order? Did I not trust my life to those treacherous monks of yours, submit to be blindfolded and led into their haunts by secret ways. For what end? Ivan told me of aspirations, of ideas, of thoughts, which only sickened my soul and filled me with shame and despair. For I am a believer in order, in moral rule, in the government of the world in accordance with the principles of religion. I told you I was willing to become a member of the order; yes, because my nature is in sympathy with its avowed tenets. But its secret doctrines, as I have heard them from you, are to me detestable. And it is for the carrying out of this unholy theory or doctrine that you propose to surrender your life? No, Fleta; you are now my queen."

"Yes," said Fleta, "I am now your queen. I know that. I have chosen the lot willingly. You need not again tell me that I have the crown I purposed to obtain."

At this moment they arrived at the Palace. There was yet a weary mass of ceremony and speaking of polite nothings to be passed through before there was any chance of their being alone again. Otto relapsed into the pleasant and kindly manner which was habitual with him. Fleta fell into one of her abstracted moods, and the court adopted its usual policy under such circumstances—let her be undisturbed. Few of the men cared to risk the satirical answers that came readiest to her lips when she was roused out of such a mood as this.

And yet at last some one did venture to rouse her; and a

smile, delicious as a burst of sunshine, came swiftly and suddenly on her mouth.

It was Hilary Estanol. Pale, worn, the mere ghost of himself, his dark eyes looking strangely large in the white face they were set in. They were fixed on her as though there were nothing else in the world to look at.

Fleta held out her hand to him; his companion—a military officer who had brought him under protest, and in some doubt, for Hilary had no friends at Court—drew back in amazement. He understood now Hilary's importunity.

Hilary bent over Fleta's hand and held his lips near it for an instant, but did not touch it. A sort of groan came to her ear from his lips.

"You have resigned me?" she asked, in a low, vibrating whisper.

"You have cast me off," he answered.

"Be it so," she replied; "but you have lived through it, and you now claim nothing. Is it not so? I read it in the dumb pain in your eyes."

"Yes," said Hilary, straightening himself and standing upright close beside her, and looking down upon her beautiful dark head. "It is so. I will not cry for the moon, nor will I weary any woman with my regret or entreaty, even you, Fleta, though it is no dishonor to humble one's self at the feet of such as you. No: I will bear my pain like a man. I came here to say good-by. You are still something like the Fleta that I loved. To-morrow you will not be."

"How can you tell?" she said, with her inscrutable smile. "Still, I think you are right. And now that we are no longer lovers will you enter with me another bond? Will you be my comrade in undertaking the great task? I know you are fearless."

"The great task?" said Hilary, vaguely, and he put his hand to his forehead.

"The one great task of this narrow life—To learn its lesson and go beyond it."

"Yes, I will be your comrade," said Hilary in an even voice and without enthusiasm.

"Then meet me at two this very morning at the gate of the gardenhouse where you used to enter."

It was now just midnight. Hilary noticed this as he turned away, for a little clock stood on a bracket close by. He looked at it, and looked back at Fleta. Could she mean what she said? But already the Fleta he knew had vanished; a cold, haughty, impassive young queen was accepting the uninteresting homage of a Foreign Minister. The guests were beginning to take their departure. Fleta and Otto did not propose to take any journey in honor of their wedding as is the custom in some places; the king opened for their use the finest set of guests' chambers in the palace, and these they occupied, remaining among the visitors until all had departed. On the next day Otto was to take his Queen home; but he had had to give way to the wishes of Fleta and her father as to the postponing of the journey.

From the great drawing rooms Fleta went quietly away when the last guests had departed; she moved like a swift shadow noiselessly along the corridors. She entered her own room, and there began, without summoning any attendant, to hastily take off her bridal robes. On a couch was lying the white robe and cloak which she had worn when she had endeavored to enter the hall of the mystics. These she put on, and wrapping the cloak round her, turned to leave the room. As she did so, she came face to face with Otto, who had entered noiselessly, and was standing in silence beside her. She seemed scarcely to notice him, but changed her direction and proceeded toward another door. Otto quickly placed himself again in her way.

"No," he said; "you do not leave this room to-night."

"And why?" asked Fleta, looking gravely at his set face.

"Because you are now my wife. I forbid it. Stay here, and with me. Come, let me take off that cloak, without any trouble; the white gown under it suits you even better than your wedding-dress."

He unfastened the clasps which held the cloak together. Fleta made no opposition, but kept her eyes on his face; he would not meet her gaze, though his face was white and rigid with the intensity of his passion and purpose.

"Do you remember," said Fleta, "the last thing that you did when you were with Father Ivan? Do you remember kneeling before him and uttering these words— 'I swear to serve the master of truth and the teacher of life——'"

"That master—that teacher!" interrupted Otto, hotly. "I reserved my reason even in that incense-scented room. That master—that teacher—is my own intelligence—so I phrased it in my own mind—I recognize no other master."

"Your own intelligence!" repeated Fleta. "You have not yet learned to use it. You did not so phrase the vow then; you only rephrased it so afterward, when you were away, and alone, and began again to struggle for your selfish freedom. No, Otto, you have not begun to use your intelligence. You are still the slave of your desires, eaten up with the longing for power and the lust of the tyrannical soul. You do not love me—you only desire to possess me. You fancy your power is all you wish it to be. Well, put it to the test. Take this cloak from my shoulders."

Otto came close, and took the cloak in his hands; and *then* a sudden passion filled him—he seized her in his *arms and pressed* his lips to hers—yet he did not do so, either, for the attempt was instantaneously surrendered. He staggered back, white and trembling.

Fleta stood erect and proud before him.

"That vow you took," she said, quietly, "you knew very well in the inner recesses of your soul, in your true unblinded self, to make you a servant of the Great Order. That vow may yet save you from yourself, if you do not resent it too fiercely. But remember this: I am a neophyte of that order, and you being its servant, are under my command. I am your queen, Otto, but not your wife."

She passed him as she said this, and he made no effort to detain her; indeed, the trembling had not yet left him, and his whole strength was taken by the attempt to control it. As she reached the door he succeeded in speaking:

"Why did you marry me?"

"Did I not tell you?" she said, pausing a moment and turning to look at him. "I think I did. Because I have to learn to live on the plain as contentedly as on the mountain tops. There is but one way for me to do this, and that is to devote my life as your queen to the same great purpose it would serve were I the silver-robed initiate I desire to be. I go now to commence my work, with the aid of a lover who has learned to surrender his love."

She moved magnificently from the room, looking much taller even than her natural height. And Otto let her go without any word or sign.

CHAPTER XII.

IT was a fragrant night—a night rich with sweet flower-scents, not only from the flower beds near, but coming from afar on the breeze. Hilary stood at the gate, leaning on it and looking away at the sky, where a faint streak of different light told of the sun's coming. It was quite clear, though there had been no moonlight; one of those warm, still nights when it is easy to find one's way, though hard to see into the face of one near by; a night when one walks in a dream amid changing shadows, and when the outer mysteriousness and the dimness of one's soul are as one. So with Hilary; so had he walked to the gate. He waited for the woman he loved, the only woman any man could ever love, having once known her. And yet no fever burned now in his veins, no intoxication mounted from his heart to his brain. Standing there, and regarding himself and his own feelings very quietly in the stillness, it seemed to him as if he had died yesterday when that wild cry had been unknowingly uttered; as if his soul or his heart, or, indeed, his very self had gone forth in it.

A light touch was laid on his shoulder, and then the gate was opened. He passed through and walked by Fleta up the flower-bordered pathway. She moved on without speaking, her white cloak hanging loose from her neck, and her bare arms gleaming as it fell back from them.

"You who know so much, tell me something," said Hilary. "Why are you so wise?"

"Because I burned my soul out centuries ago," said Fleta. "When you have burned out your heart you will *be strong* as I am."

"Another question," said Hilary. "Why did you fail in that initiation?"

Fleta stopped suddenly, and fixed fierce questioning eyes upon him. She was terrible in this quick rush of anger. But Hilary looked on her unmoved. It seemed to him that nothing would ever be able to move him again. Was he dead indeed that he could thus endure the scorching light of those brilliant eyes?

"What makes you ask me that?" cried Fleta, in a voice of pain. "Do you demand to know?"

"Yes; I do wish to know."

For a moment Fleta covered her face with her hands and her whole form shrank and quivered. But only for a moment; then she dropped her hands at each side and stood erect, her queenly head poised royally.

"It is my punishment," she said in a murmuring voice, "to discover so soon how absolute are the bonds of the Great Order; how the pupil can command the master as well as the master the pupil."

Then she turned abruptly upon Hilary, approaching him more nearly, while she spoke in a quick, fierce voice.

"Because, though I have burned out my soul, I have not burned out my heart! Because, though I cannot love as men do, and have almost forgotten what passion means, yet I can still worship a greater nature than my own so deeply that it may be called love. I have not learned to stand utterly alone and to know myself as great as any other, with the same possibilities, the same divinity in myself. I still lean on another, look to another, hunger for the smile of another. O folly, when I know so well that I cannot find any rest while that is in me. O Ivan, my teacher, my friend, what torture it is to wrest the image of you from its shrine within me. Powers and forces of indifferent Nature, I demand your help!"

She raised her arms as she uttered this invocation, and

it struck Hilary at the moment how little like a human being she looked. She might have been the spirit of the dawn. Her voice had become unutterably weird and mournful, like the deep cry of a broken soul.

Without pausing for any answer she dropped her arms, drew her cloak around her, and walked away over the dewy grass. Hilary, as silent, as mournful, but seemingly without emotion, dropped his head and quietly followed her track. Of old—only yesterday—what an age ago!—he would have kept his eyes fixed on her shining dark hair or the movements of her delicate figure. Suddenly Fleta stopped, turned and confronted him. He raised his eyes in surprise and looked at her.

"You are no longer devoured by jealousy," she said. "You can hear me speak as I did just now without its turning you into a savage. What has happened?"

Her eyes seemed to penetrate his impassive and languid expression, looking for the soul beneath. She was longing that his answer should be the one she needed.

"I am hopeless," answered Hilary.

"Of what?"

"Of your love. I understand at last that you have a great purpose in your life, and that I am a mere straw on a stream. I thought I had some claim on you; I see I cannot have. I surrender myself to your will. That is all I have left to do."

Fleta stood meditatively for a moment. Then she looked up very sadly in his face.

"It is not enough," she said. "Your gift must be a positive one."

Then she again turned and went on her way to the house. Here everything was silent and even dark, for the shutters were all closed, and evidently the place was deserted. Fleta opened a side door with a key which was attached to her girdle; they entered and she locked it behind them. She led the way through the quiet dim house to the door of the laboratory; they entered the room in silence. It wore quite a new aspect to Hilary's eyes, and he looked round in wonder. All was pale; there was no incense burning, no lamps were lit; the color had gone from the walls; a faint grey light through a skylight, which had always hitherto been curtained, dimly broke on the darkness of the room which still lurked deeply in the lower part. But Hilary found enough light to see that the thing he so hated was not present; that lay figure which was to him always such a horror was gone.

"Where is it?" he said, after a moment, wondering at the sense of relief with which its absence filled him.

"What?—oh! the figure. Again you ask a question which I am compelled to answer. Well, I cannot use that power at present; I have again to win the right."

"How did you win the right before?" asked Hilary, fixing his eyes on her; a fierce desire to know this possessed him.

Fleta started, turned toward him, and for a moment the proud imperiousness which ordinarily characterized her came over her form and her features. But in another moment it was gone. She stood before him, pale, gentle and sublime.

"I will tell you," she said, in a clear yet very low voice. "I did it by taking your life."

Hilary looked at her in complete perplexity and bewilderment.

"Do you not remember," she said, "that forest, that new earth and sky, all so sweet and strong, that wealth of apricot blossom that came between us and the sky? Ah, Hilary, how fresh and vivid life was then, while we lived and loved and understood not that we did either? Was it not sweet? I loved you. Yes, I loved you—loved you."

Her voice broke and trembled. Hilary's numbed heart suddenly sprang again to life. Never had her voice contained such tones of tenderness and passion before.

"O my Fleta, you love me still—now!"

He sprang toward her, but she seemed to sweep him aside with one majestic action of her bare arm.

"With that passion," she said, with a pale solemnity, "I can never love now. I have not forgotten entirely what such love is—no, Hilary, I have not forgotten—else how should I have found you again among the multitudes of the earth?" She held out her hand to him, and, as he clasped it, he felt it was soft and tender, that the warm life blood of a young creature responded to his touch. "I knew you by your dear eyes, which once were so full of pure love for me that they were like stars in my life."

"What came between us?" asked Hilary.

She looked strangely at him, drew her hand away, folded her cloak round her, and then answered in one word:

"Passion!"

"I remember it now!" cried Hilary in sudden excitement. "My God! I see your beautiful wild face before me, I see your lips as lovely as the soft blossom above us. Fleta, I loved you as men love—I hungered for you—what harm lay in that?"

"None," she answered, standing now motionless and statue-like, wrapped in her long, white cloak, seeming like a lovely ghost rather than a living woman. "None—for men who care only to be men, to reproduce men, to be and to do nothing more than that! But I had another power within me, that seemed stronger than myself—a stirring of a dumb soul within. When that moment came, Hilary, then came the great decision, the fierce struggle between two souls hurled together out of the dimness of life, and finding light in the fever of love—yes, light!—the fire *that is love* makes it possible for men to live. It gives them hope, it animates them, it makes them believe in a future, it enables them to create men to fill that future.

"In those old days beneath those apricot blossoms, you and I, Hilary, were but children on this earth, new to its meaning, knowing nothing of its purpose. How could we guide ourselves? We were ignorant of the great power of sex, we were only at the beginning of its lesson. So it must be with all. They must go through with the lesson, they cannot guess it from the first! Nor could we. I did not know what I did, Hilary, my lover, when I took your life. Had I known, I should only have been like a beast of prey. But I did not know. You asserted your power —you claimed me. I asserted mine—I conquered. I wanted power; and killing you as I did with that one emotion only stirring within me, I got what I longed for. Not at once—not till I had suffered patiently, not till I had struggled hard to understand myself and the force that was at work within me. And this for life after life, incarnation after incarnation. You not only loved me but you were mine—I conquered you and used your life and love for my own ends—to add to my power, to actually create the life and strength I needed. By your life, by your strength, I became a magician, read by my insight the mysteries of alchemy and the buried secrets of power. Yes, Hilary, it is so. To you I owe myself. I have become free from the common burdens of humanity, its passions, its personal desires, its weary repetitions of experiences till their edge grows blunted by long usage. I have seen the Egyptian and the Roman, men of the old superb civilizations, trying to reproduce their past pleasures, their past magnificence to-day, in this modern life. It is useless, life after life full of selfishness and pleasure, ends in the weariness of living that kills men's souls, and darkens their thought. But you and I, Hilary, have escaped from this dismal fate. I would not be content **to live again as I had** lived before, to use the life principle which lies in love, only for pleasure or the bringing of eidolons on to the earth. I determined to rise, to raise myself, to raise you, and out of our love perpetually to create something nobler than we ourselves. I have succeeded, Hilary, I have succeeded. We stand now before the gate of the first initiation. I tried to enter it and failed for want of strength — for want of strength, Hilary! I could not pluck my master's image utterly out of my soul—I looked for him to lean on—at least to find comfort in seeing that face I knew. Give me strength, Hilary! Be my comrade! Help me to enter and your strength shall come back to you a hundredfold. For your reward shall be that you too shall enter with me."

She had changed from moment to moment as she spoke. She looked like an inspired priestess—like a Divine being. Now she stood like a flame with a strange appearance, as if her whole soul and self, spirit and body, rose upward in adoration. The dawn had come; the first rays of the sun shot through the skylight and fell on her transfigured face and gleaming hair.

Hilary looked at her as a worshipper might look at his idol.

"I am yours," he said; "but I know not how to prove it."

She held out her hand to him, and lowered her eyes from the light to which they had been raised until they met his.

"We must discover the great secret, together, Hilary. No longer may you give yourself to me without knowledge. Hitherto our lives have been but the lives of the blossom; now we must be wise and enter the state when the fruit comes. We have to find out what that power is which the sun represents to us; to discover the pure *creative* power. But we have not strength, yet, Hilary;

alas! I dread and fear sometimes. More strength means more sacrifice."

She drew her cloak closer round her, the light faded from her eyes and face, and turning away, she went and sat down on a couch which was back in the shadow. Hilary felt a profound sense of sadness, of sympathy, of sorrow, sweep over his being. He followed her and sat down beside her. One pale hand lay on the couch, outside her cloak. He laid his upon it, and fell deep into thought. Thus they sat, silent, breathing softly, for long hours, till the sun was high. But still, even then, the room was very dim and cool, and full of shadows.

CHAPTER XIII.

ON the next day, the same day rather, for they sat together in the laboratory till long after the sun was high, Hilary, to his own amazement, found that he had an official post in the household of the young Queen which would keep him continually about her. Indeed, he had to pack up instantly on being informed of the fact in order to follow Fleta to her own dominions. How this had been effected none could tell—Hilary, least of all, for he saw immediately on presenting himself in King Otto's presence that he was regarded by him with dislike and distrust. Before, Otto had scarcely noticed him. The present state of things was decidedly a change for the worse. However, Hilary had already perceived very clearly that to serve under Fleta was to serve under a hard master. And he had no longer any kind of choice. Life was inconceivable without her—without the pain caused by her difficult service. He had rather suffer that than enjoy any other kind of pleasure. And, indeed, pleasure apart from Fleta did not appear to him to exist.

And yet he was still capable of doubting her.

Fleta had chosen a companion of royal birth to travel with her; a young duchess who bore the same family name as Fleta herself. This girl had been reared in a nunnery, and then taken to court, where she took part in all the pageants, and immediately found herself surrounded by *suitors.* She was not very pretty, and certainly not at all *clever.* To go with Fleta seemed to her delightful, as it would introduce her to a new court and a fresh series of suitors. It struck Hilary as quite extraordinary that Fleta should choose this child as her companion—not that the Duchess was any younger than Fleta—indeed, they were almost of an age; but Fleta appeared to carry within her beautiful head the wisdom of centuries, while the Duchess was a mere school-girl trained in court etiquette.

These three were to travel together in Fleta's own favorite travelling carriage. She simply refused to travel with her husband. When he addressed her on the subject, she merely replied:

"You would weary me; and, moreover, I have work to do."

And so they started; and as Hilary took his place, he thought of that strange drive when he and Fleta, and Father Amyot, had been the three. Recollecting this made him wonder what had become of Father Amyot; for the priest had not returned to his duties in the city. He asked Fleta, while the thought was in his mind, why Amyot was not with her now. .

"He is of no use to me," she answered, coldly.

The journey was a very long and a very weary one to Hilary; for the Duchess, finding no one else to flirt with, insisted upon flirting with him; while Fleta lay back in he corner of the carriage hour after hour, with her eyes closed. What was the work she had to do? Hilary, who had overheard her answer to the King, wondered very much. And yet, as he watched her intently he saw that her face changed. It grew darker, more inscrutable, more set in purpose.

Late one evening, and when they were, indeed, travelling later than usual, hoping to reach their destination that same night, a curious thing happened. All day long Fleta had been silent, seemingly buried in thought; but sometimes when Hilary was watching her he noticed her lids move as if in speech. He sat opposite her whenever he could; this was not always possible, as the young Duchess would talk to him, and the carriage being very large and roomy, he had to change his position, and go nearer to her in order to carry on a conversation with any comfort. But as it grew dark the Duchess grew tired, and leaned back half asleep, for indeed they had had a long day's journey.

Hilary withdrew himself to the corner opposite Fleta. It grew so dark he could no longer see her; they had a swinging-lamp in the roof of the carriage, but he did not want to light it unless Fleta wished it so; and, indeed, he longed for the quiet and the darkness very much. It made him feel more alone with her, he could try to follow and seize her thoughts then without the perpetual disturbance of the little Duchess's quick eyes on him and her light voice in his ears.

He sat still and thought of Fleta—Fleta herself in her glorious beauty—sitting there opposite him shrouded by the darkness. He could endure it no longer—the man rose up in him and asserted itself—he leaned forward and put his hand upon her. He had scarcely done so when the Duchess uttered a shrill cry.

"My God!" she exclaimed, in a voice of horror, "who is in the carriage with us?"

She flung herself across and knelt upon the floor between Hilary and Fleta; her terror was so great she did not know what she was doing.

Hilary leaned across her and instantly discovered that she was right—that there was another man in the carriage beside himself.

"Oh, kill him! kill him!" cried the little Duchess, in an agony of fear; "he is a thief, a murderer, a robber!"

Hilary rose up and precipitated himself upon this person whom he could not see. A sense of self-defence, of defence of the women with him, seized him as we see it seize the animals. He discovered that this man had risen also. Blindly and furiously he attacked him, and with extraordinary strength. Hilary was young and full of vigor, but slight and not built like an athlete. Now, however, he seemed to be one. He found his adversary to be much larger and stronger than himself.

A fearful struggle followed. The carriage drove on through unseen scenery as fast as possible; Fleta could have stopped it had she thrown the window down and cried out to the postilions. But Fleta remained motionless; she might have fainted, she was so still. The little Duchess simply cowered on the ground beside her, clinging to her motionless figure. This terrified girl had not the presence of mind to think of stopping the carriage, and so obtaining help. She was too horror-struck to do anything. And, indeed, it was horrible, for the swaying, struggling forms sometimes were right upon the two women, sometimes at the other side of the carriage; it was a deadly, horrible, ghastly struggle, all the more horrid for the silence. There were no cries, no exclamations, for indeed, so far as Hilary was concerned, he had no breath to spare for them. There were only gasps and heavy breathings, and the terrible sound that comes from a man's throat when he is fighting for his life. How long this hideous battle lasted none could tell—Hilary had no idea of the passage of time. The savage in him had now come so entirely uppermost and drowned all other consciousness that his one thought was he must kill—kill—kill—and at last it was done. There was a moment when his adversary was below him, when he could use his whole force upon him—and then came a gasp and an unearthly cry—and silence.

Absolute silence for a little while. No one moved, no one stirred. The Duchess was petrified with horror. Hilary had sunk exhausted on the seat of the carriage—

not only exhausted, but bewildered, for a host of other emotions besides savage fury began to rise within him. What—who—was this being he had destroyed? At that moment the horses were urged into a gallop, for they were entering the city gates. Hilary threw down the window next him with a crash. "Lights, lights!" he cried out, "bring lights." The carriage stopped, and there was a crowd immediately at the windows, and the glare of torches fell into the carriage, making it bright as day. The little Duchess was crouched in the corner on the ground in a dead faint. Fleta sat up, strangely white, but calm. Nothing else was to be seen, alive or dead, save Hilary himself; and so horror-struck was he at this discovery that he turned and buried his face in the cushions of the carriage, and he never knew what happened whether he wept, or laughed, or cursed—but some strange sound of his own voice he heard with his ears.

There was a carriage full of servants behind Fleta's carriage; when hers stopped so suddenly they all got out and came quickly to the doors.

"The Duchess has fainted," said Fleta, rising so as to hide Hilary; "the journey has been too long. Is there a house near where she can lie still a little while, and come on later to the palace?"

Immediately offers of help were made, and the servants and those who were glad to help them carried the poor little Duchess away.

"On to the palace!" cried Fleta, and shut the door and drew down the blinds. The postilion started the horses with all speed.

Suddenly the blood in Hilary's body began to surge and burn. Was it Fleta's arms that clung round him? Fleta's lips that printed warm, living kisses on his neck, his face, his hair? He turned and faced her.

"Tell me the truth," he said. "Are you a devil?"

"No," she answered, "I am not. I want to find my way to the pure good that governs life. But there are devils about me, and you have killed one of them to-night. Hush, calm yourself; remember what we are in the eyes of the world. For we are at the palace door, and Otto is standing there to receive us."

She stepped out, the young Queen.

Hilary followed her, stumbling, broken. He said he was ill, to those who spoke to him; and stood staring in wonder at the brilliant sight before him.

CHAPTER XIV.

THE great hall of the palace was illuminated gloriously by huge dragons made of gold, placed high up on the walls; within these strange creatures were powerful lamps, which shed their light not only through the eyes and opened mouths, but from the gleaming claws. The whole place was filled with a blaze of light from them; and the dresses of the household assembled below seemed to Hilary another blaze of light, so gay were they. Yet this was only a domestic reception. It was late, and Otto had refused to allow any more general demonstration to take place that night. But Fleta, when she threw off her travelling cloak and hood, might have been the centre of any pageant. She showed no trace of the weariness of travel, or even of the strange excitement she had passed through. She was pale, but her face was calm and wore its most haughty and unapproachable expression. Her dress of black lace hung about her slender form like clouds. Otto was filled with pride as he noted her superb dignity and beauty; with hatred, as he observed that her eyes never met his own, that she treated him with just the same civility as the steward, or any servant of the establishment. No one could notice this but himself and perhaps Hilary, supposing the latter to be capable of regarding any one but Fleta herself; for she was too much a woman of the world, this mystic, this wild girl, to admit any one even to the most evident of the secrets of her life.

After a few moments passed among the little crowd as-*sembled in the* great hall, Fleta proposed to go to her own rooms for the night, and a stately little procession formed itself at once to conduct her there. But before going she beckoned to Hilary.

"The Duchess must come to me to-night," she said. "I wish her to be in my own room. Send a carriage and servants to fetch her."

How her eyes glittered! Had he ever seen them shine so vividly before?

"Tell me one thing," he said, hoarsely. "I believe you have taken to yourself that creature's life and very body that I killed for you. Is it not true?"

"You are shrewd," she said, with a laugh. "Yes, it is true. My whole being is stronger for his death; I absorbed his vital power the instant you wrenched it from him."

"And he?" said Hilary, with wild eyes.

"Was one of those half-human, half-animal creatures that haunt men to their ill, and which fools call ghosts or demons. I have done him a service in taking his life into my own."

Hilary shuddered violently.

"You doubt me," said Fleta, very quietly. "You still doubt if it is not I who am the devil. Be it so. I am indifferent to your opinion of me, Hilary, you cannot help loving and serving me. We were born under the same star. Now go and give orders about the Duchess."

Under the same star! Those words had not come to his mind for a long while; yet how horribly true they were. For he, Hilary, it was who had actually done this dreadful deed and killed this unseen, unknown, unimaginable creature. Horror made him clutch his hands together as he thought that he had touched this thing, more, had killed it hideously. Might it not have been some good thing striving to baffle Fleta? Ay, yes! he still doubted her. And yet to doubt her so completely made the very earth to sink away from under his feet. He himself, his life, his all, were given to her, be she good or evil! Staggering and overpowered by the terrible thoughts that crushed his wearied brain, Hilary found his way to a supper-table; and too exhausted to think of anything else but recruiting his strength, sat down to drink wine—and to try to eat. This latter seemed impossible, but the wine revived him; and presently he remembered that it was his business to look after the Duchess.

By-and-by she was carried into the palace; she could not yet stand, for she had only come out of one fainting fit to fall into another.

And now came a strange and dreadful scene—one which only a few witnessed, Hilary as it happened being among those few, for he saw the Duchess taken to the suite of rooms Fleta occupied. In the corridor Fleta came out to them, she was still in her travelling-dress, and looked very quiet and even subdued. But at the sight of her the young Duchess screamed as if she saw some awful thing; she would not let Fleta touch her, she absolutely refused to enter her room.

"But you must be with me," said Fleta, in a low voice.

"I will not," answered the Duchess, with a firm resolution which amazed every one who knew her. She rose up and walked unassisted along the corridor and down the great staircase; she met the young king coming up it; he had heard her shrill cries and came to see what was happening.

"What is the matter, little cousin?" he said, seeing her tear-stained and agitated face.

"Fleta wants me to be in her room all night! I would not do it for all the world! She is a devil—she would kill me or make her lover kill me, and then no one would ever *hear of me or* even find my body. No! No!"

And so she ran on, down the wide stairs, leaving Otto *thunderstruck.* He noticed that a number of persons were gathering on the landing and stairs, and so, with a stern and quiet face, he passed through the little throng, making no observation. He went down the corridor and straight into Fleta's room. Here he found her standing silent, dark, like a sombre statue. One other person was in the room—Hilary Estanol. He was in the most extraordinary state of agitation, pouring out words and accusations; some horror appeared to possess and blind him, for he took no notice of the king's entrance. Fleta did, however; she looked up at him and smiled—such a strange, sweet, subtle smile! Seldom, indeed, had Fleta given him a look like this. Otto's heart leaped within him, and he knew himself her slave. For he loved her increasingly with every passing moment; and she had but to turn her face on him softly to make the loving soul in him burn with ardor. But that burning was fiery indeed. He turned upon Hilary and stayed his words by a sudden sharp order:

"Leave the room," he said. "And you had better go and see Doctor Brandener before you go to bed, for you are either in a fever or mad. Go at once."

Hilary was in a condition in which an order given in such a tone took the place of the action of his own brain, and he mechanically obeyed it. This was the best possible thing that could have happened to him; for he was in fact in a high fever, and if he had not, without thinking about it, done as he was told and gone to the resident doctor of the palace, he would probably have wandered raving about all night. As it was he was obliged to drink a strong sleeping draught, and was placed in his bed, where he fell at once into a sleep so profound it seemed like death.

Hilary gone, Fleta closed the door behind him.

"Do not let there be any struggle of will between us to-night," said Fleta, very softly. "I warn you, I am much stronger than I was; I am very much stronger than you are, now. And you found before that you could not even

come near enough to touch me. Let me rest, and that
quietly; I wish to retain my beauty, both for your sake
and my own."

Otto paused a few moments before he made any answer
to this extraordinary speech. Then he spoke with difficulty; and as he did so raised his hand to brush away some
great drops of sweat which had gathered on his forehead.

"I know I am powerless against you to-night, Fleta," he
said. "I cannot even move nearer to you. But be warned;
I intend to probe the mystery of your being. I intend to
conquer you at last. I will do it if I have to visit hell itself
for the magic which shall be stronger than yours."

Fleta threw aside her travelling dress and put on a white
silk wrap her maid had brought to her; she loosed her
hair, and let it fall about her slender figure. The wrap
was made with wide sleeves, that fell away from the shoulder
and left her arms bare. She raised them over her head
and clasped her hands; and as she did so laughed like a
child. How beautiful she looked! The large soft bed
with its silken sheets all bordered with foamings of lace,
and its coverlet of golden embroidery, was close beside her,
She threw herself into it, and the white lids fell heavily
over her eyes, the long black lashes lying like pencil marks
on her cheek. In a moment she was buried in a slumber
more profound than even drugs can produce; for a magician knows how to take the soul away from earth on the
instant, and leave the body without dreams or any uneasiness, free to rest and recover like a babe. And Otto
standing there looking on this lovely sight felt his brain
turn to fire and his heart to ice within him. He loved her
so desperately and yet so hopelessly, this woman who was
at this moment actually his wife. No effort of his will enabled him to approach an inch nearer to her. She was
absolutely protected, perfectly isolated from him. And it
seemed strange indeed that she could rest there like an in-

nocent child while within only a few paces of her stood a man
—and that man her husband—within whom burned all that
fiery passion is, who suffered the fulness of longing and
hunger insatiable. At last—for the dawn was creeping in
at the window as he did so—Otto turned and left the
room, and went softly down the stairway and along more
corridors and down more stairs, till he reached a little doorway which he opened with his own key. It was a side
entrance from the great garden and the park beyond. In
the breathing of the soft, keen, morning air, in the roomy
freshness of the early sky, his maddened spirit seemed to
find some hope of bathing and recovering himself. He
strode away through the park, and climbed a hill which
rose beyond it. From its summit he could see all over the
city, and some extent of the surrounding country. The
sight sobered and strengthened him. He knew himself to
be no petty prince playing at state. True, his was a small
kingdom, and his capital could be seen from end to end
from this hill top. Yet the great Powers of Europe
watched him with interest.

Fleta was out in the morning light not long after him,
dressed in white; she wandered alone through the gardens
and plucked some rich roses to wear at her waist. The
bloom of supreme youth and beauty was on her face when
she came back from among the flowers; she had gathered
dew from the grass, and wetted her soft cheeks and lips
with it. Some dewdrops from a rosebush she had shaken
gleamed in her dark hair, more beautiful than diamonds.
She sent messages of inquiry for the Duchess and Hilary
by the first servants she encountered; and she stood waiting for the answers, leaning against the side of the sunny
window by which she had entered—a brilliant figure that
shone the more brilliantly for the strong light, as a jewel
might. And, indeed, this Fleta was a jewel of the world
—*whether her light be baleful or beneficent, yet a jewel.*

The answers were brought to her presently. The Duchess had been very ill all night, and the doctor was even now with her, and would not allow her to be disturbed. Hilary was still wrapped in the profound slumber which had already lasted many hours.

"Wake him," said the young queen, "and tell him I shall be waiting for him in the magnolia arbor in about an hour."

She wandered out into the garden again, moving to and fro in the sunlight. It was an entirely secluded garden this, which had been highly walled and sheltered by trees, so that here royalty might have sunshine and fresh air in freedom. And all this sheltering, it being a very sunny spot, had made it a perfect golden land of flower. Fleta was deeply happy for the moment here; she became like a child when her mind was quiet, and when the beauty of nature appealed to her senses. She gathered here and there yet another beautiful rose that specially caught her fancy, and fastened it on her dress; so that at last, when it was time to go to the magnolia bower, she looked like a queen of roses, so fantastically was she dressed and decked in them.

The magnolia bower was the great beauty of the palace garden. It stood right opposite to the windows, though at some little distance across a smooth belt of turf. Originally, an arbor had been built, and at the side of it a quoits alley was arranged, filling one half of the wall of the garden. It was all open to the house and lawn, and roofed so that it was protected from rain and wind. Otto's grandfather had built this, and had planted many different kinds of rare trees and creeping plants to grow over it. But the place had in some way suited the magnolias best of all; they had grown so richly that at last they had claimed the whole as their own; and all the winter the roof and pillars of it were beautiful with great green leaves in climbing masses; when the magnolias began to flower, it was lovely beyond belief. And now the arbor and alley were all, by common consent, called the magnolia bower. Fleta had been fascinated by the beauty of this place when she first came out, and had questioned a passing gardener about it. She felt curiously happy and at home within its shelter; and here Hilary found her pacing slowly to and fro. He paused as his eyes fell on her. She seemed to him the realization of all possible beauty. She was younger, fairer, yet stronger in expression than he had ever seen her. And the pure richness of the flowers about her dressed her as no diamonds, no rich gowns, could do. For this strange creature was essentially natural—at home among the flowers or on a mountain-top, strange and haughty among courtiers and in the ordinary life of men and women.

"Sit down here," said Fleta, taking her place on a deep, well-cushioned couch in a shadowy corner. Ah! how still and sweet the air was!

"You are better," she went on, "I can see that. You have slept like one dead, and have found a new life this morning. It is well; it is what I expected; but what might yet not have been. Now, I want to talk to you. Our work is close at hand. By noon I have to be dressed, ready to go to the great Cathedral and be crowned. From that time I shall be in public all day till late in the evening. But I have learned how to live alone in a crowd, and to play a part unknown by any one. And you must do the same. For our work begins to-day. And we have gained the necessary strength for it."

Hilary shuddered, even here in the sunshine and amid the flowers. He knew she referred to that awful scene in the dark yesterday when he had killed——what?

"Fleta," he said, with tolerable quietude, "do you remember what I was saying to you last night when I was told to leave you? Did I not demand an explanation before I did any more work for you?"

"Yes; you did. And that is why I sent for you here that I might explain all that you can understand." She paused just a moment; and then went on speaking rapidly, yet clearly.

"We have spoken of the lives of long ago, when we were together before, Hilary; when we loved, and lost, and parted, only to meet again and love and lose again. Like the flowers that yearly bloom and then die away till another season gives them another life, so once in an æon have we flowered upon this earth, brought forth the supreme blossom which earth can produce, the flower of human love. You do not realize this, Hilary, because you will not claim your knowledge and experience; you are weak, and easily content, lacking in faith, and still filled with love of life. That is why you are my servant. The power I took when first our souls met on this earth you have never wrested from me. I have remained your ruler. Now I urge you to use all the will that is in you and step nearer to my side in knowledge and in power; for I no longer have need of you as a servant. I want a companion. You know that a little while ago I essayed the initiation of the White Brotherhood, that stately order which governs the world and holds the reins of the starry universe in its hands. You know that I failed. I do not regret having had the courage to try; I should have been a coward indeed to draw back when Ivan himself was ready to lead me to the place of trial. But I was a fool to over-value my efforts and my work as I have done. I had served so sore and so long an apprenticeship, had grown so weary, through many lives, of lovers and of children, that I thought all human love, all love that clings to one person in the world, had been forever plucked out by its very roots. I thought it *is gone from* me forever, that, though I would work for humanity, that though I would gladly give all that was in me to any one who desired help or knowledge, yet that I myself could stand alone, leaning on none, looking for none. It seemed to me it was so—that the mystery was solved for me. That the problem of human love, of the life of sex, of the mystic duality of existence, was all set at rest forever. Oh, if that had been so! Then, Hilary, I should have blossomed on earth for the last time; I should have found in myself the fruit, the divine fruit that gives new life, another life, a divine knowledge, an unshaken power. But I failed, I entered among them, Hilary—I saw them. No other woman has seen these strange, austere, glorious beings. But——

"You saw me next. You found me. You know how I was crushed and broken. Before you came to me I had heard words, spoken, as it were, by the stars, echoing in the heavens, that told me my fate, and showed me my work; and bade me be strong to rise up and do it. Afterward I desired to see one of the White Brotherhood and obtain a confirmation of my order. But I could not. And then I understood that I alone was to be judge and compeller of myself."

She rose now and began to pace up and down in front of him. She began to speak more slowly, her eyes fixed upon the ground.

"Sweetheart, wife, mother, these things I can never be again, for the love of any man. I am alone in the world; I can lean on no man, I can love no man any more throughout the ages that I may wander on this earth. That life has gone away from me once and for all. I stand above it. Are you still ready to devote yourself to me, to stand at my side, to be my companion?"

A great sigh burst from Hilary. It seemed to him that he was *bidding* farewell to his dear, dear love, to his one *hope in life,* to all that was fair in woman, to all that he had ever desired or could ever desire. And then he saw before him the shining white face of a priestess. Fleta for the moment was transformed as she gazed upon him. A great light gleamed from her eyes. He saw that a finer thing, one infinitely more desirable and satisfying, must take the place of the fair blossom of love in his heart. All this came to him in an instant; and as the sigh burst from him he uttered a "Yes" that seemed to shake his being. And then on a sudden—on the instant—the white blinding face of the priestess of life had gone from before his eyes, and he saw instead the young, fresh, lovely face of the woman he loved. A groan as of physical anguish passed his lips.

"Fleta, I cannot do it," he said; "I canot resign you."

"You have done it!" she said, and laughed.

It was a strange laugh, not womanly, and yet with a ring of gladness in it.

"You cannot go back from the pledges given by your spirit because your heart protests!" she said. "Your heart will protest a thousand times: it will seem to dissolve your very body with its suffering. Do I not know? I have lived through it; I have died from it. But the pledge once taken, has to be fulfilled. I am satisfied; for I know now that you will work with me."

She walked to and fro a few moments in silence; then came and sat beside him, talking in her first manner, rapidly and clearly.

CHAPTER XV.

"I CANNOT go in alone. I cannot go in for myself. I have to learn the supreme lesson of selflessness. I must take a soul in each hand to the door, ready, purified, prepared for offering on the altar, so that they shall even become members of the Great Brotherhood; while I must be content to turn back and sit on the outer steps. I have thought it out; I understand it; but whether I can live it out, whether I can do it, is another thing—a very different thing. Ah, Hilary, where shall I find those two hearts, those two souls, strong enough to pass the first initiation?"

"When it comes to that doorway," said Hilary, in a strange dull tone of misery, "must these two be ready to go on without you, leaving you outside?"

"Yes," said Fleta. "Certainly yes."

"Then I will not be one of them," he said passionately. "I love you, and I do not want to lose you, even for Heaven itself. I will serve you, if you choose; but I must be with you."

He rose and went away across the lawn, as if he could not endure any more of the conversation; in a moment or two he had disappeared among the trees. Fleta sank back with a weary dejected air; a pallor took the place of the brilliant fairness, which but a moment since had made her face so beautiful. Her eyes, wide open, yet apparently seeing nothing, remained fixed on the grass straight in front of her. She seemed scarcely to breathe. A kind of sad paralysis had fallen on this beautiful vivid form.

"What am I to do?" she exclaimed at last, bringing the

words out by a great effort; "how can I live through the struggle and the suffering? I will live through it. I have invoked the law of pain. Pleasure is no longer mine, even if I desired it."

She was silent for a little while after this, and very quiet. Then she rose and began to walk up and down slowly, evidently in deep thought. Her mind was working rapidly.

"I cannot do it alone," she said at last, desperately. "Who is to help me? I cannot yet even guess who is to be my second companion, the other soul that I am to take to the door of the temple. O mighty Brotherhood, it is no easy task you have set me."

She drooped her head while she was talking thus to herself. When she raised it again, she saw Otto standing on the grass, in the sunlight, watching her. His face was softer than it had been for a long while as he gazed at her. She stretched out her hands to him with the same sweet subtle smile with which she had greeted him before. He immediately approached her.

"I have been thinking," he said, "up there on the mountain, ever since I left you last night. I have been thinking earnestly. Fleta, I do not consider myself pledged to that Brotherhood to which you profess allegiance."

Fleta's look became amazed, and then almost stern.

"How is it possible you can so deceive yourself," she said, "when you have so recently felt the bondage which is placed on the novice?"

"What—in my inability to approach you? You are a magician, I know well; it is quite useless to try and hide that from myself, because I have seen you use your power. Those brothers have taught you some of their unholy *secrets*. No doubt you could make a circle round yourself *now into* which I could not enter. In fact, I believe you *have done* so. But what of that? I have read, I have

thought, a great deal on these subjects. The supernatural
is no more extraordinary than the natural when once one is
used to its existence. That it does not exist, that all nature stops at a given point, could only be maintained by a
blind, foolish materialist. And I am not that. But I am
not awed by the supernatural. I have always been used
to believe in it, having been educated by Catholics. But
your Brotherhood is a very different matter. This claims
to be so positive a thing as to be a force in Nature, a power
which every man has to be with or against at some period
of his development. Is not that what you would say—
what Father Ivan would say?"

"Yes," answered Fleta.

"Well, there I cannot follow. I do not see that the
Brotherhood has any right to set up such a claim."

"It does not set it up," said Fleta. "There is no need
to parade a fact. Wait and see. You will find it is
a fact. I would rather not discuss the matter with you.
It is like talking to a man as to whether the earth is flat
or round."

For a moment a red flush of anger came into Otto's
face; for there was no doubt that this speech was delivered
with an indifference which savored of royal insolence,
and should only be used by a queen to her subjects, not
to her king. But he conquered himself after a moment's
thought.

"After all," he said, "I can just fancy that it may seem
like this to you. It is useless to argue such a point. But
to me the existence of such a Brotherhood is a purely
arbitrary statement. I know that Ivan is extraordinarily
superior to most priests. What makes him so?—Intellect,
I should say, for the first thing."

"No," said Fleta, "it is the White Star on his forehead
which marks him out from among men and makes him
divine. He lives for the world, not for himself; like all

the Brotherhood, he is passionless and desires no pleasure. Otto, I have to win that star. Will you help me?"

"How?"

"A great piece of work has to be done. I have to form a school of philosophy, and turn the thoughts of men toward the subtler truths of life. It is a mark given me, and I need aid. But that aid can only be given me by one who makes no claim on my love, who no longer looks on me as a woman, but as an instrument of the White Brotherhood; who is ready to serve and to suffer without any wages or compensation; one who in fact desires to reach the door of the great Brotherhood."

She spoke quickly, enthusiastically, a great hope in her eyes; for his face had been full of gentleness all this while.

"I came to you," he answered, slowly, "with an offer, a request. I will make it. I am prepared to be your true lover till death, your friend, and even your servant, in all that is human and natural, if you, Fleta, will put aside these unnatural aspirations and be my wife and helpmeet."

It was a manly speech and said well. The tears gathered in Fleta's eyes as she looked at him.

"I have never loved you, Otto," she answered. "Nor ever can as you mean it; yet you can move my being to its depths, and stir my soul. For you are very honest. But you might as well try to change the courses of the stars as alter the shape and pathway of my life. It is written irrevocably; I myself have inscribed it in the book of fate by my steady desire through long past ages. But that I under-rated the difficulty I would now be beyond your knowledge, within the great gateway. But I had no real comprehension of the deep unselfishness needed for that great effort. I see now that I may never live for myself again, not even in the inner soul of love. I have to work—I ask you to help me."

Otto looked at her gloomily.

"I ask for a helpmeet," he said. "And so it seems do you. This is not as it should be between husband and wife. One must give way to the other."

Fleta looked at him and her eyes glittered; she seemed to be measuring her strength. Suddenly she turned away with a sigh. At the moment the Palace clock struck. She remembered that it was time to go in and prepare for the ceremonies of the day. She paused and looked again at Otto. She was looking very pale now, so that the roses seemed more bright by contrast.

"Do you wish me to be crowned your queen?" she said. "Or would you rather it were not done now that you know me better?"

"I have no choice," said Otto, rather bitterly. "You are in fact my queen already. But you have your own conscience to deal with in treating me as you are doing."

"My own conscience!" The words repeated themselves in Fleta's mind, as she went slowly across the grass to the open window, without making any answer to Otto. "Have I what he would call a conscience? Do I reproach myself for misdeeds, or regret past follies? No; for how could I live did I do so? I that have the mystic memory, the memory denied to ordinary men, and can see myself travelling through lives and see how I lived them, and what my deeds were! Otto will suffer. He is not strong enough to claim his memory, he loves the world of healthy human nature, where the inevitable is not recognized and Destiny is a force despised even while it works steadily to its ends. Ah, my poor Otto! 'husband, lover, friend,' would that I could save you the suffering!"

She had reached her own rooms now, and was surrounded at once by maids, who were preparing for her toilette, and by great ladies who were selected as her companions. She was gracious to all alike, but so deeply buried in thought that she scarcely distinguished one from the other, and

spoke as gently to the maid who dressed her hair as to the
court beauty who paid dutiful respects to her. This
seemed to them all very strange, and coupled with the sad
look on Fleta's face, filled them with wonder. Had she
already quarrelled with her husband?—or had she been
married to him against her will?

The ceremony of dressing was made on this occasion
much more formidable than was Fleta's usual toilette; and
she grew pale and weary before the end of it. But she
looked almost unnaturally beautiful when she stood up in
her sweeping robes; there was an expression of such stern
resolution and power upon her delicate features. She
conquered her weariness by an effort of will; and when she
entered the great cathedral and became the chief feature
of the pageant within it, she was once more the brilliant
young queen, dazzling the eyes of those who looked upon
her, and conscious of her great beauty and her royal power.

And yet, within, her heart was dull with sadness.

For the gateway seemed fast closed! The two who loved
her would only love like other men. She could not give
them any gleam or momentary vision of the great love
which does not desire gratification, but which is divine,
and gives itself. Where was she to look for other souls?
Not in this Court, where the men seemed to her more
empty-headed and self-seeking than those she had left behind. Nor could she ever hope to begin her larger work,
to create any school of philosophy here. Was every door
shut to her? It seemed so. And with that conviction
came the strengthened and more profound resolve to
conquer.

CHAPTER XVI.

EVERYTHING was closed, the world was dark to her; there was no turning either to the right or to the left. We have all experienced this; even to young children this bitterness comes, when the darkness falls on their souls. In the grown man it is so great a thing that it blinds him and blackens his life sometimes for years. In one who is treading so dangerous, so difficult a path as was Fleta, it comes as a horror, a shame, a despair. For she had more knowledge, more intelligence, than ordinary human creatures, who have not yet raised their eyes or their hopes beyond the simple joys of earth. She had a knowledge so great that it weighed on her like a terrible load and crushed her very spirit when, as now, she could not tell how to use it.

She knew perfectly what it was she had to do; but in what way was she to do it? She, the supreme, the peerless, the unconquerable one, who rose up again unaided after every disaster, and who could not be held back by any kind of personal difficulty or danger, was now paralyzed. Paralyzed because she had to influence, to guide, to lead, some other human being. Alone she could go no farther; another soul must stand beside her, and yet another. And as yet none were ready! None!

She hardly noticed what passed around her, though she mechanically fulfilled her part; and she gave no thought to the events of the day until she found herself at last in her own room again—once more at peace, once more undisturbed except by those who waited on her. Even these she sent away, and sat still in her chair, alone, yet so full of wild and passionate thoughts that the very air seemed full of their vibration, and to be quivering with life.

The queen was alone. How utterly alone none but herself could tell. One of her maids looked into the room and saw the beautiful young queen sitting there so completely motionless that she supposed she had fallen asleep in the great easy chair, and would not disturb her. Fleta's face was turned aside, and laid on the silken cushions, and it was so still and expressionless that one might fancy it a thing carved in ivory rather than of flesh and blood. For all color had died out of it, and there was no faintest fleeting shadow of changing expression.

Fleta was alone with a terrible reality, a fearful problem, and one which she well knew she must solve, or else die of despair. And this offered her no thought of escape as it does to most, for she knew well that if she died it would only be to live again, and find herself again face to face with this problem.

For all nature follows laws; and as the plants grow, so does man. Life must progress, and none can stay it. And Fleta had entered into the great rush of intelligent and vivid life which lies above the animal existence with which most men are content. No natural triumph, no power of her beauty, no magic of her personal charms, no accomplishment of her brilliant intellect could please or satisfy her any longer, for she had come into a keener consciousness, a knowledge of things undying. And she knew herself to be undying, incapable of death; and that she must suffer and suffer till this terrible point was passed.

It seemed to her impossible to pass it.

She might not ever hope to near the gate she longed to reach, unless she brought with her other souls, souls purified and ready. Her strength, her power must be used to *save them,* not herself,

But there were none who would be saved.

These two men who stood on either side of her, and who through many lives had stood on either side of her, even now, even yet, after so long, they were blinded by their love for her. And as she fully realized this a deep sigh passed all through her frame and made it quiver faintly like a dying thing in pain.

That love! with which she had held them and led them so long—the love of her, which had guided them so near the gate. Was it possible that now they must fall away, and because of that very love! Was it possible?

Suddenly Fleta rose and began to pace the room to and fro impatiently. "Shall I use my power?" she said to herself, half aloud. "Shall I make myself hideous, old, a withered and faded hag? Would that kill this passionate love in them? Would that make me their guide and not a thing which is beautiful, and which each desires for himself? I must think—I must think!"

Moving to and fro in her room she thought silently for a long while. But there was no ray of gladness or light of conscious strength on her face.

"I must try it, I suppose," she said aloud, at last. "I must throw aside my youth and my beauty, and see if they can either of them discover the soul within. But it is a great risk—a terrible risk."

This she said quietly, and as one in deep thought. But suddenly something seemed to touch, and rouse, and sting her, as if a knife had entered her flesh.

"Great Powers!" she exclaimed, in a voice of agony. "What do I see in myself? Risk—risk of what? Of their souls being lost because I am not able to help them. Folly! If they are to be saved, some aid will be given even if it is not mine. Risk!—risk of what? Of my losing their love. There is no longer any disguising it. I have been fooling myself. Hilary! Otto! forgive me, that I should ever have spoken as if I were wiser or more unselfish than you. The mask is torn away. I am deceived no longer. I never dreamed that I must serve or save any but these two who have been to me friends and companions through ages. And this is Fleta, who fancied herself free, able to enter the hall of truth, able to stand before the great masters and learn from them! Is my soul never to be purified? Can my heart never be burnt out? Oh, fire of agony, come and kill this weakness!"

She staggered to her chair, and sat there, staring fixedly at the floor before her with wild eyes.

"How am I to burn these last ashes out of myself? How? And to think of it!—to know, as I see now, that for lifetime after lifetime I have fancied myself a saviour, free in myself, only helping these others! And all this sad while I have but been leaning on their love, clinging to them as any frail thing might. If these did not love I should fancy love was not; if these did not follow and aid me I should fancy the world empty. And love, true love, the love that gives utterly and asks not, is not yet born in me! Well, I am punished—I have punished myself before I knew my fault! The world is not empty, indeed, but I am alone in it. Yes, utterly alone. My master has left me—my friends have left me. I have done wrong to each and all, and they are gone. Can I wonder that this is so? No, for I deserved it—and I deserve it."

Fleta drew a cloak round her that hung on the back of her chair. She drew it over her face and head and her whole form, so that she lay back like a mummy in its wrappings. For hours she sat like this, and quite motionless. Several times persons came into the room and looked at her, but she lay so still, and had so evidently arranged herself in this way, that no one liked to disturb her, thinking she must be asleep. For there was nothing ceremonial at which it was necessary for her to appear; the

king and the queen were to have dined alone quietly. But
when Fleta did not come, the king did not ask for her.
And so the evening passed and the night came.

Then Fleta rose, and hastily putting on a dark robe and
cloak hurried out of the room when there chanced to be
no one to observe her movements. She stole down the
stairs quickly, like a passing shadow, and succeeded in
reaching the garden unseen. The strong fragrance of the
magnolia flowers attracted her, and for a moment she
stood still, seeing in her mind's eye the scenes of that
morning re-enacted. But at last she broke away, and
hurried across the dim lawn, till she reached the boundary
of the garden. Then she passed along swiftly and silently,
keeping by the wall. Her object was evidently to find a
gate, or some way out of the inclosure. It was not to
meditate under trees, or to smell the sweetness of the flowers
that she had come here. It was only that she did not
know how else to get to the city—she had not liked to try
the great front entrance to the palace, for she did not
want to be noticed or followed. At last she came to an
iron gate, high and well spiked. She looked at it for a
moment, and then suddenly sprang on it and climbed it
quickly, passing over it in some swift adroit way that was
rather an effort of will than any skill of body. Just as she
descended, she heard the sentry on his beat approaching
her. Like a serpent she glided away into the shadow of
some opposite trees. But, for all her swiftness the sentry
had seen her. He knew it was a woman, this fleet shadow;
he had a single glimpse of this pallid face, and its wild,
strange expression; and he was afraid to follow. For he
did not think it a creature of flesh and blood like himself.
And yet poor Fleta's heart was beating so hurriedly when
she reached the shade that she had to stand still a little
while to stay it.

But at last she recovered her nerve, and went steadily

onward toward the lights of the city. Either instinct
or some mysterious knowledge seemed to guide her, for
she went direct to the part of the city she wanted—its
worst quarter, where all night long there was a glare of
light and a crying of strange and discordant voices. For
the gypsies were constantly here, in the heart of this city;
nomads though they must be always, yet here they most
frequently returned as to some place resembling home.
And they so inflamed the passions and the love of excitement which was in the people, that round the shanties
and hovels in which they dwelled, an orgy was held perpetually.

Fleta walked on through the narrow and crooked streets
of the poor district, and walked so quickly and steadily
that no one spoke to her or delayed her, though many
paused and looked after her for a long while. She could
not altogether hide her star-like beauty. At last she
reached the place she wanted. Here there was a three-
cornered open space, paved, with a fountain in its centre.
When this part of the city was built, it had been intended
for better purposes than those it served; work people were
the class the houses had been planned for. But the whole
quarter was now taken possession of by the race of ruffians,
thieves, and murderers; a race which lives alone in every
city because none dare be in its midst. This three-cornered
square was its centre, a meeting point of many ways: and
in it was held at night an open market. It should have
had trees around the pathway, and shrubs beside the fountain in its midst, but all traces of such civilization had
long disappeared from it. It was given over to squalor
and dirt. When Fleta entered it the market was just becoming lively. It was a strange mart indeed; at one stall
rags were sold and old cooking vessels; at another jewels
of some considerable value. But anything of beauty which

might be for sale here, was well hidden under the dingy covering squalor which overshadowed the whole.

Fleta walked straight across the square to the fountain. Beside it, at the point which she approached, was placed a rickety, dirty old tent. On the ground inside it was a sort of bed of rags, on which sat an old woman. The tent was but just big enough to shelter her; she sat facing its opening. By her side was a wooden stool, on which she told fortunes with a filthy old pack of cards. A woman was leaning over her now, watching the cards with breathless anxiety as she dealt them out.

Fleta drew quite close and then paused, leaning against the side of the dry fountain, and regarding this sordid scene with her beautiful eyes.

The old woman looked up after a moment. "Ah, it's you?" she said.

"Yes," answered Fleta; and that was all. The old woman told her cards, and pocketed her silver with elaborate care. Then, her customer leaving her and no other appearing for the moment, she looked again at Fleta.

"Want your fortune told?" she said, abruptly. She always spoke with a rough abruptness and many abbreviations; but it is almost impossible to give any adequate idea of her peculiar terseness of style, since she spoke (at all events, to Fleta) the true Romany tongue. To the woman whose fortune she had told she spoke in a rough dialect of the country.

"Yes," said Fleta.

The old woman laughed aloud, a queer, cackling laugh, and then got out a little black pipe and began to fill it. Suddenly she put this aside again, and looked up.

"I begin to feel as if you mean it. That can't be possible."

"Yes," said Fleta, for the third time. And her face

grew whiter every time she spoke. The old witch peered at her out of her small eyes.

"Then it's come to hard times with you, my dear! But you're queen here, aren't you?"

Fleta only nodded.

"Then how do you manage to be in a place like this alone? Oh, well, I know you are clever enough for the devil himself. But what has happened that you come to me?"

"I have lost my footing," said Fleta, very calmly. "I do not know which way to turn; and you must help me to find out."

"I must, must I?" growled the old woman, her unpleasant amiability suddenly turning to a virulent ill-humor. "So you keep your airs? How did you find out I was here?"

Fleta did not answer.

"You're clever enough for that still, are you, my dear? Then why can't you look into to-morrow and next year for yourself?"

Fleta clasped her hands and held her peace.

"I insist upon knowing," said the old woman, with a flare of fury, "or I'll not do your bidding, not even if you fill me with pains from top to toe. I know what you are; I know you'd rack me with torments, as you've done before now, to get knowledge out of me. Go on, do it if you like. I've got a new trick that'll help me bear it. I'll not do a thing for you unless you tell me why you come to me for help. I thought you were now white as a lily, sitting on a throne, talking with angels. What's the reason you're here?"

Such a speech would have made most people smile. But Fleta knew with whom she had to deal, her old companion and instructress, and regarded it very seriously, weighing *her words* as she slowly answered:

"I tried to pass the initiation of the White Star, and I failed. My powers are gone, and I am blind and alone."

The old woman uttered an extraordinary ejaculation, something between an oath and a cry.

"You tried for that, did you? Why, no woman has ever passed it. You deserve to be blind and dumb too, for your insolence."

And then the old wretch burst out laughing, Fleta standing by quietly watching her.

"I know quite well what you're set to do now," the witch said at last. "You're set to save souls, just as I'm set to send them to hell, as we both did in our last lives. Well, you won't find it easy. Nobody wants you now you've started into that business."

"I've found that out already," said Fleta.

"And they *do* want me," cried the witch. "Only think of that, and remember how pretty you are, and how ugly I am! People like their souls lost for them; they hate having them saved. That's the common herd that I'm talking of. But there's somebody wanting to be saved now—somebody wanting help."

Fleta remained standing quite still, her eyes fixed on the old woman.

"Shall I tell you who it is?"

"Tell me the truth, Etrenella; I command it."

After a moment the old woman spoke in a low voice, less harsh than before.

"It is your master Ivan. If you must go saving souls, save his. He needs somebody to help him."

Fleta involuntarily started, and retreated a step; the fixed gaze she had kept on Etrenella relaxed.

"Do you mean this?" she exclaimed, utterly deceived.

Etrenella laughed, and dropped into her original manner.

"You needn't pretend you don't know when I'm telling the truth," she said; "you're not gone back to be a baby,

I'm sure of that. Now look you here, my queen; I can give you something much better than your throne, or your king, or your kingdom, or anything else on this earth for you; I can make Ivan love you more dearly than the White Star itself; he's half way to it already, and does but want a touch. I can do it if you give me the word—ah! I see your face, my white queen; I see your hands trembling—so that's why you failed, is it?"

And this terrible Etrenella took up her little black pipe and proceeded to fill and light it; while Fleta leaned against the fountain sick and faint, as if unto death, with the tide of emotions which rushed over her. It was the greatest temptation she had ever met.

After one shrewd, cruel glance at this quivering figure Etrenella went on speaking.

"You needn't hesitate. You've got crimes enough on your conscience. I can see them in the very air round you. What was that you made Hilary Estanol kill for you, you vampire? You made him commit murder, and you know it. The thing was nearly human!"

"You sent it!" cried Fleta, suddenly finding strength to speak.

"Yes, I did. And why not? I'd heard you were married, and I sent to hear about you. It was quick and clever of you to kill him and take his life for yourself. You'd be in a fever now if you hadn't done it, and very near death. That little Duchess will die after awhile; you scared her so that she can't get over it. And how about Hilary Estanol? Isn't his soul very near lost through this beauty of yours? And so you can't have your laboratory now? Ah!"

"Speak to me as you should speak," cried Fleta, recovering herself and quickly taking the command again. "Tell me where to look for my master."

"*I can't tell you that*," said Etrenella. "You've got to

get much more hungry than you are yet before you find him; so much I know. And I'll tell you this, for it's quite plain, and you might read it yourself; everything will crumble away from you—not only your friends, but your throne and your kingdom. You will be just as much neglected as if you were as ugly as the old father of devils. My trade's a better one. Come, now, isn't it so?"

Fleta turned and walked straight away without once pausing or looking back or hesitating. It was evident she did not look upon Etrenella as a person toward whom it was necessary to use politeness. When Etrenella saw that she was really going, she half rose off her rags and flung a screech after her.

"You'll have to go to hell's door to find him, I can tell you that!"

Fleta walked on, seemingly unmoved. But the words repeated themselves again and again in her ears, and seemed to echo along the streets. The whole city appeared to Fleta to be full of her own woe—there was none else, and nothing else in it—or, indeed, in the world.

CHAPTER XVII.

ON the very morrow—or, rather, indeed, on the same day, for the dawn came as Fleta walked through the city—Etrenella's predictions began to be fulfilled. Fleta had entered the palace safely, though how this had been accomplished she could not even recollect. And at an hour when she was usually out among the flowers, she lay on her bed in a stupor of exhaustion and despair. A message came that the King particularly wished to see her. It sounded so urgent a message that Fleta thought it best not to deny herself to him, weary though she was. She rose, put on a loose white lace robe, and went into a little sitting-room that looked on the garden, to wait his coming. The singing of the birds worried her, and she retreated from the window—to which she had gone from habit—to the back of the room. She was standing there when Otto entered, and he paused a moment, startled by her appearance. The morning freshness, which no midnight labor had ever taken from her face before, was not on it now; she was as white as the dress she wore, and with her black hair falling unbound upon her shoulders, she looked like a spectre rather than a living woman.

"You are ill, frightfully ill!" exclaimed Otto.

Fleta deliberately walked to a mirror, and looked into it. And then she smiled—such a bitter smile.

The thought in her heart was this: "I am fading already—the human mechanism goes always the same weary old round, and he will very soon tire of me now. It is over."

And with this dull sadness in her heart she turned away

without any answer, and sat down on a couch in the dimmest corner of the room. The appearance of this action was as of indifference which actually amounted to insolence. Otto was a little nettled by it, and said no more, for the moment, as to Fleta's illness.

"I intruded on you," he said, stiffly, "merely because it was my business to do so. Last night war was declared between two great Powers. My position and that of my kingdom is simply that of a gnat between one's forefinger and thumb; the allied powers are so strong, and so situated, that I must be crushed. Of course, I must fight it out, though the end is a foregone one, and inevitable. But you must not stay here. You must go at once. I cannot guarantee your safety after another twenty-four hours are passed. And I owe that much to your father. Go, now, and get ready and leave this place. Do not delay an hour or a minute. You have been my queen for a day—no doubt that has been long enough for you."

"Quite long enough," answered Fleta, quietly; "and yet the fall of the curtain seems a little hurried. I knew your position, of course; but I thought you expected to save it, and hoped for my assistance in so doing. That, in fact, it was still a matter of diplomacy."

"So it was till last night," answered Otto. "I had no idea that any such sudden action was meditated. I had intended that we should both visit London and St. Petersburg within the next two months, and I fully admit that I expected great help from you in dealing with these powers. But everything has been taken out of my hands and it has all been finished without my knowledge."

He walked to the window, and then, standing with his back to her, said, in a tone of deep feeling:

"Is it any of your cursed witchcraft, Fleta? Did you stir these men in their dreams, so that they should combine to crush me?"

162   THE BLOSSOM AND THE FRUIT.

For a moment Fleta seemed about to answer fiercely; but she controlled herself by an effort, and then said, in a very low voice:

"As your queen I am loyal to you."

There was something extraordinarily impressive in the way she said this. It convinced Otto instantly. He turned on her with a sudden swift flash of interest and vivacity in his face. It was the first gleam through the cloud that had been on him all the time he had been with her.

"Will you show yourself to the army before you go?" he exclaimed. "It would make all the difference. The men have no heart in them."

"Not!" cried Fleta, rising instantly. A spot of color was on each cheek, her eyes glittered.

"When shall I come?" she said.

"Now," answered Otto, responding to her spirit. "On the great plain outside the city they are holding parade. Will you come?"

"One moment!" cried Fleta.

She swept past him, and shut the door of her own room. No one was there, and quite alone she made her toilette. This was so much the better, for it made her task easier. For three minutes she stood perfectly motionless inside the shut door. Her face was as set as that of a statue; every line was marked and rigid, and her eyes were like the eyes of a tiger. Her fierce will, roused into action, passed through all her frame and powers, and called out all the latent vigor in them. And so she worked a miracle, as many a clever conjuror does. It seemed like a conjuring trick to herself, when, the three minutes over, she advanced to the mirror, and saw her face all alight with life, her cheeks flushed, her eyes vivid and sparkling, and youth returned more dewy than before. She hastily coiled up *her hair*, and fastened it by jewelled pins; she passed her hand over her face, with the same sort of result that women produce with crême, and rouge, and powder, and half-an-hour's labor—the whole sparkling effect was blended, softened, made more beautiful. She threw aside her white robe, and hurriedly found in a wardrobe a dress of cloth of gold, over which she drew a long cloak all of white and gold, and lined with crimson.

Then she went to the door, opened it, and said, "I am ready."

"My God!" exclaimed Otto, "you are indeed a witch. You are well, you are brilliant, you are twenty times more beautiful than ever. O Fleta! listen to me. I will never leave your side, I will serve you like a slave if you will only let me love you."

"Love *me!*" exclaimed Fleta, with the most burning scorn. "No—don't deceive yourself. You only love my beauty—a thing of the moment only. If instead of making myself beautiful I chose to make another woman so, you would transfer your love to her. Come, take me to your soldiers. They, at least, are honest. They like a woman while she is young and pretty, and weary her with their love; and when she is old, they let her cook for them and carry the loads like an ass. You kings are the same, only you have not the courage to say so. Come—I am ready—lead the way."

Her manner was so imperious, Otto had no choice but to obey without further words.

And now came the one brief hour in which Fleta ever felt herself a queen; for yesterday's pageant had not touched her. As she moved among the soldiers it was like a torch carried along that lit fire wherever it went.

Seeing the young queen in her triumphant beauty among them the men rose to the wildest enthusiasm.

Now and again, when it was possible, she spoke a few words to the men round her, who stood devouring her with their eyes and listening as though her voice was heaven-sent. The old General who rode by her carriage looked twenty years younger when he saw his men's faces all aflame.

"I wish your Majesty would go into the field of action with us," he exclaimed, suddenly.

"So do I," answered Otto, from the other side.

"Well, I will," said Fleta, quietly.

"What do you mean?" exclaimed Otto, in a different tone. He had no idea of her taking his words seriously, he had simply expressed the enthusiasm which the sight of her influence excited in him.

"Tell the men, General," said Fleta, "that I am going to the battle-field with them. I shall return to the palace at once and make my preparations. It is of no use for either of you to remonstrate now my mind is made up. I am going."

She ordered her coachman to turn back to the palace, and to drive quickly; so that no one had time to consider or to hesitate. She was gone; but not her influence. And when it spread about among the men that she was going with them, the excitement was something extraordinary.

The first move was to send a large detachment to the frontier, where there was a great plain on which the army was to camp. Here it was anticipated that the first blows would be struck. The King and the General both went with this party of the army; and now Fleta was to go too. Everybody envied these lucky men, who were pretty certain to lose their lives, but would nevertheless be smiled on by the young queen; so wild are the sentiments of war when once roused. They were all awake in Fleta herself. She found a fierce relaxation in this excitement which had entered her veins and made her blood grow warm again; it was a reprieve, a rest from the terrible anxieties *of her life*, and it seemed to her as if it had perhaps just come in time to prevent the strain under which she was suffering from driving her mad. As the thought came into her mind she paused in what she was doing at the moment and raised her hands to her head. "It is possible," she said to herself, "it might have been a lifetime wasted in a mad-house. This war-fever has come as a rest; I will not let myself think while it lasts—I will take the passion and live in it." And so, with fresh vigor, she hurried the maids who were packing and arranging for her. The hour of starting from the city had not given her very long to get ready in; but she was more than punctual—she was in her place some minutes before she was expected. She stood up in her carriage to bow in answer to the enthusiastic greeting she received. By the side of the carriage rode a servant leading a very spirited young horse. It was Fleta's favorite, the one she had ridden to and fro from her garden house at home into the city; it had been brought with her to her new home. She had given orders that it was to accompany her now. Otto inquired why she had brought it; but she made no answer. The march was not a long one; it only lasted a day and a half. Fleta's carriage was closed when they started on the next morning; no one had seen her since they had departed for the night, not even Otto. Nor did any one see her till the midday halt was called, when she stepped out of her carriage, wearing a riding-habit of very soft, fine crimson cloth. Her non-appearance had somewhat dulled the spirits of the men; but now that they saw her, and dressed in this way, moving about among then, it was just as if the sun had suddenly burst out in the heavens, so the old General told her; and he begged her not to shut herself up again at once.

"I am not going to," cried Fleta, who seemed to be in her gayest and most gracious humor. "I am going to ride the rest of the way."

What a march that was, that afternoon! None of the men who survived the night could ever forget it; they talked of it afterward more than of anything else. The slender figure in its crimson dress, riding so gayly between the King and the General, was a kind of loadstone to which all eyes were drawn. It was extraordinary to observe the swift subtle influence which Fleta exercised. Her presence inspired the whole troop, and the feeling everywhere was that of courage and success.

Late in the day, when the twilight began to fall, Fleta fell into a dim reverie. She was not thinking of anything in particular, her mind appeared to be veiled and asleep. She forgot to turn her face from one side to the other as she had done during the afternoon, firing the men with the light from her brilliant eyes. Her gaze was fixed before her, but unseeingly, and she simply rode on without thought. As it grew darker she became aware that something was happening around her; but so buried was she in the abyss of thought or imagination she had entered that she did not pause nor did she give her attention in any way. Possibly, she could not, for her eyes were as set and strange as those of a sleep-walker. She rode rapidly on through the gathering darkness, and at last her horse grew uncontrollably terrified and darted away at a tremendous pace. Fleta kept her seat, swaying lightly with the movements of the maddened horse, over whom she no longer attempted any guidance; indeed she let the reins fall from her hands, and simply grasped a handful of the long flying mane in order to steady herself.

A wild cry reached her ear at last, and roused her partly from the abstraction in which she was plunged. A wild cry, in a familiar voice, and yet one that was unrecognizable from the terror that filled it. "Fleta! Fleta!" came to her on the wind. At the same moment her horse reared, *stumbled* and fell backward. He gave a shriek of agony

as he did so that almost stunned Fleta's senses, it was so
terrible. He was dead in another moment, for he had been
shot, and mercifully the shot was immediately fatal. Fleta
rose to her feet, and looking round her discovered the
most extraordinary scene. She was right under the
enemy's fire, and near her were only a few dying men and
horses, who had been shot down in their attempt to fly in
the direction in which she had been riding. There was a
blurred moon, half hidden by clouds, but enough light
was given by it for Fleta to see very plainly that her own
soldiers were flying from the scene in every direction; and
also that the ground was cumbered with dead bodies,
further back. She stood perfectly still, gazing round her
in a kind of frozen horror; and she was still a target, for
the shot fell all about her. But she seemed to bear a
charmed life; and she stood unmoved. A horse, urged to
its wildest pace, was approaching her with thundering
hoofs; and the cry rang out again: "Fleta! Fleta!" Then
in another moment the horse was at her side, stopped suddenly, and stood panting and trembling. Some one leaned
down toward her. "Make haste, spring up behind me,"
cried a hoarse voice, thick with fear for her. She stared
at the face. How long had she known those eyes? Had
they not spoken love to her through ages? And yet they
were strange to her now, for she had indeed forgotten the
very existence of this man who loved her so dearly.

"You, Hilary?" she exclaimed.

"Spring up," he exclaimed. "Don't you see you are
being shot at? Make haste!"

She obeyed him, without any further words, and in another moment the great horse he rode was tearing away
with them through the gloomy night.

When they were in moderate safety, Hilary slackened
speed, for he knew that unless he was merciful to the horse
now it would fail them later on.

CHAPTER XVIII.

THE dawn broke in the sky at last, to Hilary's great relief; for he had had no easy task to guide the horse while it was dark. Now they could ride on quietly, and his greatest anxiety for the moment was allayed. In the strange stillness of the first few moments of the light he turned in his saddle and looked at Fleta. She returned his gaze very quietly, but she seemed preoccupied and absorbed in some hidden thoughts of her own. "Safe!" said Hilary, aloud. He alone knew the torturing anxiety he had suffered about her, the frenzy of despair he endured when he saw her standing coolly beneath the fire of the enemy.

"Oh, you of little faith," said Fleta, with a smile.

"You might have been shot!" he answered, with a quiver in his voice. "Your courage is indomitable, I know; but it is madness to stand as a target, not courage."

"I have some work to do yet," answered Fleta. "I am in no danger of death. You have buried all the knowledge you have ever acquired beneath so deep a crust, Hilary, that you cannot even find a little faith to work with."

She spoke in a tone of cool contempt, undisguised. It nettled Hilary, whose irritable nature had suffered severely from the terrible anxiety he had been through.

"The shot has been hard at work on your men, the men you led on to their destruction, Fleta; and you don't even think of the poor wretches, apparently. I think you are *utterly heartless.*"

"The men *I* led on?" exclaimed Fleta, in unfeigned amazement. "I wonder what you can mean?"

"Why, you know well enough. They would have turned and run away long before if you had not always kept ahead, for it was perfectly plain that nothing but destruction could come of going on. But the men would have followed you anywhere—they followed you to their death."

"Merciful Powers!" exclaimed Fleta, "and I let myself go a thousand miles from that battle-field—I know absolutely nothing of what went on through the evening and night, Hilary, till you found me—absolutely nothing. Those deaths are on my soul, I know it—I do not try to evade it. But only through thoughtlessness. I was away on what was to me the first and chief work I had to do—I was out of my body the whole time. And that body, that mere animal, that physical presentment of me led these unfortunate men to death. What demon was it that held the reins of my horse? It was not I—no, I was far away. If I had stayed, we should have won the battle."

Hilary was sobered and subdued by the extraordinary tone of excitement and the deep seriousness with which she spoke.

"Is that true?" he said. "Had you the power to win that battle?"

"No," answered Fleta, "for you see I have failed. I thought of one soul that I love, and forgot the many to whom I was indifferent. This is a fearful sin, Hilary, on the path I am treading. I must suffer for it. I failed for want of strength. I should have had patience till the battle was over."

"But," said Hilary, "perhaps we had to lose that battle."

"There was the national destiny to reckon with, I know," answered Fleta, "but I was strong enough, at one time to-day, to reckon with that. For you know very well,

Hilary, that a being who has won power at such cost as I have can control the forces which rule the masses of men."

Hilary made no answer, but fell into a profound fit of thought.

"We must get to a town, and to a station, as soon as possible," said Fleta, presently. "We have a long way to go."

"Where are we going?" inquired Hilary. "I did not know we had any goal but to reach a place of safety."

"Safety!" said Fleta, impatiently.

"Well, where are we going, then?" said Hilary, repeating his question with an air as if he were determined no longer to express surprise or even anxiety.

"To England," replied Fleta.

"England!" Hilary could not help repeating the word, this time with great surprise. "And why?"

"We have to do some work in England. At least, I have."

"It is my place to take care of you," said Hilary, in a rather strained voice, as if he were endeavoring to control himself under great emotion. Fleta noticed it in spite of the fact that her thoughts were even now elsewhere—very far away from the country road they were traversing.

"Why do you speak so strangely?" she asked.

"Do I speak strangely?" said Hilary. "Well, I have been through a good deal to-night. I have seen you right under fire—that was enough by itself. But I was never on a battle-field before, and it is no light thing to see, for the first time, hundreds of men shot down." A faint sigh from Fleta interrupted him here, but he went on, apparently with an effort. "I have seen more—I saw some one with whom I had been very much associated shot, and die in agony."

Fleta leaned forward and looked into Hilary's face, putting *her* hand on his shoulder, and compelled him to turn toward her. To Hilary it seemed as if her eyes penetrated his brain, and read all that was in it.

"I know," she said at last, very quietly, yet with a vein of anguish in her voice that cut Hilary to the heart with grief for her grief. She let her hand drop from his shoulder, and took her eyes from his face.

"I know," she said. "You need not tell me. 'Everything will crumble away from you, your friends, your king and your kingdom.' It has come, and come quickly. You spoke well, Etrenella. Otto is dead. And his death is at my door. My destiny sweeps on so fiercely that men die when their lives touch mine. It is horrible. 'Your friends,' too, she said. I think I have no friend, Hilary, unless I reckon you as the only one. I hardly know, for I think love in you drowns all friendship. Well, you will leave me, at all events, and that soon. And Otto is dead!"

She relapsed into thought or some mood of feeling which was so profound Hilary could not determine to address her; it required some courage to do so when she wore the severe and terrible look that was on her face now. What did it mean? Was it grief? Hilary had no idea. She was close to him, and he felt her form touch him with every movement of the horse. And yet she was as far removed as a star in the sky. She was an enigma to him, unreadable. That her words were unintelligible did not trouble him; he often found it impossible to follow her as she talked. But he resented this heavy veil which fell between them, and left him a whole world away from her, so far that he knew she was unconscious even of his physical neighborhood. Could he ever make her feel him? Could he ever make her love him? This heart-breaking question seemed to come upon him as one quite new, and also as one unanswerable. He forgot how long he had been striving to win her love—he only knew that now, this moment, his need of it had become a thousand-fold intensified. He succumbed to the pain with which he became conscious that his love was a hopeless one—for how could he make this star, this creature so far removed from any ordinary forms of life, how could he make her give him any part of her heart? And so they went on, each buried in sad thought, and removed from each other by a wide gulf. For Fleta's soul was set on one great thought, one all-absorbing aim; it rose up and obscured all else, even the memories of the horrors of the night, just as it had obscured them when they were actually happening.

And that thought was of the star of her life, the other soul toward which all her existence was set. Ah, unhappy child of the lofty star! Why is it that your human nature must drag you back to the dark place of feeling where the great light is invisible and only another soul, any individual life, can shine to you with any powerful brilliance? Fleta felt herself tottering—knew her soul to be standing on the brink of a terrible abyss. But one thoughtless step, and she would find herself loving as other women love—adoring, concentrating all thought on the object of adoration, and so limiting the horizon of her life to the span of that other's soul and intellect. Suddenly a quiver passed through Fleta's form which shook her like an aspen. "Is it true what Etrenella said?" she was asking herself. "Do I already love him? Is the fate on me, not merely a thing possible to happen? And was he, too, that great one, on the verge of this abyss, so that he needed but one touch? Is it possible to fall from such a height?" This she thought of with a deep shame, sadness, and humility. For though her own heart was being torn by a fierce human longing, yet she knew well what standard of unselfishness was required of the members of the White Brotherhood; and she felt Ivan's possible failure to be a thing inconceivably greater than her own, so much greater that the *idea awed and* shamed her even in the midst of her longing. The idea of Ivan was a religious one to her; the thought of his failure was to her as the thought of sacrilege. So that she got not one gleam of joy from the thought that possibly he might have learned to love her. Not one gleam—strange though it may sound, when she had reached a state of feeling in which his image filled all space and stood alone. For she understood, in her sad heart, that to love her would be to him despair and pain, while to her it would mean endless remorse, should she be the instrument to drag him from his high estate. Such was her folly—so deep the delusion she was plunged in! A deep sigh escaped her, so deep that it made Hilary turn to look at her face; but no answering look came to him, and he turned away again. Thus they went on till they reached the neighborhood of a small town.

"We can take the train from here," said Hilary. "But I do not see how to get into the town while you wear that dress. I don't know whether we are safe here or not. Can you think of any other way to get some different dress?"

He stopped the horse, and Fleta sprang to the ground. She discovered, now that she was roused, how tired she was.

"I must have some breakfast before I even try to think," she answered; "let us go to the nearest house and beg food first of all."

She set off on foot without waiting for any answer. Hilary followed her, leading the tired horse. For some distance she hurried on, with quick steps, then stopped by a gate in a thicket hedge. The house was invisible. Hilary had no idea there was one there. But Fleta used finer senses than those which men usually employ; she had followed her instinct, as we say when we speak disparagingly of the animals, creatures still possessed of actual knowledge, because their development has not yet brought them within the light of intellect, which, like a powerful lamp, makes darkness deeper beyond the reach of its rays.

Fleta opened the gate and entered, not staying to think, but obeying her instinct; she walked up a narrow pathway thickly bordered by flowers which shone and glittered with the morning dew. This path seemed to end in nothing but a thicket of trees. Yes under these trees, when she reached them, lay a widening way which turned suddenly aside; and the entrance to a tiny cottage was marked by two grand yew trees. Fleta stopped suddenly, clasped her hands together, and it seemed as if she breathed either a prayer or a thanksgiving. Hilary had reached her side by now, having fastened his horse at the gateway and hastened after her. He was puzzled that she did not advance, and asked her why she paused.

"My fate," she said, "is for the moment blended with the fate of the noble one I go to. I have only just understood this; and I understand also that this can only continue while I think and feel without any dark shadow of selfishness in my thoughts and feelings."

"What makes you say this now?" asked Hilary, controlling a certain impatience that rose within him at what seemed to him complete irrelevance. But he now knew enough of Fleta to feel that if he could see and hear as she saw and heard she would never seem irrelevant.

"What makes me say it? A very simple thing. I have committed a great crime in this murderous thoughtlessness of mine; a crime which must be punished sooner or later by Nature's immutable laws. Is it likely then that of my own fate I should encounter, in the moment of need, with a servant of the White Brotherhood? No; it is the fate of that other whose servant I am. That you may never again be so ignorant I tell you this—that yew trees mark the entrance to the home of every one in the world who is pledged to the service of the silver star. And why? —because the yew tree has extraordinary power and prop- *erties.* Come, let us go in."

They went on, Fleta leading the way. The cottage door stood wide open. Within was the most simple and primitive interior of the country. The cot evidently consisted of but two rooms, one behind the other; in the farther one all domestic work was done. In the larger, the one into which the front door opened, the resident slept, and lived, and dined, and studied. This last was an unusual characteristic of peasants, and therefore one unusual feature appeared in the room—a small shelf of books, the volumes being very old. No one was in the house; two glances were sufficient for the search of the rooms. Fleta, after these two glances, went straight to a corner cupboard and opened it. Before Hilary had quite recovered from his surprise at this she had half laid the table, putting first on it a white cloth and then producing cheese and bread and milk, and a jar of honey.

"Come," she said. "This is food freely given us. Let us eat."

Without staying to question her assurance, as he might have done had he been less hungry, Hilary sat down and assisted with a great sense of comfort in this impromptu meal.

They had appeased the first pangs of hunger when a shadow suddenly darkened the doorway.

"It is you!" cried Fleta, in a tone of the greatest amazement.

Hilary, who was sitting with his back to the door, started and turned round. He recognized immediately, in spite of the present dress he wore, the monk, Father Amyot.

CHAPTER XIX.

"YES," said Father Amyot. "Are you surprised to see me?"

"I am, indeed," replied Fleta, slowly.

"Then you are losing knowledge fast. Can you have forgotten that there are duties to perform at the death of even a blind slave of the Great Brotherhood, much more so of one who actually has taken an elementary vow?"

Fleta looked at him as he spoke with the same puzzled air she had worn since his entrance. Then suddenly she cried out, "Ah, you mean Otto!" and suddenly, leaning her head on her hands, burst into a passion of tears.

Hilary felt numbed, as if some blow had struck him dumb. He had never seen Fleta weep like this—he had never conceived it possible she could do so. He had come to regard her self-reliance and immovable composure as essential and invariable parts of her character. And now, at the mention of her dead husband's name, she broke down like a child, and wept as a woman of the people might weep when reminded of her widowhood.

But it was only a fierce, passionate storm, that passed as quickly as it came. With a quick movement Fleta rose from her bowed attitude, and started to her feet. Amyot's eyes, a great severity in them, had been fixed on her all the while. He now held out his hands, both filled with *flowering* herbs, a vast bunch of them.

"Who is to do this?" he asked. "You know what it *is.*"

Fleta looked at the delicate little flowers and shuddered.

"Yes, I know what it is," she answered, in a voice of pain. "I shall do it. That work is mine. I have power and strength left me to do this difficult work. I will recall my knowledge."

She advanced toward him, and, with a fierce, proud gesture, she took the herbs into her own hands. Father Amyot surrendered them, without any further word. Then he crossed the narrow floor and stood in front of Hilary.

"Your mother," he said, "is ill, very ill; and her sufferings are greatly increased because of her anxiety about you. It is your business to go to her."

Hilary did not reply, but turned his head and looked at Fleta. Amyot answered the gesture. "She is my charge," he said.

Thoughts came with an unwelcome swiftness into Hilary's mind. Father Amyot would not only be as devoted an attendant upon Fleta, but one far more fitted; and he had, moreover, mysterious powers at command which Hilary lacked. He knew all this in a second of thought. And then came the wild outcry of his heart, "I will not leave her!" and the desperate pang of knowing it to be the wrench from Fleta which made his duty impossible. More than once had he left her in anger and vowed never to return to her; yet he found himself always at her feet again, helpless, hungry, unable to live without her voice and her presence. Poor human soul that lives on love and passion, and mingles the two so that one cannot be told from the other. But this it is, this mixture of the beast and the god, the animal and the divine, which is humanity. A hard place to live through truly; but once we were as innocent as the gentle brutes, and later we shall be pure as our own divinity. But the blur has to be *lived through* and learned from, as the child has to go through youth to manhood, and in that space of youth learn the powers and arts which make manhood admirable.

And Hilary was learning this fierce lesson at its hardest point. For the facet of the many-sided soul of man which is turned most nearly on his earth-life is that of desire. Sex is its most ready provocative; and so the world goes on without pause, the creation of forms being the easiest task for man. Then come the hundred-eyed shapes of desire, filling the soul with hunger of all sorts; making even the tender mother's love into passion because it asks return and knows not how to give generously unless it is repaid by love for love.

Hilary did not answer Amyot, or ask any further question. He accepted the truth of his news and the reasonableness of his command without doubt. For Amyot had been the example of a saintly life and a holy character in the city which was Hilary's birthplace ever since he could remember.

He did not hesitate about obedience. He rose from his chair ready to depart, and to yield Fleta up to the monk's guardianship. But he did not know how to go without one word, or look, or touch, from the woman he worshipped —yes, worshipped, in spite of the fierce efforts he had himself made to tear himself from her. He knew now, as he stood for a long minute gazing at her, that he had been held high in hope and delight at the idea of being the companion of her flight, of shielding her, so far as he could, from the dangers of her path, even though the object which she pursued actually separated them and destroyed all sympathy. He advanced a step nearer to her.

"Good-by," he said in a choked voice; "you don't need me now."

Fleta turned and looked at him, and a sudden deep *softness* passed into her face and added deeply to her **beauty.**

"You know that I need you always," she said quietly, yet with a ring of sadness in her voice that seemed to touch Hilary to the very soul. "I have told you so; you do know it, Hilary. Because duty separates us for a while do not look at me like this, as if you were leaving me forever. That can never be, Hilary, unless you forcibly separate your destiny from mine. We were born under the same star. Willingly we had entered on the same fate. Try to look afar and recognize the great laws which govern us, the vast area of life in which we have to move, and then you will not suffer like this for a mere sorrow of the moment. It is like a child with whom the grief for a broken toy becomes so great that it seems to blot out all the possibilities of his future life. So with you, Hilary; you let your passion and longing of the passing moment blot out the giant way you have to tread. Do not be so delayed."

She spoke this little sermon-like reproof with so much gentleness and tenderness, that it robbed it of that appearance, and Hilary, who had often resented her words before, did not resent them now. The tender look within her beautiful eyes touched him in some obscure place of feeling, which until now, she had never reached. A deep sadness seemed to suddenly come upon him like a wave; for the first time a dim sense reached him of the fact that it was not Fleta who refused him her love, but fate, inexorable, and without appeal, which forbade it to him. It was not Fleta's to give—and yet her soul melted toward him. He saw it in her eyes, he heard it in her voice. What was this tenderness? He could not tell; but he knew it was not the love he desired, and a fierce grief, a devouring sadness, took possession of his heart—never again to be dislodged, though it might be, perhaps, forgotten in the absorption of work. It was the first yielding of himself to the fates, the first giving up of all hope of joy which *was possible to* him in ordinary life.

With a heavy sigh he passed out of the cottage without any word of farewell. Then he stood for a moment outside, stupefied at his own barbarism. "Because it hurts me to say good-by, I leave her without a word, like a savage!" He flung himself back to the doorway.

"May you have peace, my queen," he said. Fleta looked up from the flowers in her hands. He saw that starry tears stood shining in her eyes. She only smiled, but the smile was so sweet that it was enough. Hilary hurried away, not pausing another moment lest his courage should forsake him.

Amyot followed him.

"Can you walk," he asked, "or are you worn out?"

"Not as far as walking is concerned," answered Hilary. "It will be the best thing for me."

"Then leave us the horse. He is spent now, but will recover with a day's rest. There is a cart here in which I can harness him, and so carry the queen. It will be better so, for we must keep in the country and go a long way before we can take any other kind of conveyance. But you have only to walk into the next village, where you will find a diligence starts which will take you on your way home."

"Tell me which way to turn," said Hilary, as he stood at the gate. Amyot gave him directions, and then, just as Hilary was starting, caught his shoulder in a strong grip.

"My son," he said, "I have tried to teach you religion. I want to teach you that there is something beyond all religions, the divine power which creates them, the divine power of man himself. It is in you, it is strong and powerful, else you could not be loved as you are. Grasp it, make it part of your consciousness. You must suffer, I *know*; but try to forget that. Growth in itself is sometimes scarcely distinguishable from pain. Go, my son, and face the duties of your life. And remember, when you are in need of knowledge, that your one-time director is known to you now as the humble servant of great masters; come to me if you want help."

"And how," inquired Hilary, who was outside the gate, but pausing to listen to the priest, "am I to find you?"

Amyot drew a ring from his finger. A single stone of a deep yellow color was set in a gold circlet.

"Never use it for any other purpose," he said, "but if you really need me, look intently into that stone. Goodby."

He went back up the narrow pathway to the cottage; and Hilary started on his walk.

Fleta stood between the yew trees of the doorway.

"I am ready," she said, with an abstracted air, as he approached, looking at her inquiringly.

"I will leave you now," he answered. "You know your work better than I do; I must attend to the horse and to other matters. At sundown we will start. I shall accompany you; it has been made my business to watch you through this test. Are you still entirely confident in your own knowledge?"

"Entirely," answered Fleta.

"I shall go with you," he repeated. "I know a straight way which will enable us to reach the spot we want when the moon has risen."

Fleta retired into the cottage and closed and fastened the door. She would be alone here now for some hours. But she had plenty to do which would occupy her; and she commenced at once upon her task.

It would have puzzled any one who could have observed her now, that she seemed to be completely at home in the cottage. She opened certain well-concealed cupboards and put her hand unhesitatingly upon vessels or other things she might need, even though these were hidden in the dark recesses.

But there was nothing extraordinary in this, after all, for these cottages which have yew trees at the porch are all built after a certain fashion and adapted for certain purposes; once having been shown the uses of such a place one is the same as another. And Fleta had several times been in these obscure sanctuaries and knew well their contents. She passed on into the room beyond, and here by a few touches effected an extraordinary transformation. The little kitchen, which had the appearance of the very simplest peasant's kitchen possible, was altered by a certain re-arrangement of its furniture, a putting away of certain vessels and bringing forth of others, into a primitive holy of holies containing a plain altar. Over this altar a strangely-shaped copper vessel hung above a vase of burning spirit. And in this copper vessel a liquid of dark color boiled and threw up a white scum. Fleta had obtained this liquid out of various great glass jars, securely stoppered and hidden in a secret cupboard. She had taken different quantities from the several jars, deciding these quantities with no hesitation. Only sometimes pausing with her hand to her forehead, before commencing some new part of the business she had in hand, as though anxiously testing her memory.

When the liquid had thrown up a quantity of scum which Fleta had carefully taken from it, and had become almost clear, she began to throw in the herbs, which Father Amyot had gathered. These she had sorted and arranged in various heaps upon the altar; and now she gathered one here and one there from the heaps, seemingly taking each one up with a definite purpose. As she threw each small and delicate flower or leaf into the seething liquid, she became more and more enrapt, and her face grew unlike *its natural* self. Gradually her movements between the *different* bunches took a dancing or rhythmic character, *and she* began to sing in a very low, almost inaudible voice. The rapidity of her movements increased, and they also became more complicated, so that at last the dance had acquired a perfectly marked character. When the last of the herbs was cast in, she whirled away from the altar, and plunged at once into the most fantastic and elaborate figures. Her consciousness seemed altogether gone, or so one would have fancied from the death-like expressionlessness of her face; but yet her eyes were kept always fixed on the deep recess of the chimney, where now a great volume of gray smoke was ascending from the vessel.

Suddenly she stopped and became quite motionless, standing in the front of the altar. To her eyes there was a shape now visible amid the gray smoke.

CHAPTER XX.

STANDING there in silence and alone, Fleta waited the complete working of the spell. Its fruition needed a deep and profound quiet following upon the vibration of the air which she had artfully produced.

The whole of the little room seemed full of a gray smoke now. And then the shape her eyes perceived stood close in front of her.

"It is thou?" she demanded.

"At your bidding I am here," answered a voice, which seemed to come from a long distance. "But it is torment. Why do you stop my effort to enter bliss?"

"Come nearer," was the answer, spoken in so positive a tone that no demur from the command seemed possible. Nor was there any. In another moment the shape which had seemed but a darker cloud of smoke became definite, and Otto, the dead King, stood before her, dressed as he had been for battle, and with his face covered with blood from a wound in his head.

"Let me go," he said angrily; "you bring me back to the pains of death. I want rest and pleasure. There is a pleasant place which I had nearly reached—let me return there. Why torment me?"

"I torment you," replied Fleta, in an even voice, "because I have to keep you from that place of pleasure where the spirits of the dead waste ages in enjoyment. This is not for you, who have taken the first vow of the White Brotherhood. Unceasing effort is now the law of your *being*," she added, assuming in her great illusion and fierce pride a power and knowledge which were beyond her. "You are no longer of those who pass from earth to Heaven. You have entered on the great calling—consciously you work for the world, consciously you have to learn and grow. I would be willing to warn you only, that in Heaven every cup of pleasure would be to you poison, and let you choose. But I cannot do that. I am no longer your wife, nor even to you one you love, or a friend; at this moment we stand in our true relation; you a neophyte of the Great Order, bound only by its earliest vow, yet bound inexorably; I, a neophyte also, but having passed all early initiations and standing at the very door of supreme knowledge. To you I am as a master. And I am, in fact, an absolute master at this moment, for it is the whole Brotherhood which speaks in my voice. I command you to take no rest in any paradise or state of peace, but to go unflinchingly on upon your path of noble effort; enter at once again upon earth life, and set yourself in humility and with unflinching courage to learn the lesson that earth life teaches. Go, soul of the dead, and become once more the soul of the living, entering on your new life with the resolution that during it you will take the next vow of the neophyte."

She had raised her left hand in a gesture of command as she spoke the latter part of her speech. The gesture was a peculiar one, and full of an extraordinary unconscious pride almost Satanic in its strength. The shade drew back before it and made no further protest. Some overpowering spell seemed to hold his will in check. As her last words were uttered, the form became merged in the gray smoke. Fleta flung up both hands, and waved them above her head. The cloud cleared away from her, and slowly the smoke began to disappear altogether from the room. Fleta threw herself upon the ground with an air of complete exhaustion, and lay there, as still as though she too were one of the dead. The time passed on, and all the little house remained still and silent. The quiet was intense. At last Fleta sighed; a sigh of great weariness and sadness. She moved a little, and presently raised herself, with some difficulty as it seemed. But she did it, and then, standing up, looked round the room. She was faint and dizzy, and her great beauty had paled and grown dim. But she sustained herself by resolute will for the tasks which lay before her. They were heavy ones, as she well knew, and she had not recovered herself in any measure from the ordeal of the past night; but this only intensified her resolution.

It was dusk now, and she could but just see to rearrange the little room so that it should again present its ordinary appearance. The full day had gone in the effort she had made. She set about removing all traces of it, and when this was done, she went through the front room, opened the door of the house and passed out into the air. This seemed to be a great relief to her. She stood for awhile beneath the yew trees breathing the soft air of the twilight as if it gave her life. While she stood thus Father Amyot came up the pathway. He gave her a keen searching glance.

"You are ready to go?" he said.

"Yes," she answered; "I am ready to go."

She turned back into the house and stood hesitating a moment on the threshold.

"Shall I wear this dress?" she asked doubtfully, looking down at her scarlet habit.

"No," he answered; "I have a peasant's dress for you. It is outside, in the cart which is ready to take us. I will fetch it for you, and you had better lay aside that dress at once. Indeed, I think, if you will give it me I will bury *it so that it shall be safely concealed.*"

When all this was done, Amyot led the way to the gate

where the horse Hilary had ridden stood harnessed to a small peasant's cart. Some of the horses which had run riderless from the battle-field were taken care of and used by the peasants, so Amyot hoped that using this horse would not attract any attention. The animal usually used in the cart was a small mule, and he was anxious to do what they had to do more quickly than they could if they drove this.

They got into the cart and drove off, retracing the steps that Fleta had come on the previous night. To any passer-by they would at the first glance wear all the appearance of two ordinary peasants; and yet only the dullest could have avoided a second glance at the strange faces; Father Amyot's so skeleton-like, so spiritual in expression Fleta's so beautiful, and so full of the marks of absorbing thought.

It was not until quite late at night that they reached the battle-field. The moon was at its full, and shone in a clear pale sky, lighting up the ghastly scene with terrible vividness. Father Amyot fastened the horse to a tree when they had come to the spot he wished to reach; and then they set out on foot, searching among the dead.

Presently Amyot, looking up, saw that Fleta was walking steadily on in a definite direction; he immediately gave up his general search, and followed her.

Her steps did not falter at all, and Father Amyot had to walk very rapidly in order to reach her side. When he was close beside her he looked into her face, and saw there the abstract expression common, as a rule, only to sleep-walkers. He appeared at once quite satisfied, dropped his eyes to the ground, and simply walked as she walked. He was roused after some half hour, or perhaps a little less, by Fleta's stopping quite suddenly. She passed her hand *over her face* and heaved a deep sigh.

"Well," she said, "I have found him."

She looked down as she spoke on to a confused mass of human bodies which lay at her feet. In a heap, easily distinguishable at a glance, was the young king's figure; it looked heroic and superb as it lay there, the arms spread wide, the face upturned to the sky, and on the face was an expression which had never been on it during life, one of profound peace, of complete contentment.

Fleta dropped on her knees and looked at the face for a long moment, but still, only a moment. Then she quickly arose, and turned to Amyot.

"Now," she said, "what is to be done? Must we carry him into the woods?"

"No need for it," said Amyot. "This spot is the loneliest in the world just now. No one will visit this battlefield at night. There is a place there, see, where the shrubs grow thickly."

"Be it so," said Fleta. "But we must make a circle to keep away the phantoms and ghouls."

"You can do that quickly enough," answered Amyot. "I will carry him there first."

Fleta stood back. She would very willingly have helped in the task, but she knew that Amyot, who looked so worn that most persons imagined him to be very frail, was in reality a perfect Hercules. He had undertaken physical labors and achieved heroic efforts, which only a man of iron frame could have lived through. Fleta knew this well, and therefore gave her sole attention to her own special part of the task they had in hand. Having watched Amyot separate the body of the young king from those of the soldiers and officers it lay among, she moved away to the shrubbed space Amyot had pointed out. Here there lay no bodies of horses or men; partly, perhaps, because it was somewhat raised above the surrounding ground, and partly, also, because of the shrubs. She stood for a short time in the centre of the spot; remained there almost motionless until Amyot, carrying his heavy burden, was close beside her. "Lay it there," she said, pointing to a piece of rough ground where there were scarcely any shrubs, and which was almost in the centre of the shrubby space. Amyot laid the young king down, gently enough, but letting the weight of the body crush beneath it the few plants which were in its way. Fleta came near and bent over the prostrate figure. She did not close the eyes, which with most persons is the first instinctive action. She left them open, staring strangely at the moonlit sky. But she raised his hands and clasped them together on his breast. As she did so she noticed the signet-ring on his finger. She looked at it for a moment, and then drew it off and placed it on her own finger above her wedding-ring.

"I was your queen for a day only," she said, "but never your wife. Still this is mine. You had no other queen; and alas, poor Otto, I think had no other love. Poor Otto, to love such a woman as I am, who has no heart to give you back!"

She fell on her knees by the side of the figure, and buried her face in her hands. Scarcely a moment had passed before Amyot touched her on the shoulder. She looked up and saw him standing, tall and gaunt, more like a spectre than a man, at her side.

What was that strange look on his face? Was it horror or disgust at this fearful magical rite in which she was engaged.

"Beware," he said, "this is no time for emotion. I speak knowingly, for could I kill out the feelings of my soul I should not be the slave I am. You run a thousand-fold risk in yielding to them now, when you have but just defied the demons that throng this battle-field. Rise up and be yourself and keep them back; else you may be overpowered, yes, even you, a chosen child of the White Star."

Why did he speak these words with such ironic emphasis? She could not stay to conjecture; her chosen work lay before her.

Fleta rose without a word, and without any hesitation. Her face changed; the softer lines gave place to strong ones; a fierce vigor shone from her eyes, which but a moment before had held tears in them.

She looked round her with a haughty glance, as a princess might look on a rough mob which threatened to close in upon her; yet to the ordinary sight there was nothing visible in the flooding moonlight but the motionless forms of the dead men and horses who lay intermingled in so ghastly a manner. Fleta smiled a little as she turned from side to side.

"Stand you here, father," she said, "keep watch on this spot."

She went slowly from him, moving very easily; yet it was evident after a little while that she was guiding her steps so as to form a figure. It was a complex figure, and Amyot, watching her, though he knew well what it was her movements shaped, wondered at the ease with which she did it. In fact, she had forgotten her body; the magic figure was written in her mind, and her footsteps followed the lines which lay before her inner sight.

As she moved, she sang, in a sort of monotone, some words which Amyot could not hear, close though he was to her; and every now and then flung out her arms with an imperious gesture. At last, when she had moved all round, and returned to the place from which she had begun to move, she drew the signet ring from her finger, and described some shape in the air before her with it.

"Are you willing for the torment?" she asked. She *kept her* eyes fixed on the ring, and whence she drew her answer, Amyot could not tell; but evidently she was satisfied, for a moment later she said, "Be it so."

Then she stepped to Amyot's side, and drawing a jewelled box which hung by a chain from her waist, into her hands, she opened it and took out a primitive flint and steel. Amyot stood like a statue, apparently absorbed in thought or in prayer, while she struck a light and set the shrubs and dying ferns on fire. At first, no flame came, and it seemed as though no fire could be kindled in the green wood; and Fleta, starting up, spoke some fierce words as she struck a light afresh. Then the flame rose, and leaped from side to side; and in a few minutes there was a great blaze. Fleta stood with her hands over it, seeming to draw it hither and thither, and always leading it toward the body of the young king. And as the tongue of flame touched him and licked his face, a strange thing happened. It seemed as though the fiery contact had galvanized the body, for it half rose, and a strange groan broke the deadly silence. But this was all. The head and shoulders fell back into a lake of fire, and silence followed, save for the noise made by the fire itself. The two living forms stood perfectly still watching the horrid sight, till Fleta at last moved, turned toward Amyot, and said, "We may go now."

She led the way quickly from the fiery ground; but suddenly stopped as she reached the line of the figure she had made.

"What am I to do?" she said, wildly. "I cannot go on! I am not strong enough to meet these devils! See Otto himself stands here waiting to kill me."

"Otto himself?" repeated Amyot, in a voice of amazement.

"No, no," said Fleta, hurriedly. "Not Otto, but that animal part of himself which has become separated. Now I have to deal with it. Ah, but it wears his very shape and face—Amyot, it is awful."

"*You* a coward!" said Amyot in a tone of disdain and disbelief.

"But do not hurry me on!" exclaimed Fleta. "I must have time to think, to know how to meet this. Do you not see that this fiend has power to dog my steps?"

"You must go on," said Amyot, "unless you would die a miserable death. The fire is close on us. Have you power to check it?"

Fleta looked back and uttered one word in an accent of despair.

"No," she said.

"Neither have I," said Amyot. "I am willing to stay with you and die, if there is no other course for you."

"Oh, it would be so much the easiest," said Fleta, "but I cannot. How is it possible? My life is not my own. Ivan needs me. No, I must go on. But how can I quell this monster, this animal which stands here? Am I to be killed by a ghoul if I escape the fire?"

As she spoke the fire leaped up and caught her cloak, and rushed upon her right arm. She sprang forward and flung herself into a great pool of blood, which quenched the fire, while Amyot, snatching his cloak from his shoulders, threw it upon her, and pressed out the sparks.

Rise up," he said, hoarsely. "Come on, now that you have decided. The fire is spreading quickly."

"It will not go far," said Fleta, in a strange, feeble voice; "there is too much blood." But she rose up as she spoke. What a figure was this standing there in the moonlight? Even Amyot, whose eyes were always turned inward, looked wonderingly at her. In the white light her beauty was more extraordinary than ever it had seemed in a brilliantly-lit room. Her face was perfectly white, and her eyes shone like blazing stars. She held out, to gaze at it, the cruelly burned arm, all stained most horribly **with blood.**

"I cannot restore that," she said, with a strange smile.

"It is the mark of the deed you have done," said Amyot. "Perhaps that disfigurement may gain you admission when next you try to enter the Great Order."

Fleta made no reply, but turned and walked rapidly away, Amyot following her quickly and silently.

CHAPTER XXI.

IT was broad daylight when they had again reached the gateway of the cottage. Amyot had not been able to drive rapidly, for the movement of the rough cart was not easy, and he was afraid of Fleta's being too weak to bear it. She fainted several times during the journey, and at last fell into a deep swoon, from which she could not be awakened. Father Amyot lifted her from the cart when at last they had reached their temporary shelter, and carried her in his arms up the path and between the yew trees. He placed her very gently on some rugs upon the ground, and put a cushion beneath her head. Then hastily he took the horse and cart into the rough shed which served for stables, gave the horse a feed, and then hurried back to the house. He applied no restoratives to Fleta, as another person would have done. He knelt down beside her, after an earnest look at her face, and took her hands in his. Almost immediately he rose again, with an abrupt, heavy sigh.

"She will be very ill," he said aloud. "I wonder if she is to live? It seems hardly possible now. But what is to be, is to be."

He went into the inner room and opened one of the hidden cupboards, from which Fleta had taken her materials for the rite which she had gone through there. Slowly, and with much thought, Amyot took out certain phials, from each of which he dropped a few drops into a curious square glass. When the mixture was made a very faint smoke and a scarcely perceptible perfume rose from it. He held it in his hand and looked at it, as if in doubt, for some minutes.

"Dare I give it her?" he said, speaking aloud to himself. He had acquired this habit in his monastic life in the city, where he dwelled in a far more isolated manner than he did when in the remote monasteries, or indeed under any other circumstances.

"Dare I give it her? Is it my province to decide whether she is to live and face this terrible fate she has brought on herself? I cannot do it. This is a decision she alone may make. May she make it rightly!"

He poured the precious drops from the glass upon the ashes of the hearth. A bright light, almost a flame, vividly blue, leaped up for an instant and was gone. Amyot replaced the glass, closed the door of its keeping-place, and went slowly back to where Fleta lay.

Certainly she appeared now like one dead. No faintest tinge of color was on her face or lips, no faintest sign of breathing showed. He put his hand on her pulse. It was still.

"She alone must decide," he said, in a low tone, in a voice of intense pain. It was as if he found himself compelled to face the fact that she might choose to die, and as if that thought were agony.

"And yet," he said, suddenly, "why should I doubt that she will live? She, who is always ready for action and never stays for rest or for pleasure? Of course she will wish to live—fool that I am! Why do I not help her?"

And after turning to look at the white, statuesque face, he moved quickly again into the farther room, evidently with the intention of once more mixing the medicine which he had flung on the ashes.

But before he had time to move more than a step or two across the floor he heard a sound at the doorway of the cottage. He paused and looked back. A figure stood there—tall, wrapped in a long travelling cloak, and with a wide hat on, which almost concealed the face. But Amyot recognized the outline of the form, and immediately made a profound obeisance.

"I have already mixed the potion once and then threw it away, thinking it too great a task for me to take upon me, to deal with her for life or death. Yet now I have thought that she is certainly determined to live, and I was about to mix it again and give it her. Shall I do so, Ivan?"

"No," was the answer, "not now. Come, and we will watch beside her. She has enemies we may save her from."

Ivan put off his hat and cloak, and showed himself in a plain monk's dress. His face wore marks of sternness and profound thought, which were not on it when Hilary saw him at the monastery in the forest. They were new, too, since Amyot had seen him last.

"You are tired, my master," said Amyot. "Let me get you food."

"Not now," repeated Ivan. "We must guard her. I have come a great distance in order to be by her side."

All through the long morning they sat beside Fleta's body, with gaze fixed intently on her, without moving, without speaking. Probably neither of them was conscious of time, whether it passed quickly or slowly. It was just noon when Ivan moved. He rose suddenly and yet very quietly, and touched Amyot. Together they went slowly out through the sheltered doorway into the sunshine.

"She will live," said Ivan. "I know that now. Do not you?"

"Yes," said Amyot. "But I have never doubted it since I thought seriously for a moment. At first I was blinded by my distress."

"Let us break our fast out here in the air," said Ivan.

"We commenced our watch at nine this morning, we will begin it at nine to-night. Before midnight her soul must have passed on, or returned."

He began to walk to and fro up and down the pathway to the cottage. Amyot seemed to take the post of servitor as a matter of course. He accomplished his tasks with the same austere earnestness with which he undertook anything he had to do. Nothing trivial seemed to be any trouble to him, or subject for thought or discussion. While he moved to and fro his soul appeared to be as remote and as buried in ecstasy as when he lay on the altar steps of the city cathedral. In a very short time a table stood on the grass and a white cloth was spread on it; and coffee and bread and fruits were placed ready. A passer-by who might have looked into the cottage garden would only have seen two poor monks, and would have guessed that they were being hospitably entertained by the cottager. The meal did not take long; neither spoke, for it seemed as if each had too much thought within his mind to have much time to spare for expressing any of it. And yet, perhaps, this silence was only a return to monastic habits, which came naturally when these two found themselves sitting at table together. For they had been reared side by side; and when Amyot called Ivan "my master," it sounded very beautifully from his lips. It had in it all the profound reverence due to a superior; but the expressive "mine" added an affectionateness which could only be shown from an elder to a younger man.

All through the long bright day Fleta lay like a corpse, just as Amyot had first placed her. She was never left alone for more than a few minutes; either Ivan or Amyot came and sat beside her. At last the evening came. At nine o'clock the two took their places one on each side of her. It was a strange vigil, for all was so perfectly still and silent that it seemed only like watching beside the dead; and yet there was a purpose in it which religious watchers beside the dead know not of. Whether Fleta had lived or died this watch would have been observed. When the body has only just loosed hold of the spirit it is in these hours that danger is at hand.

Until eleven o'clock there was no sound or movement; the group might have been cut in marble. But then Ivan stirred slightly, and placed one hand on Amyot's arm. The priest looked up quickly, and was about to speak; but instantly his gaze became rivetted and he gazed in silence.

Behind Fleta's head hung a deep, dark shadow, which from moment to moment seemed more clearly to take some form upon it. There were different figures shaping themselves out of its vague substance. At last three outlines were clearly seen. Fleta herself, pale, gray, ghost-like; and beside her, Otto—strong, dark, powerful. Amyot started when he recognized the other face; it was Hilary's. He stood there, dark, and strong as Otto; and Fleta's pale shape rose like a dim flame between them, wavering a little to and fro, as if from want of strength.

"Why is she so weak?" asked Amyot, in a piteous whisper.

"Do you not know?" said Ivan. "Because this is her shade, her animal soul. She is compelled to rouse that stronger than ever into life in order to speak to these two so that they will understand. For they live unconsciously in the world of shades, while she lives in it knowingly."

At this moment the form of Fleta became suddenly stronger and more clear; and Amyot heard her voice quite clearly, yet with a peculiar remoteness and distance about the sound. The words came slowly, too, as if she were not sure of her strength.

"I summoned you," she said, "I summoned you both *that* you should speak to me face to face before we go on into a new chapter of life. Can you remember, you two, that long ago, when first you loved me as men love on earth? When first this soul, this human life, awoke to consciousness? Do you remember, beneath those wild apricot trees, how passion and desire and selfish purposes over-mastered us each and all? Yes, even I; for in me the animal soul was even then tempered by the growing power of the divine spirit in me, yet selfishness, a love of myself before all created things, prompted me when I killed the man who first desired to win my love for himself. I have expiated that sin; and by its force I won the power by which I work now. The chains that unite us were forged then in those old savage days; they unite us even now. But now they must change and alter, or be broken forever. I have suffered long ages through you both; suffered until this very hour. But now I have a right to be free. I have a right to be free, not from you, because your companionship is precious to me, but from your love, your human love, which kills and destroys the divine life in you and fetters it in me. Otto, you know that in my last effort for you I called upon myself the anger of this animal soul which now represents you here and assumes your shape; I drove it from you and left you free to pass on purified into other lives. Is this thing to follow me through my life and madden me by memories of your cruel love? Otto, from your place of quiet I call you; come, kill this thing and free me! Let me remember you as one who had gentleness for me, not that devouring thing which men call love."

A profound silence followed this speech, and the two who watched saw the figure of Otto waver and grow fainter. At last it flung itself on Fleta, as if to catch her in an embrace; but the movement was only like that of a flickering flame, and as Fleta stood motionless, gazing intently on the quivering form, an unutterably sad and terrible cry sounded on the air, and the thing had vanished. Ivan drew a long, deep breath as of intense relief. Fleta stood as statue-like in her shadow form as in that unconscious body which lay upon the floor, until Hilary approached nearer and touched her.

She immediately turned to him, and again her voice was audible, now with a sweet tone in it which had not been there before, and a strangely mournful tone also.

"Hilary!" she said, "listen to me. I ask of you, as I have asked of Otto, death in your present shape. I have been asking it of you all this lifetime, since I have known you as Hilary. Do you not know that your love is a burden to me, and that it scorches your own spirit, and makes it blind and helpless? Free yourself from it, Hilary! Know me for what I am, no longer a woman to be loved, as of old, but a disciple of the light—one who is striving to pass on to a larger life. It is time you came and stood beside me; you are ready for it, but for this blind passion which still makes your eyes dim. Come, Hilary, let this savage self of yours die, and pass back into the nature from which it rose. You have used it, learned from it, experienced it to the full. You lie asleep now, in your bed at home; I see your body much more clearly than this shade which stands before me. Be as courageous as Otto, who has conquered. His spirit is in a place of quiet, till the swift moment comes when he will wake to a new life of work, unhampered by that shade just now destroyed. Your spirit stands back and lets the shade be king. Come to me in your divine self and be my friend and companion; do this now, and banish forever this shade with hungering eyes. Then, when you wake in the dawn, the disorder of your mind and the fever of your soul will have passed away. You will love me no less, Hilary; but it will be a love that will help instead of paralyzing you. We have *used the blossom*, Hilary; it has come to its full flower;

its petals are ready to fall. It is time now to see the fruit! Come, Hilary, I must pass on! Come with me——"

The shadows changed and melted suddenly away. In their place came new and confused forms, which by degrees shaped themselves into a room. Then Amyot saw that the figure of Hilary Estanol lay in it, locked in sleep. But suddenly Hilary started from that sleep, and Amyot heard his voice as if from an immense distance cry out, "Fleta, did you call me? I am coming—I am coming!"

And Hilary sprang from his bed and hastily began to dress.

"She has failed," said Ivan, mournfully. "Poor child, she must carry her burden yet farther." The darkness closed in round them; the lights and shadows all had died away.

A faint fluttering sigh reminded them of the dead Fleta, who lay so helplessly. Was life returning to her? Ivan rose and struck a light, and bearing a taper in his hand, came and stooped over her. Yes, she was stirring a little; a faint flickering of her eyelids ended suddenly in their opening wide, and her glorious eyes looked straight into Ivan's. The vacant dim glance changed instantly into one of rapt adoration and deep delight. Stooping over her he could hear the faint whisper that came from her white lips.

"Ivan! Ivan! You will help me!"

He rose, gave the light into Amyot's hand, and passed out through the porch into the darkness of the night. Here, he stood still, in the cool air, deeply thinking. . . . This is why she failed just now with Hilary! This is why she must have failed in her initiation! Not pride, nor self-consciousness, not anything a mask would hide, but simply because she leaned on him because she looked on him as a god. Proud soul, how bitter must her failure have been! The fearless, resolute heart, to face the awful White Brotherhood before the time! What could he do? Her suffering must yet be bitter; for she spoke truth when she said that with her the time for the blossom-life of pleasure is over. It is the hour for the divine fruit to shape itself. And neither nature nor super-nature can be stayed by any adept's hand, nor any spirit's prayer or command.

His head bowed, his thoughts deeply at work, he went away in the darkness and wandered far into the forest. And Fleta, the frail, broken, worn-out body of Fleta, lay, after that first moment of joy, in such pain and weakness that delirium soon came and blotted out all knowledge and all thought.

CHAPTER XXII.

FLETA awoke to consciousness again to find herself lying on the cottage floor; her head had slipped from the pillow placed for it, and was upon the flags. Probably the extreme discomfort of her position had helped to rouse her. She tried to lift herself, but found she was too weak. With great difficulty she raised her head to the cushion. Then she looked round the room in a dim wonder. Brilliant sunshine came in through the small window and the half-open door. The air that reached her was soft and pleasant. In a feeble contentment she looked at the sunlight playing on the floor. A profound, child-like happiness filled her soul. She desired nothing, knew nothing, thought of nothing. But the brain refused to remain inactive; the first stir of its machinery brought to her recollection the horrors of the battle-field—dim, confused, unintelligible, but horrible. She cried aloud in a strange, shrill voice—at first incoherently, making no definite sound. Then she called Amyot's name over and over again. But there was no answer; no one came; she was alone. She ceased to cry out, and shut her eyes from sheer weakness.

But memory proved too strong for her. The recollection of the last awful episode came back to her mind, and instantly she opened her eyes to learn the truth. Had it all been a nightmare—that fire, that blood? No; it had all been real, for her right arm lay beside her, scorched, maimed, blasted, hideous to look on; and the stain of blood was on it and on her dress. This last fact seemed to fill her with horror more than anything else; staring with fixed eyes at the blood, she tried to raise herself. It was a long time before she could succeed, and when at last she was on her feet it was only to totter to a chair and sink down again. The change of position at first brought the fierce overwhelming consciousness of weakness, and nothing more. But afterward it seemed to restore her more to herself; in a few moments she had begun to realize her position.

She sat there on a straight wooden cottage chair, against the wall; her figure was half in the sunshine and half in the shade. Who would have recognized in this broken, wan-faced, maimed woman the splendid young queen?—she who had been so royal in the consciousness of her own inner power.

She looked down at her disfigured arm.

"This could not have happened had I not failed in my trial," she murmured.

"Ah! Fleta, poor soul," she murmured, a moment later; "how sick and weak thou art! Have you lost the secret of power, of youth, of immortality? Is it gone? Is all gone because of that failure?"

She sat more upright, and seemed as if summoning her own strength; the fierce determination on her face took from it all softness, all delicacy. No one had ever seen her look like this, even in her most resolute moments. It was the face of a soul struggling for life, of a strangled thing striving for breath. Then, quickly, the look altered; softened and grew stronger, both. She raised herself from her chair and stood upright, as if vigor had begun to return to her body. And so it was. She moved across the room, slowly, but resolutely, and without wavering. She went into the inner room and approached the secret cupboard. And now she herself proceeded to mix that draught which Amyot had prepared for her and cast away after it *was ready*. She had no hesitation or doubt; she drank it after a long look into it, and some words murmured faintly under her breath.

Courage, fire, vitality came to her from that draught. She stood still, letting the blood surge up and color her cheeks and fire her brain.

"I am alive again," she said to herself; "now I must act. I must accomplish the purification."

She looked about her for her peasant's cloak, and presently found it thrown upon a chair in the outer room. It was unstained, and when put on covered the disorder of her dress. She drew it about her as well as she could, not yet being used to have but one arm and hand. There was a hood attached to it, and this she drew over her head. As she did so something fell out and fluttered to the floor; a paper, folded. She stooped to pick it up, and opened it. There was nothing inscribed on it but a star; no writing of any sort. Fleta trembled a little as she looked at it.

"They watch me, then!" she said to herself; "the awful brotherhood watch me. Who has been here? Who has left this? It was not Amyot, for he does not know the sign that burns in its midst. The White Brotherhood! Cold abstractions, men no longer!" She began to walk to and fro in the narrow cottage-room while she spoke, holding the paper before her. "Human no longer! It withers my soul to think of them. Yet to become one of them, to be like them, is my only hope. Passion, life, humanity, these are the fires of death for me. I have no home but in the White Brotherhood."

She stopped abruptly; folded the paper again and placed it within her dress, and seemed to immediately become rapt again in the object she had had in view before finding it. She stepped toward the porch and out beneath the yew-trees. Here she paused a moment, closely scrutinizing the trunks of the trees one after the other. On one she found some marks cut in the bark which appeared to be what she was in search of; for after studying them very carefully and murmuring to herself as she did so, she hastily walked down the path, into the road, and then left it again as soon as possible by striking across some wild land. Evidently she knew what direction to follow quite clearly; but as evidently she had never trodden the way before. For sometimes she was much perplexed to find the crossing over swollen streams, though always after much search she reached a place where it was easy to pass over. Sometimes she found herself near houses, apparently to her great annoyance, for she would make a circuit round to avoid them, and then return to her direct path. At last she entered the forest, following the track of a stream which struck straight into it. It was not easy to follow the water-course for the brush-wood which grew along its side, and overhung it; but she persevered in keeping close to it, even in its windings, so that now it was evidently her guide.

The afternoon wore away while her long walk lasted. The sun had set, and it was gray twilight outside the forest; within its shadow it was dark as night. Fleta followed the gleam of the water as it caught rays of light here and there. At last something shone darkly before her like a black pearl. She uttered a cry of delight and thankfulness. It was a wide deep pool, surrounded closely by forest trees which grew to the very edge. But it was large enough to have room to reflect the sky. And it was still, as if it were a pool of death. But to Fleta it seemed to mean life. She pressed eagerly on till she reached its very brink. Then she threw her cloak aside, and after that her dress. Her dress she washed in the water wherever it was stained, rubbing it as well as she could with her one hand. The effort was useless; and finding it so *she rolled* up the dress and flung it away among the brush-wood. She stood now like a ghost, in a fine white linen robe which she had worn under her riding habit; it was richly bordered at all its edges with needlework. The peasant's dress cast off, the figure was that of the young queen again, clothed in purple and fine linen. This dress was unstained, as she found to her great pleasure; she took it off and laid it with her cloak, and then completely undressed. A moment later, and a gleaming shape flung itself into the deep waters. Her long hair lay spread on the surface. Fleta was a remarkable swimmer, one who loved the water; and often when living in the garden house which had been her home, she spent hours of the summer nights swimming in a lake which was in its grounds. But now she had but one arm to use. Yet she was so well practised, and so accustomed to the water, that she was able to keep herself afloat, and guide herself hither and thither; though she could not strike out boldly for the midst of the pond nor dive as she would have done otherwise. A long time she remained in; when at last she returned to the shore there was a smile of strange contentment on her face. She wrung out her dripping hair, and dressed herself quickly. Drawing her long cloak over the white linen dress, she instantly set out on her return journey. She walked easily and lightly now, seeming impervious to cold, and insensible to the clinging damp of her hair.

It was nearly midnight when she regained the cottage.

She looked anxiously at the moon a moment before she entered.

"It is not too late!" she said.

Quickly entering, she closed and barred the door behind her. The moonlight shed a long direct ray across the room through the small window. Fleta threw aside her cloak, and knelt down directly within this ray.

"Come!" she said, aloud. "Come, thou that art myself, I. myself, my own supreme being. Come, I demand to speak with you that are myself, to know the meaning of my life, to know what path to take!"

The moon-ray appeared to shape itself; Fleta looked up. A form, no more materialized than the moonlight stood over her. It was herself—yes, her own face, her own dark hair. Who that has once achieved this terrible moment can again be as other men? Fleta looked—yes; it was her own face, but how cold, how white, how implacable! Her own dark hair, but bright with gleaming roses. Words came.

"Ask me not to speak with you, for you are still in the mud of earth while I am crowned with flowers."

Fleta uttered a strange cry, hardly articulate, and then fell forward, insensible. She lay a long while like this, directly in the moon-ray, its white gleam on her face. Then consciousness came back to her, and she began at once to speak, talking with herself.

"How dare I summon that starry spirit which I degraded and dragged back from the very door of initiation? No wonder that my own shame has prostrated me like this. But I have learnt much in this dark hour of unconsciousness—yes, Fleta, you have learned, now profit. Chain that lofty, flower-crowned part of yourself to the maimed and ignorant Fleta of earth! How? By doing her will. She is more heroic, more terrible, more severe, than any other master could be. I have seen my master's face soften with pity—but this one is implacable. I am bound to her from now—I obey her.

"What was it she showed me? What was it I saw, and heard, and learned? That I, Fleta, the Fleta of earth, am not free, and cannot enter the gate of the initiates. And till I can do so, she stands at the gate waiting for me, waiting to become one with me—and then her crown *will be* mine.

"Her crown! At what a cost! To tear the last human feeling from my soul.

"Yes, my master, the scales are fallen from my eyes. I know why I am desolate, why you have left me utterly alone. I have loved you, I have worshipped you, only as a disciple may love his master, still it has been love, longing, leaning, hunger for your grand presence and your fine and spirit-stirring thought. Life had no savor and no meaning without the superb and delicate perfume of your presence to gladden it. All this is over. I will yield to it no longer, for I desire it not, neither do you desire it. That it burns in my veins still—yes—burns—makes it the more necessary that it shall be conquered. I will be alone henceforward, and look for no help or comfort save in myself.'"

She rose to her feet as she uttered the last words, and drew herself up to her full height. Her bearing was erect, as though no weariness or sickness had ever befallen her; yet she looked very sadly at the arm which hung withered at her side.

"How weak I was to fear that thing! How is it that I did not have more confidence in my power? Well, be it so; I must bear the mark of my cowardice."

The cottage was still utterly deserted save for herself. It was very lonely; she had tasted no food for a long time. Yet she seemed indifferent to the discomfort and solitude of her position. She walked across the room, and in doing so, recognized that she had exhausted all her strength in the strange struggles and efforts she had gone through. She went to the cupboard, and again mixed a vitalizing draught. That taken, her power returned; a faint color came into her face; she looked like the Fleta of the palace, the young queen full of strength; only that there was a new intensity in her face, something which greatly altered its expression. She returned to the larger room and began to pace up and down, thinking very earnestly as she did so.

"Your Master Ivan—if you must go saving souls, save his—you'll have to go to hell's door to find him!" She murmured these words of Etrenella's over and over again to herself. Presently she stood quite still, looking through the narrow window at the quiet scene without, but not seeing it. She was absorbed in internal questioning.

"How could I be so blinded as to believe her, that witch, that traitress?" she exclaimed aloud, at last. "What made me wish to go to her? Was I actually blinded by love? Oh! how ready I was to brave the terrors of hell's door. Fool! to be so readily deceived. Insane pride, that could prompt me to believe such folly. Of my master there is no need to ask pardon, for my mad thoughts could not injure him; but I ask pardon of the Divine humanity, the White Brotherhood, that I could have dreamed that one who is a part of its divinity could fall from that noble place——

"How is it that I have purified my thoughts and heart, so that now I see my folly? What have I done to get this light?

"I understand. I have begun my work. I have saved Otto from himself. But there were two for me to bring with me to the gateway. Who is the other? Hilary! He with whom I have failed so many times? He whose touch is like death to me from the memories of dead loves it brings? Ah! Fleta! Yes, you are still in the mud of earth. Come, be brave and go to work! The blossom has fallen and is decaying; its over-sweet scent sickens and disgusts me. I must look for the fruit."

Her whole manner suddenly changed now. She busied herself in coiling up her long hair, and finding her cloak to wrap herself in. Then, for the first time during the ordeals she had been passing through, she thought of food.

She found bread and fruit in the little pantry, and of this ate almost hungrily. Then she drew her cloak round her, and leaving the cottage, closed the door behind her.

CHAPTER XXIII.

WHAT a long and terrible journey was that on which Fleta entered! The horse and cart had gone from the stable; she had no money with which to obtain any sort of conveyance. But she had a number of valuable rings on her fingers, and round her neck was a string of uncut jewels of all kinds, a favorite necklace of hers because of its barbaric simplicity. She wore it always under her dress in order to carry about with her a little locket which held in it some treasured possession of hers. When she reached a large village she succeeded in disposing of one of her rings for a twentieth of its value, and with the money she purchased a complete peasant's costume. Thus dressed, and wrapped in her cloak with its hood drawn close over her face, she could walk along the roads without exciting much comment. She bought food as she went, for she found her strength very insufficient for the task before her; but she could not bring herself to sleep or rest beneath any roof, and walked on by night as by day. She went a long distance out of her course in order to avoid the battle-field, the scene of her great fault, when her longing to find Ivan and the rapt thought of saving him from some great danger, had caused her to forget the task she was then engaged in and so sacrificed the army and the king. It seemed as if she dared not tax her strength by passing through the scene of such associations. At last she reached a large town where there were jewellers to whom she could offer the stones of her necklace for sale. They were of great value, being so large, though rough and uncut. She sold three of these for a mere nothing, considering what the jewels were; but it was a fortune to her, for it was enough money for her to travel all the rest of the way in coach or carriage. She professed to have found the stones on the battle-field, for the jeweller, looking at her peasant's dress and her carefully concealed face, seemed very suspicious of her. Lest his curiosity should prompt him to have her watched, she hastily engaged a carriage at the nearest inn, and left the town, scarcely pausing to taste food.

That evening she drove through the city where for one day she had reigned as queen, and which she had left triumphantly at the head of her army. It was desolated; the shops closed, the streets empty, signs of mourning everywhere. Fleta shrank back into her carriage, white and horror-stricken. This was her work! For a moment it seemed as if remorse would sweep over her and postrate her utterly. But she fought the feeling with a fierce courage.

"I will not regret the past," she cried aloud. "I have to redeem it."

And now she passed over the road which she had last driven over when with Hilary and the young Duchess and that other nameless thing she had entered the city. Her blood grew cold at the memory. Why had she let Hilary kill that creature of the devil? Surely she could have kept it far from her by her own strength had she not already begun to fall. It must have been so. Her atmosphere must have lost its purity before that thing could have approached her so closely; her soul had not cognizance of its strength when she could let Hilary be her defender. She sat thinking of these strange things and striving to learn the meaning of the past. They were heavy lessons that she learned in these memories, and her face blanched to a more deadly white as she thought of them.

At last she saw the towers and gleaming roofs of her
own city, her native home. She dismissed her carriage
some distance before the gates. She wished to enter altogether unobserved. It was dusk, and by drawing her hood
close over her face she succeeded in passing through the
streets without attracting any attention, though here she
was so well known that she feared even her walk and bearing would be recognized. She soon reached the long and
wide main street, close to the cathedral. Here all was
bright; it was as gay as ever, perhaps gayer, for all who
feared war and its terrors and preferred the pleasures of
life had hurried here from Otto's city at the first note of
disaster. It was thronged with carriages; evidently there
was some great excitement on hand. Many of the ladies
were still shopping; coming from flower shops with
bouquets, from milliners and jewellers, on all kinds of business intent. Fleta knew them nearly all by sight; a faint
amusement rose within her as she passed on through the
crowd, a mere unnoticed peasant. How different it used
to be when she walked down this street. As she wandered
on, looking hither and thither for the face she wanted, she
drew near her father's palace, and saw at once what was
the event of the night. The whole palace was illuminated
and *en fête;* evidently there was to be a state dinner and
a ball afterward. A thought came quickly into Fleta's
mind. Hilary would certainly be at the ball; she too
would be there. Without thought of fatigue, or of distance, she immediately turned her steps on to the road
leading out of the city to her own dear garden house. She
had rested so far in the carriage that she could walk this
distance without any trouble. She found the house, as
she expected, quite deserted. Oh, how sweet was the
familiar fragrant scent of the garden! It seemed as though
she had passed through a lifetime of experience since she
had last been here. And so, indeed, she had. It made

no difference to her that the house was shuttered and barred, for she had a secret mode of entrance to her laboratory which she could always use. In a few moments she stood within it, and paused awhile in the darkness to enjoy the faint lingering perfume of the incense. A sense of power came upon her as she stood here.

"Oh, if I am recovering my lost place!" she exclaimed to herself. "If my powers return to me! But I must not think of this; I must go on with my work."

She easily found her way in the dark, for the place was so perfectly familiar. In a few moments she had struck a light, and then she lit a large hanging lamp which made the whole room brilliant. The empty incense vessel stood beneath it. She looked at this a moment longingly, then turned away with a sigh. "I may not," she murmured. She quickly set herself to the task she had in hand. A large deep cupboard, almost as big as a room, was in one of the thick walls. She opened this and carried in a light. It was all hung with dresses; not ordinary dresses, but rather such as one sees in the property-room of a theatre, only that all of them were of the most rich character, except in cases where this was contrary to their style. She took out first a white robe, one that she had worn when Hilary had come to her at the garden house, and when, finding her in the garden, he had thought how like a priestess she looked, blinded though he was by love. It was, in fact, the dress of a priestess of an ancient order long since supposed to be dead.

Before the great mirror in the laboratory she performed a careful toilette. All travel stains disappeared; she restored to her skin, by perfumed waters, a delicate freshness; she brushed out her hair, and coiled it round her head like a crown. She dressed herself in the white robe, and fastened it at the throat with a very old clasp, which she took from a locked casket. As she did so, a flame leaped into her eyes, a light came into her face. "Yes, I am that one again, I have her fire and her courage; I am the priestess of the desolate woods, looking to the first dawn-ray for my guidance, not to any human intelligence. So be it. I am as strong in that personality as in the Princess Fleta's; let me take and use the strong courage of that pure nature worship. Let me dedicate myself to it anew, but also with a new intelligence. I cannot again be taught by the spirits of the air and water, but I can be as indifferent to man as I was then. Come, with your strength, my past self of the solitary woodland altar!"

So saying, she moved away from the mirror, and, as she went, broke into a low, monotonous chant. Monotonous —yes! But how full of magic! It made the blood in her veins grow fiery.

From the great cupboard she took out another dress; that of the old fortune-teller, which she had worn when she first met Hilary. With the large cloak and hood she completely concealed her white dress; and she masked her face so as only to show her eyes, which looked the more marvellously brilliant when thus isolated.

CHAPTER XXIV.

TWO hours later she presented herself at the door of the palace. The dinner was over, and guests were crowding into the ball. It was not a masque, as on the occasion when she wore this dress before, so that she had to resort to a more complicated plan of obtaining entrance.

She recognized all the servants standing round the broad entrance and upon the great oaken staircase. She selected one of the group and went straight up to him.

"Tell the king," she said, "that I wish to speak to him."

The man looked at the crooked figure of the old gypsy, and laughed. "Not to-night," he answered.

"Yes, to-night," she said, and she looked straight at him with her wonderful eyes. The smile faded off his face, and he answered seriously:

"It is impossible, indeed," he said. "Come in the morning."

"I wish to go into the ball-room," said Fleta. "I will amuse the guests if his Majesty pleases."

The servant shook his head.

"Not to-night," he repeated; "the people are too grand."

"I'll tell them tales of themselves that will make them stare!" said Fleta, with a curious laugh that made the servant look wonderingly at her.

"You mustn't stand here," he said, as a new group of guests arrived at the door. The old gypsy's red cloak made her a conspicuous figure. She curtsied deeply as a tall handsome lady passed her.

"You will have your wish, Duchess," she said, in a low voice; "but not as you would like it. Your husband will lose all he has at the cards to-night, and stab himself before he leaves the tables."

The lady stopped, stared at her with wide-open, horror-struck eyes, and then hurried away, speechless and white.

"Come, you must go," said the servant, rather roughly. "This will never do."

Fleta quickly hurried after the lady she had spoken to, and put her hand on her dress.

"If you will help me," she said, "I can help you. You play to-night and let me sit near you; and you shall win more than your husband loses."

"Impossible!" said the Duchess. "How can I do it?"

"Tell the king I would speak with him. I have news of his daughter. She is found."

The Duchess looked at her for a moment; then the terror left her face, and she burst out laughing.

"You have overshot the mark, my good woman," she said. "I think I will manage without your help to-night."

Fleta stood back against the wall, silent and amazed. The servant again came, and said she must go. She drew a ring from her finger, and held it out to him.

"Take this to the king," she said, "and tell him its bearer wishes to enter the ball-room."

The servant hesitated, looked at the ring, and was evidently struck by its value and beauty. He turned and went up the wide stairway. It was quite a quarter of an hour before he returned. Fleta remained motionless, where he had left her.

"Come," he said; "the king says you are to enter." The bent figure of the old red-cloaked woman went up the flower-decked staircase and entered among the throng of *courtiers* and splendidly-dressed ladies. Everybody stared at her; immediately they supposed it was some surprise of the king's, to give an added amusement to the night. A lady who was standing by him said so, as she saw the quaint figure approaching. The king turned hastily. He was troubled and anxious to know who it was carried this ring, which was his daughter's and had belonged to her mother.

"I understood this was masque to-night, your Majesty," said Fleta, in a very low voice, as she appoached him. "That is why I wear this dress. Let me pass as a fortune-teller, and amuse some of your guests. Presently I will tell you my errand."

"As you please," said the King, seeing no better way out of the situation. "You shall have the little gold boudoir, and hold your reception there."

"Give me back the ring," said Fleta, in the same low voice. He hesitated, evidently uncertain what to do. She put out her left hand from under the cloak, and held it toward him as if to take the ring. He started violently, and uttered a sort of suppressed cry. It was a hand that no one could mistake, having once seen it; and he knew the rings on the fingers. He dropped the ring he held into the open palm of this hand, at which he gazed so strangely. Fleta hastily drew it under her cloak; she could not understand his manner, and it was time to put an end to the situation, which was beginning to attract attention.

In the same moment everything was explained to her. For there, on the other side of the King, just approaching him, she saw herself, beautiful, triumphant, radiant, dressed with the greatest splendor, and shining with diamonds. Instantly she saw it all, realized everything, and marvelled at her recent blindness. This was Adine.

And the man beside her, the handsomest man in the whole room, young, tall, with his face alight with love and pride; the man on whom Adine leaned, resting the tip of her gloved fingers on his arm? It was Hilary Estanol.

The group of which the King was the centre was standing just at the entrance to the ball-room. At this moment some exquisite waltz music began, and Fleta saw these two figures pass away down the room, the first, and for some moments the only, couple dancing. Together they moved marvellously, like shapes in a vision of rhythmic movement. Fleta looked after them, and then turned quickly away.

"Myself, and not myself," she thought. But her thoughts were quickly stayed by the words she heard around her.

"What a sight!" said some one close by her. "The Princess always seemed to me mad, but I never thought she could do this. Imagine her refusing to wear a widow's dress, or even to stay quietly in her rooms, just because the king Otto's body has not been found, though there are two or three officers here to-night who saw him fall. It is disgraceful; I cannot understand how the king allows it."

"Oh, he never had any influence over her," said some one else. "She is a witch, and he is obliged to let her do as she chooses. But to flaunt her love affair with Hilary Estanol before every one's eyes at such a time as this is in execrable taste."

A great deal more was said, but she could not stay to hear it. Some one was showing her the way into the little gold boudoir. Here she sat down alone, thankful for even a moment's peace. She took off her mask, and, leaning her head on her hand, tried to think. But in a moment there was a sound at the door. She hastily put on her mask. Two or three court ladies came, one after the other, and then some of the courtiers. Every one went out startled and white. Each had not only been alarmed at the gypsy's knowledge, but had received some severe words. Presently there was a little pause, some laughter; then the doorway opened wide to show Hilary and Adine standing together there. Fleta fixed her eyes on the image of herself, never even glancing at Hilary. The door closed, and Adine advanced into the room alone.

She seemed disinclined to do so, and the smile died away from her lips. Fleta threw off the mask and cloak and rose to her feet, a terrible look on her face. Thus they stood opposite each other for a moment of silence. Then Fleta spoke, in a cold, stern voice:

"You have betrayed my trust, and this masquerade must come to an end. I do not need you any longer."

Adine shivered and turned very pale.

"I thought you were dead," she said, stupidly, as if she could think of no other words to say. Fleta flung a look of scorn at her.

"As if I should die while you live!" she said. "It is enough that you have had these days and nights to use my power and name and to darken both name and power. Go, now; it is full time. And you go forever. You will never take my place again. You cannot return to the convent; you have no claim there now. Go back to your home with the peasants."

Adine uttered a sharp cry of pain, and staggered back as if struck. But she said nothing. All power appeared to have left her.

"There is no time to lose," said Fleta, after a moment's silence. "You have done wrong and I have to make it right. Come, throw aside my likeness, throw off that dress, put away the mad follies which have been turning your brain and making your soul too great for you!"

As she spoke Adine stepped back and sank into a chair. A kind of stupor seemed upon her, a helplessness. Yet she obeyed Fleta in a mechanical way that was piteous; she drew the jewels out of her hair, unclasped the diamonds from her neck, with slow fingers began to unfasten the gorgeous dress she wore. Fleta watched her steadily, without relaxing her gaze. The strangest thing in the whole scene, could there have been any on-looker to appreciate it, was that the likeness between the two grew momently less. As Adine obeyed she seemed to alter visibly. She stooped forward so that her stature appeared to be lessened; her eyes narrowed and contracted; her mouth lost its firmness, and the lower lip took on a droop that changed her whole face. No one could have mistaken her now for Fleta, though the shape and coloring of the two women was still the same. But from one the spirit had gone, while in the other it was stronger. Fleta had never looked so powerful, so completely herself, as at this hour. All her courage and confidence had returned to her in the moment she discovered the urgent need of action.

She approached Adine and stood close to her. "What are you doing?" cried out Adine at last, in a voice choked by distress and fear.

"I am reading your sins," said Fleta." "I see very plainly that unless I can blot those sins out you will have the death of a struggling soul to answer for. You!—that are not strong enough to answer for yourself! How dared you play with Hilary Estanol? Do you not know that he is a chosen one, not like the other men you meet? Could you not have been content with making my name a shame to me and a thing for men to laugh at, without tampering with one chosen by the Great Brotherhood? You knew he was chosen—you saw him there in the forest. Traitor! Ingrate! You are capable of nothing but to be a fool—you cannot grow a spirit within your vicious body. Go—it is not I who condemn you, but the Brotherhood. You have betrayed the trust placed in you—you must suffer for it."

Fleta ceased speaking, and the room was quite still. Adine leaned back in her chair and uttered no word.

Fleta herself was buried in profound thought; she stood like a statue, her eyes fixed on some terrible thing which was in reality visible only to her mind.

Again she saw her own crime acting through the folly of some one weaker than herself. "For these wild hours of infatuation," she murmured at last, in a kind of whisper, ".how much have I to pay! Fool! Because the actual image of my master had come before my eyes and blinded them to all else—because I had let that witch pour maddeningly sweet poison into my soul, and make me dream my master needed me—only for a little while—only a little while was I mad enough to let the dream darken my sight—yet in that time an army is crushed, a king is sacrificed, and now it is I myself, that part of me which I had impressed on this poor ignorant girl that has forgotten all that is good and remembered pleasure only. I have much to do!—and I have to do it alone. I have no master now. How is it possible I should have, I that have thus sacrificed his confidence? O Fleta, Fleta, be quick to learn the horrid lesson, the first that must be conquered. Learn that there can never again be for you man or woman to love or lean on. Quick! not even yourself—only your aspiration!"

She spoke out loud now, and vehemently. As she uttered the last word she went to the door, opened it but an inch, and said to the person nearest it that the princess wished for the king to come to her at once. In two or three minutes her father pushed open the door and entered. Fleta quickly closed and locked it. The king stood amazed, looking in silence from one figure to the other. Both were transformed, and the situation was inexplicable.

CHAPTER XXV.

"HER day is over," said Fleta, after a minute or two. "She must go!"

"But who is she? What does this mean? What mad folly is it now that you are engaged in?"

"You know," said Fleta, quietly, "that this peasant girl has taken my place here before."

"You have told me so, but I never believed it."

"Surely you believe now. You saw my hand, and knew me when I entered disguised."

"It is true. Why indulge in such masquerades?"

"It is not my doing that she is here. It is her own hardihood, for which she must suffer."

"But how is the thing possible, that my own eyes and senses could be deceived? Fleta, you are cheating me!"

"You have been cheated, certainly," said Fleta, coldly. "If you would listen to the voice of your higher instincts you would not be so easily cheated. Adine might easily deceive the world, even might readily deceive Hilary Estanol, because he is blinded by longing. But I do not think she could have deceived you save for the fumes of wine. You would know your daughter, did you not sacrifice all right to your relationship with her. Come, now, let us put this scene to an end. You must contrive some mode of sending Adine out of the palace unseen; and for me to go to my own rooms unseen. I am worn out with hardships."

"It is impossible!" said the king. "There is no way *from* this room.

"Positively none?" said Fleta. "Think!" She had lived so little in the palace that she knew nothing of its construction. It was well-known to contain many secret passages and doorways.

"Positively none," said the king.

"Then I must act for us all," said Fleta. "Come, Adine, make haste, and take off that dress and give it me."

Adine did so tremblingly and with nerveless hands. Her face was as white as the dress. The king stood watching her face. Suddenly he turned to Fleta.

"How had that girl the power to make herself your image till just now?"

"The power was given to her," said Fleta, "and she has abused it."

The king turned away with an impatient movement.

"You always talk enigmas," he said.

"I answer plainly," said Fleta, "as I will answer any question you ask me."

"Where is your husband?"

"Dead. I myself have seen his dead body, have seen it burned to ashes, have seen his spirit freed from it."

"It is true, then!" said the king, mournfully. "I had hoped against hope."

Adine was now dressed in the fortune-teller's cloak, and masked. Fleta had not put on her the priestess's robe she had worn herself, but had put the cloak over the white lace-decked under-dress which Adine wore. She was completely disguised.

"Now stoop, as I did," said Fleta. "Come, you can imitate me well enough. Now, father, open the door and let her go. Hasten, Adine, go to your home and repent. And do not forget that unless you keep a close watch upon your tongue about all that you have known and seen, the Dark Brothers will visit you with instant death. Be warned!"

The king opened the door, and Adine passed through it, entering at once into a crowd, which was greatly surprised to see her come out. She was questioned on every side, but would return no answer. Without speaking she hurried through the rooms and down the great staircase.

"What has happened?" said the guests one to another. "Why are the king and the princess shut in there together still?"

"What are we to do now?" asked the king, shutting the door and turning again to Fleta.

"You go," said she, putting hastily on Adine's brilliant dress; "tell them the gypsy came to bring me the certain news of Otto's death, that she brought me the signet-ring from his finger. See, I have the ring here; I took it myself from his dead hand. Let the guests go. I shall go to my rooms; I shall take my place as his widow, returned to you."

"You are right," said the king. "It is the best way. Are you ready?"

"Yes," said Fleta. "Go. Leave the door open to me when you go, and let any one come to me that wishes."

She sat down on a chair by the table, rested her arm on it and her head on her hand. She was utterly worn out, and she knew that if she simply let herself feel her complete weariness and heart-sickness, no acting would be necessary to present the appearance of grief. The moment she relaxed her effort the light fled from her face, her eyes grew dull, and she had all the look of one crushed under a heavy blow.

Instantly that the king left the doorway Hilary Estanol appeared in it. But when he caught sight of Fleta's figure he did not enter; he paused horror-stricken; he heard the king speaking and turned to listen to him. Some of the court ladies came to the doorway and pushed past him.

He let them go in. An hour ago, maddened by his love for Fleta, he would have dared any comment and approached her first had he seen her in trouble. But a strange chill had fallen on him when first his eyes met those of the gypsy when she entered; he had not recognized her—was it likely, so completely deceived as he was?—but he was terrified by her, and had lingered near the door of the room in great fear. Now that he saw her figure sitting there so rigidly, with that terrible death-like look on her face, he staggered, overpowered by something he could not understand. It was as though an ice-cold hand had caught at his heart and checked its very beating. Ah! poor Hilary!

In half an hour the palace was almost deserted. While still there were a few guests in the rooms Fleta rose and walked through them. Stately, sorrow-stricken, with darkened eyes she passed.

"She must have cared for him, then!" they whispered one to another, "and really would not believe him dead. And we all thought her heartless!"

So the young uncrowned queen, the young widow, went to her own rooms, followed by sympathy. And who could guess at the deep solitude, the hopeless sorrow, of that heart? The neophyte, who had failed and lost all that made life dear in the failure; the would-be initiate, who knows all love and companionship must be laid aside for all time. This is the darkest hour of human life, this fearful moment of shadow before the dawn, when passion and love, and all unequal friendship or companionship, must be forever surrendered for the hopeless and absolute solitude which darkens the door of initiation. Into such an hour of despair and agony none dare penetrate. It was easy for Fleta to wear the appearance of a widow grieving for her husband, when in her heart was the awful grief which every candidate of the White Brotherhood who fails carries in his heart forever. The grief of complete surrender, not of one love, or one loved, but of all, does not touch the soul nor pollute the thoughts of him who has made himself ready for the Hall of Initiation.

CHAPTER XXVI.

FLETA bore out the character of one overcome by grief only too easily. She found herself close to the crisis, the bitterest suffering of her life; and the fierce regret for the past stood in her way. In the morning, when she rose and stood before her mirror, she saw a worn, wan face, eyes deeply bordered with shadows, and a new line of pain on her smooth forehead. She saw these things, but without thought. It was just what she had expected to see, for she had let the storm rage in her soul through the night. And now she stood there muttering to herself:

"The expiation is close—I have to begin the expiation."

It was a cool, fresh, clear morning; Fleta had risen very early. She set her window wide open, and stepped out on to the balcony. From it she could see over the city and away to the blue hills beyond. For a long hour she leaned here, drinking in the morning freshness, and a dim, faint peace came to her soul from the clear skies. At last her attention was attracted by a sound in the room, and she turned to look back into it. A figure stood there; she looked doubtingly at it. Yes, it was her father, the king.

He regarded her very earnestly as she re-entered the room. She wore a loose white gown, on which her dark hair fell in a tumbled mass. It was a sad figure.

"Do you wonder at this early visit?" said the king. "I have not rested at all; and just now I was wandering in the garden when I saw you standing here. I have come to ask you a strange question. Who are you? What are you?"

"Why do you ask me these things?" said Fleta, in a very low voice.

"Because you cannot be my child, nor yet your mother's. Last night's experience convinced me of your extraordinary powers. You divested Adine of her likeness to yourself. How, I cannot tell. I would never let myself believe you to be a magician until now; but it is useless any longer to hide the truth. I have been looking at you from the garden. There is no mark of my family or your mother's in your face or figure. I saw you as I have never seen you before, without a mask. You have always worn one for me. Just now I discovered a profound unfamiliarity in you which has roused my curiosity into a passion. Your face, divested of its softer charms, is that of a man; through it looks a spirit which suffers. Tell me what you are."

"I am your daughter," said Fleta. You need not doubt that, or fancy me changed in my cradle. My heritage is true, unlike though I may be to you and the others who have gone before me."

"Your heritage! It is not mental, nor physical; it is not in any way visible."

"That," said Fleta, "is because I have moulded myself for my own ends."

"Now you speak as you look. You have some strange power. Whence do you get it? I say, what are you? You are no ordinary mortal."

Fleta smiled; a smile of such sadness as can hardly be imagined.

"No; I am not an ordinary mortal. The difference is only this. I had found out that there is a straight path to divinity, and I was treading that path: but lost my way."

"You have not begun to tread it since I have known you," said the king. "You began before." He spoke in a changed voice.

"Yes," said Fleta. "I began before. I began in a prehistoric age, when the world was a vast wilderness of savage beauty. I marked out my destiny then by a fierce act of rebellion against the passion which makes human life possible, against the blind hunger of man for sensation which drives him into this dull world of matter and compels him to live innumerable ignorant lives, worthy only of animals. I hated it! I rebelled! I raised my hand and took life. It was the first step into power, and it has darkened the sun for me through ages. I have lived it out, I have expiated it only after many lives of pain. But in taking power I took knowledge. I began to climb the great ascent of life toward the divine. And in every rebirth I have gained more power and more knowledge."

She ceased. She had spoken passionately, from her heart. The king had never taken his eyes from her face. The soldier, rough, almost devoid of sentiment, stood there spell-bound. He was facing a reality.

"Tell me more," he said. "Why do you suffer so now?"

"Why do I suffer?" said Fleta. "Must you ask me this?"

"I desire very much to know," said the king, in a low voice.

"You have a right to ask me," said Fleta, sadly. "Not your right as my father, but your right as a servant of the White Brotherhood. You are but just within their influence, and you have never been conscious of it, though you have obeyed it. I have been possessed by an arrogance which convinced me I could by my strength obtain the right to enter the order. My longing to enter it gave me the privilege of birth in your house. I have had great opportunities, but," she concluded, in a tone of infinite sadness, "I have failed!"

"Is that why you suffer?" said the king.

"No," answered Fleta. "I suffer because those who loved me long ago love me still; they have been in the marvellous orchard of life where Nature flowers in superb lavishness. The orchard is beautiful, yes! Nothing can be more beautiful. But there is a force always at work, a force which demands progress. After the blossom the fruit. To be man and woman, to love, to live each for the other, this is glorious, as is everything in nature. But it comes to an end. The miracle of transmutation must be worked. The sweet softness of the blossom, mere beauty, that must pass, and the hard fruit come and ripen to its harvest. The lesson must be learned, and the soul pass on. Oh! there is one who holds me from the gate by his love. But I must purify him, I must take him to the gate, or else lose all hope myself of ever reaching it!"

She hardly seemed to remember who she spoke to. Her pent-up feeling had hardly broken into words, and emotion made her speak on without pause till she ceased. There was silence for a minute or two; then the king approached her.

"Tell me," he said. "What am I to you?"

"A friend," she answered; "always a good and true friend. Nothing else. Your lessons in life have lain apart from me. We have never even been father and daughter save in circumstance."

"It is true," he answered; with a sigh. "Yet I would it were not so. You are far beyond me. Help me."

Fleta held out her hand. The king took it, and so they stood for a few moments in silence. Then she gently took her hand away, and turning from him, sat down in a chair. Her pallor was so extreme the king was alarmed. And, indeed, she looked more like death than life. He hastily left the room, returning in a few moments with a slender glass full of a dark wine. He put it to her lips. She opened her eyes, smiled faintly, but pushed back his hand.

"I need it not," she said as the king held the glass in his hand. "Though it is more than mortal brain can endure to look back over the stairway of life. Reason seems to reel on its throne before such a sight. So deep is the abyss, so great the height, so incredible the ascent. My mind is worn out. I must rest, I must sleep, or I shall lose my senses. Let no one disturb me till I call; but do one thing for me, my father; let Hilary Estanol be sent for. I must see him when I wake."

She rose, and moving to her bed flung herself upon it. What a death-like figure it was! The king turned away. He could not bear the sight. He left the room, and calling a waiting-woman to him bade her sit by the door and watch it, letting no one enter but himself. Next he sent a messenger to Hilary. Then he went to his own writing-room, where he moved to and fro, thinking; his thoughts were running riot, plunging back into the past, leaping into the future; he was unconscious of the present moment, once having let it go.

CHAPTER XXVII.

THREE hours later Fleta awoke. She had been wrapped in a profound sleep; so deep, she was as one returning from the dead. It had restored her mind; her inner strength had returned. She knew, in the moment she woke, that she was fit now to go on with her task.

She rose, went to the door, and called. The waiting woman who sat close by came to her. When she found Fleta wished to dress she went away, bringing back with her some sewing-maids who had been busily working all the morning. In a little while Fleta had bathed, her hair had been dressed and coiled round her head, and she was robed in black mourning for her husband of a day. Her burned and helpless arm was wrapped in black silk and placed in a sling. She looked in the glass and smiled. Fleta the beautiful, the radiant, thus disfigured, thus dressed. She quickly turned away, trailing her black train after her.

She had already inquired and learned that Hilary Estanol was waiting for her in her own old sitting-room, where she had made her home when necessity or caprice had induced her to dwell in the palace for a few days together during her girlhood. It was kept as it had always been—bright, colored in gold and white, with walls lined with books, the windows filled with flowers.

Hilary started up as he heard her at the door. He uttered a sharp cry of pain as she entered. The change was indeed awful—from Adine, the flower and froth of Fleta's gayest superficial life, to this pallid trouble-stricken, sad-eyed woman. Her dress accentuated his feeling. It seemed to shock and surprise him. He had forgotten, in his recent happiness, that she was Otto's wife. He turned away and hid his face in his hands.

"Do not be so distressed," she said in a very sweet and quiet tone. "This must seem terrible to you when but yesterday you were dancing with my mocking shadow. I have sent her away from me forever, because she has too deeply betrayed my trust in her in betraying you. How is it possible that you, born under the star of true knowledge, like myself, one of the children of the life of effort, could be so cheated and pleased by a mere phantasm? Well, I know you regret that phantasm—I know you loved it very dearly. I read the pain in your heart because I show myself to you without the phantasmal appearance—without beauty or youth or gayety. My dear friend, it is not for you to choose between pain and pleasure. You have not the power. If you choose pleasure you will be forever pursuing a will o' the wisp and never reaching it; the pursuit will soon become pain. But though you have not that choice I can give you one which may seem to you very like it. You can choose between this Fleta who now speaks to you, the servant of the White Brotherhood, and that Fleta whom you worshipped such a little while ago—my mocking shadow."

"Where shall I find that Fleta?" asked Hilary, in a strained voice of pain.

"You will be mocked by her as much as you will if you choose to be so," was all Fleta's answer.

"But will *you* wear that guise?"

"Ah, you want the two Fletas in one!" she cried out—"no, that is over. You have desired that for a long time, and now and then you have almost fancied you had got it —is it not so? In that morning sunshine, on the first journey we took together—sometimes at the garden house—you imagined that without losing the priestess you could claim the woman. That is impossible—it never has been, it never can be, you must have the one or the other. I have waited for you long enough; now you must choose. I have the power to give you what you wish. If you only desire the woman, the thing that will die in a few years, then I will make this body that now speaks to you young and beautiful and gay, and leave it for your amusement; for I am very weary of it, and it is only for your sake that I now stay in it, and if you make that choice we part forever. But if you choose me as I am, the servant of knowledge, then you have to recognize in me your master, and desire nothing from me but such knowledge as I can give you."

Hilary rose and went to the window. It seemed for a moment as if his senses were about to desert him. But a moment later he turned round and faced her.

"I am not strong enough to make such a choice," he said with a sort of defiance in his tone.

"Not strong enough!" exclaimed Fleta, in a voice full of contempt. "Go then, and take your own way, followed by the darkness you have worked for yourself. Do not blame any one else, whatever you may suffer. You have invoked the false shadows that surround the man who knows not whether he wishes good or ill. It is over."

She turned and moved very slowly out of the room, her black dress trailing behind her. Hilary started forward as if to stop her, but immediately drew himself back again, and remained standing motionless, watching her go. The door closed and still he did not move. But at last, after a long silence he roused himself—for his one wish was to leave the palace without having to speak to any one again. He succeeded, although he had to grope his way almost *like a blind* man. He was stupefied, half dazed, scarcely *conscious of* what he was doing. A great loneliness was *eating away* at his heart—a hunger was at work there, as real as physical hunger. For he had more than worshipped Fleta the woman—he had lived on the thought of her, on the passion he had only for her image. And now she seemed to have been shattered before his eyes, and to be like a broken statue destroyed forever. He comforted himself perpetually with the thought that he had not chosen this so easily destroyed idol. And yet, even in the midst of this comfort, another memory would come—of Fleta's scorn, when he said he could not choose. This gave him some dumb perplexity and pain; but he was not learned enough to know that if he had chosen the woman she would have had less scorn for him, and more pity. It was the weakness of that dreadful moment, come and gone so quickly, which condemned him in the sight of Fleta and her order. Had he but found strength enough to decide positively for ill, he would have laid the foundations of such power as would have enabled him, later on, to choose positively for good in another earthly life.

The moment had indeed come quickly and gone quickly, and it appeared to Hilary as if he had had no time given him in which to decide and choose. And yet he dimly knew that if that moment could have been protracted to a thousand years he would have been no nearer a positive choice; and he dimly knew, also, that the moment which seemed to come so unexpectedly was, indeed, only a summing-up of his life—that ever since he had known Fleta he had been in this state of hopeless indecision. The great chance had been given him, and he had been unable to take it. He did not realize the blow in this form yet, though the consciousness came, keenly enough, later on. He only knew, as yet, that he had lost Fleta—all the Fleta he had known and worshipped, the woman and the priestess both.

It was over.

CHAPTER XXVIII.

THE next morning Fleta had a long talk with the king; a very quiet and serious one. During that day on which she saw Hilary she would see no one else, not even her father; she remained alone, and no one knew whether she slept or waked, whether she was suffering or at rest. But in the morning she went to her father's breakfast-room, and entered it, wearing her black robes. She was altered by the hours of solitude; at first the king thought it was her youth and beauty that had returned to her. But a second glance showed him that this was not so. The subtle, feminine charm which she had hitherto exercised was gone. She stood before him slender, fair, proud in bearing as ever; but the radiant beauty had not returned. The eyes were sad, the strange, sweet smile had seemingly left the mouth forever. Had a painter put her on his canvas he would have used the face for one of those sexless angels the early Italians knew how to paint.

"I am going to England," were her first words. "Will you help me?"

"It is my business," was the king's answer. "Tell me what you wish."

Fleta sat down beside him; and they talked for a long while. Then she returned to her room, and the king summoned his secretary and his steward and began to make the arrangements she wished.

Late that afternoon Fleta left the palace. She was wrapped in a fur cloak that hid her black dress, and her pale face was hidden by a black lace veil. She put this aside and kissed the king's hand, as she took a final leave of him in the great hall of the palace.

"Send for me instantly if you need me," he whispered to her. She bowed her head and turned away. The whole retinue of the palace was assembled to see her depart. But no one accompanied her, or entered her travelling carriage with her. On this journey she was to go alone. Not even a maid or servant of any sort was with her.

CHAPTER XXIX.

SOME parts of the north-east coast of England are singularly desolate and wild, and strangely deserted, considering how small the island is. One would suppose it hardly possible to find retreat in an over-populated small country such as the British islands. But nineteenth-century life is centred in cities, and in the present day people find no landmarks in Nature, and do not understand that by the edge of the sea, or in the midst of fields, they may be surrounded by aerial hosts who have been associated with that special spot since the wild small island was built amid its harassing seas. It has been a centre and point of a special character, for those who read between the lines during all this age of the earth of which we have any knowledge.

But there are some who know and feel the powers that are not visible to the material eyes, and who know how to use them.

In a remote, desolate, and very bleak part of the north-eastern coast there stands a small house, well sheltered by a high hill close behind it and a thick belt of trees. The land on which the house stands is part of a very large estate, which has been cut up and sold by successive spendthrift and dissolute owners. These men had Norman blood in them, and never took complete root upon English soil. The big castle which was their family house was *most often* untenanted, and so was this small dower-house *on the seashore.* It was now the property of a younger son, who had scarcely ever been seen by the people of the place; never at all since he had been quite a boy. Now and again some one visited the old house for a few days; lights were seen in the windows so unexpectedly that the peasants said the house was haunted. But at present it was in regular occupation. A foreign servant came into the village one day to make purchases, and said that he was with a friend of Mr. Veryan, to whom the house belonged, who had borrowed it to live in for some months. He told any one who was curious enough to question him that his master was a doctor of great reputation in spite of being still comparatively young; that he had come to this remote place in order to be quiet and carry on some special studies. It was not likely that his quiet would be disturbed, for the old castle was nothing but a big ruin, the elder branch of the family being represented by an agent, who was doubtful whether to make money out of converting the castle into a show-place, or to pull it down and sell the bricks it was built with. No one had any kind of positive idea where the present owner was. And this was the condition of an old and proud family. Everything had been squandered; even the beautiful old family plate had long since been packed and sent to London for sale. It was said that the worst of all the succession of spendthrifts who had dissipated the fine old property was the beautiful wife of the last lord, the mother of the two sons now the sole representatives of the name. She was a Hungarian of noble family according to the statements made at the time of her marriage. But the servants and peasants always declared her to be a gypsy, pure and simple, and, moreover, a witch. She was extraordinarily beautiful and fascinating, and in the few short years of their married life did with her husband whatever she fancied.

Her death had been a terrible one, and the poor people firmly believed that her ghost haunted the old castle in which her luxuriously furnished rooms, decked in a quaint barbaric fashion, were still to be seen, hardly touched since her death. Even the agent, whose one idea seemed to be to sell anything convertible into money, had left her many costly ornaments in their accustomed places. Some kind of superstitious feeling kept him from having these rooms stripped. He had been in great terror of the beautiful chatelaine during her life, and possibly he had not shaken off that fear even now. It was the only theory by which to account for the reverence with which these rooms were treated, for her son had given no orders about them.

The new resident at the Dower House lived in great seclusion and quite alone, save for his two foreign servants, who appeared to do for him all that he needed. He was a great rider, but the hours he spent out of doors were usually those of the very early mornings so that he was seldom seen. It was soon discovered, however, that he was an extraordinarily handsome man, in the prime of life. All sorts of rumors at once were circulated about him. A recluse is expected to be old, crooked, eccentric in manner. Why should this man, to whom life would be supposed to have every attraction possible, shut himself up in absolute solitude? He was met now and again by one of the laborers who had to rise with the dawn and go to work, evidently returning from a walk. Such habits as these, to the sloth-loving English peasant, could only indicate the restlessness of a mind diseased or guilty. Yet there was something in the face of the man which forbade this mode of accounting for his peculiar tastes from being even talked of; the dullest mind could not but recognize the power and strength shown in that beautiful face.

His servants always called him "Monsieur," giving him no name. They appeared to think the peasants of too little importance to require any more definite information; and as no letters ever came to the Dower House, no name was associated with its resident. This, in itself, seemed odd; but common persons soon get used to a custom of that kind, and think no more of it once the first shock is over.

As a matter of fact, however, it is impossible to remain *incognito* in a civilized country for long together. Some prying person, possessed of a kind of officialism, is sure to disturb the temporary peace of this form of oblivion. In this case the agent did it. He rode up to the Dower House one day, got off his horse, and sent in his name. In a few moments he was ushered into a room which he did not recognize, so completely was its appearance changed since he had seen it last. It was entirely hung with tapestry on which were worked figures of the most life-like character; warriors, women in dresses of different periods, monks, and clowns. These were not formed into groups and pictures as is usual upon tapestry, but were marshalled round the room, like so many witnesses of any scene which might take place within it. So real was the effect that the agent half misdoubted whether the interview was indeed a *tête-à-tête* one, when his host came forward to meet him.

He was dressed in a gray shooting suit, the simplest dress possible for an Englishman to wear in the country. Yet it so well suited and set off his splendid figure and face, that his visitor was for a moment startled into silence. When he found self-possession enough to speak, it was with much more than his usual gravity.

"I presume sir," he said, "that you have some reason for being here without letting the people know who you are; though it seems a strange thing to do, for you must be recognized sooner or later. I have not seen you since you were a child, but your likeness to your mother is unmistakable; as I know that Sir Harold Veryan is at present in Africa I presume I am speaking to Ivan Veryan."

"*You* are right," was the answer. "I had no serious

intention of concealing my identity, for that would be absurd. But my servants habitually call me M'sieu, finding my name a difficulty; and as the poor people here have no recollection of me, I should prefer that they remain ignorant of who I am. I wish for complete solitude here, not to assume the position of the next heir, who may be supposed to take an interest in the fate of the castle, the condition of the cottages, and the felling of the timber."

"If you wanted seclusion this seems the last place to come to," observed the agent.

"I find a seclusion here which suits me, for the time being," was the reply. "I only want one thing—a key to one of the doors of the castle, as I came here partly to use its library—unless all the books have been sold."

"The books have not been touched," replied the agent, "the library was one of Lady Veryan's favorite rooms, and none of them have been disturbed."

"Then I shall be glad to have a key as soon as you can send it me."

"And you wish no one told of your presence here?" inquired the agent, doubtfully.

"Who should care to know of it?"

"The county families——" he said hesitatingly, wishing very much for permission to retail his piece of gossip at the next market-day in the county town. There was always a middle-day dinner at the biggest hotel, where all sorts of magnates and men of property and business met and talked; and he would have interested the whole tableful if he could have informed them that one of the Veryans had actually returned to England and was living in his own house.

"If I wish to see any of my neighbors I will call on them," was the decided answer; "till then, I should prefer that nothing is said about me."

The air of command with which this was spoken made

it final. The agent said nothing more on the subject, but soon took his leave. Later in the day a messenger came to the Dower House with a key of the castle gate, and a key of one of the doors of the castle.

CHAPTER XXX.

THE old castle of the Veryans—which was a queer building, roomy, rambling, not beautiful, but very strong and amply veiled with green ivy, stood on high ground, looking well over land and sea. It was not sheltered like the Dower House, but faced all fortunes of weather, confident in its own strength. No tree stood close to it, for the position was too exposed. But gardens which had once been glorious, and even now were beautiful with the remains of their past glory, stretched on every side. They had the supreme charm, unknown to modern gardens, of never being flowerless. All the year round, even in the bitterest weather, lines and stars of color made the ground beautiful.

Along the cliff edge of the garden two high walls were built; and between these was the Lady's Walk—a place of delight to any sightseer who might stray to this deserted place. A wide gravel path went straight down its centre, forming a wonderfully dry promenade. On each side were wide flower beds full of rare plants that grew well in this sheltered spot; and the walls were covered with fruit trees and blooming creepers which flourished luxuriantly. On the side of the sea were openings in the wall, here and there; and seats were placed in sheltered, sunny nooks, from which the grand view might be seen.

It was to the Lady's Walk that Ivan went direct, as soon as he entered the castle grounds that same evening.

The flower-beds were neglected and overgrown, the creepers untrimmed and hanging in thick masses from the walls. The place was all the more beautiful from this neglect just overlying the high and careful cultivation of the past. It was like the languor of a tired beauty, her hair loose and undressed, but its richness undimmed.

Ivan wandered up and down the path for a long time, full of thought, very grave, yet sometimes smiling faintly.

It was the early spring, and small yellow flowers were peering out here and there, some on the ground, some on the walls. This color, which is so associated with the birth of the year, had a meaning of its own for Ivan. He stopped often to look at these flowers, but he did not pluck them. He never picked a flower or a leaf, except for use in some definite experiment.

At one end of the walk the common rose called the monthly rose was trained upon the wall, and on this there was one delicate pink bud, half blown. This flower appeared at last to attract Ivan's attention entirely. He sat down on a bench near it and looked at it for a long while.

It was late in the afternoon, but though the air was growing very cold the light was still strong, for the long days had begun. He sat there, apparently disinclined to move, full of thought.

A sound of footsteps disturbed him. Turning his head he saw Fleta approaching him, walking down the path with the rare, proud carriage which distinguished her.

"You left the gate open for me?" she said questioningly.

"Yes," he answered.

"Then I did right to come to you here?" she said, in a reassured tone.

"Certainly you did right," he replied. "Do not doubt your own knowledge. You have known from the first you had to meet me here."

"Yes," she answered.

Ivan had risen when she approached him, and they stood

face to face. His eyes were steadily and very earnestly fixed on her. Fleta had only glanced at him, and then turned her gaze on the sea. But in the pause that followed her answer she suddenly lifted her eyes and answered his look.

"I needed the mask," she said, speaking with an evident effort; "for I was still woman enough to worship you as a splendid being of my own race. I did right to cast the mask away, and suffer as I did, because it has made my lesson shorter, if fiercer. I know now that you are not a being of my own race—supposing me still nothing more than a woman. You are divine and a teacher, and I can be nothing to you but your servant. Teach me to serve! Teach me to so transform this love for you that it shall become pure service, not to you, but to the divine in you. I have cut all knots; I have cast aside all that dragged me back. My duty is done and utterly fulfilled. I stand freed from the past. Teach me!"

Ivan stepped to the side of the path and plucked the pink rosebud. He gave it her. Fleta held it in her hand, but looked at it as if utterly bewildered.

"Do you not know the color?" he said. "When you have entered the Hall of Learning, you will see such flowers on the altars. The purple of passion burns out to this pale pink, which also is the color of resurrection and of dawn. Sit here till I return."

He left her and walked down the path, through the gardens, to the gate. Here Fleta's carriage was standing. He bade the man take Fleta's trunks to the village inn and leave them there till they should be fetched away, paid, and dismissed him. Then he re-entered the grounds, locking the gate behind him.

He went to Fleta, where she still sat, regarding the *flower* she held in her hand.

"Are you ready for the offering?" he asked her.

"Yes, I am ready," she replied, without looking up.

"Come, then," he said, and turned to walk away over the grassy slopes of the garden. She rose and accompanied him. It was nearly dark now. He walked round the castle to a side door, which he opened. A deathly chill came from the interior of the building. Fleta shivered slightly as she crossed the threshold.

"Are you afraid?" said Ivan, pausing before he closed the door; "there is still time to go back."

"Back to what?" asked Fleta.

"I cannot answer that," he replied. "I do not know what you have left behind you."

"I have cut off everything," she answered. "There is nothing for me to return to. Let me go on. I am afraid of nothing now. How should I be?"

Ivan closed the door and led the way down a long passage. He opened a door and said, "Enter." Fleta passed through it, and was immediately aware that he had shut it behind her without passing through himself—that in fact she was alone.

Alone!—and where? She had no notion—she only knew she was in complete darkness.

For the first time she fully realized the ideas of darkness and solitude. They did not terrify her, but they presented themselves as absolute facts to her consciousness; the only facts she was conscious of. Moreover, she was vividly aware that she could not escape from them, which made them much more intensely real. She could not guess which way to move, nor did it occur to her that she would be in any way benefited by moving. She stepped back to the door through which she had passed, which was, to her fancy, the only link between her and the actual world, and stood there with her hand upon it.

The next thing she became conscious of was that there was no air. At all events she believed there was none.

which was quite as bad as if it were so. She imagined herself in some very large place, whether a room or a hall she could not guess, which was hermetically sealed and had been so for years.

Faint fancies as to what kind of place she was in formed themselves in her mind at first, but presently passed away altogether; for she had no clue or image to which to attach any picture. Her mind became quite blank. Presently she became aware that she had lost all sense of time. She could not tell if she had been standing in this way for minutes or for hours. Her sensations were extraordinarily acute, and yet to her they hardly seemed to exist, because there was nothing objective for them to be marked by. In a little while, the moment when Ivan had ushered her into this place had become removed to an immense distance in the past, and presently she found herself thinking of Ivan as a figure in her life which had entirely retreated from it; she could not imagine that she would see him to-morrow; for to-morrow appeared to her no longer to be possible. This black night looked like an eternity.

No danger or adventure which she had ever experienced had affected her like this. She was completely unprepared for such a sudden fall into the abyss of nothingness. And yet she had just strength enough to stand against it by summoning the philosophy which told her never to fear anything, for nothing could in reality injure her. She kept her mind and nerves from being affected by steadily recollecting this. But she was unable to stem a wave of exhaustion which gradually swept over her and which made her tremble as she stood.

It was the incredible completeness of the silence and darkness which baffled her and at last daunted her. No creak or groan sounded in the house, no echo of wind or sea came to her.

At last she began to doubt if she was alive or whether,

instead of passing through a door, she had stepped into some deep water and met death unconsciously. But she had too much experience, too great a knowledge of life and of death, to be deceived so easily. She would never have succumbed even so far as she, had done, so far as to be physically unnerved to any extent, but that she had been anticipating some experience of an entirely different character. She believed she had offered her heart, had lived past the mistakes which hitherto had held her back, and that she would have been able to ask direct help from her master and obtain it. Something friendly, quiet, natural, had been more in her expectations than anything else. Instead of which she found herself facing the most extraordinary experience she had ever been through.

The complete and absolute silence wrought on her physical sensibilities more than any other circumstance. She found she was watching the silence, listening to it, and that she dreaded to move, that she held her breath in some vague and unreasonable dread of disturbing it. It seemed to be a positive fact instead of a negative one, this complete and immovable silence. Then suddenly a power appeared to rise within her to oppose this fact—a power stronger than it. And as the feeling came to her, the silence broke, and a soft shower of music filled the air— something as tender as tears and as lovely as sunshine. The keenest pleasure filled Fleta's soul, and she leaned against the door and listened. But suddenly a thought darted into her mind: "The silence is here still—this music is only my own imagination, filling the hateful void!" And as the thought came the silence returned. Fleta fell on her knees. It was the first time she had moved since she had entered this place. With the movement came a whole rushing tide of emotions, of feelings, of fancies, a great passing phantasmagoria. She saw Ivan standing at her side, but she would not even turn to look at him, for she knew this was only an image created by her longing. She saw the place in which she was, suddenly lit and full of people. It was a great hall, gloomy and vast. There was a moving crowd in it of persons dressed very brilliantly.

"Ah!" cried Fleta, in a voice of despair, "that I should be so cheated by my own fancies is too terrible!" and with the sound of her voice, the darkness returned, closing heavily in upon her. She rose and drew herself up to her full height. A consciousness of what she was actually experiencing had come, and she became instantly calm and strong.

"I refuse," she said aloud, "to go through this neophyte's exercise. I am not the slave of my senses any longer. I dominate them; I see beyond them. Come you to me, thou that art my own self, and that art pure, impalpable, unsubstantial, without glamor. Come you and guide me, for there is none other and nothing else on which my consciousness has power to rest."

She leaned back against the door, for she was trembling with the force of her own fierce effort. The door and the floor on which she stood were now her only links with the actual or material world. She knew of nothing else; it appeared to her as though she had forgotten the material world and knew not whether she lived or died; certainly the power of hope or of fear was leaving her. She became indifferent to everything except the desire to hold her own higher self, her pure soul, in view; her longing to face herself, and so find some certainty and knowledge, swallowed up every other desire. She remained a long time, resolutely fixing her whole intensity of will on this, and waited, momentarily expecting to see the starry figure close in front of her. Once she saw it, quite distinctly; but it *was like* a marble statue, lifeless. She knew this was no reality, only her own imagining, and her power and strength began slowly to leave her after this cold vision.

If unconsciousness could have come to her now, it would have come like rain to a parched land. Her brain was on fire, her heart like lead.

But nothing came to her, nothing became visible. And then she knew that she had offered up not only the physical senses and emotion, but the psychic senses and power.

Again she fell on her knees, and clasping her hands fell into an attitude as if of prayer. In reality she was in profound meditation. As in a long series of pictures, she now saw herself passing through innumerable experiences. She saw herself, and without anger, regret, or pain, suffer and enjoy. She watched her slow separation from those who loved her, even until now when Ivan left her in the hour of trial.

She had passed through fiery trial and all the tests of the passions and emotions. But these were as nothing beside this mysterious blank, this great chasm of darkness, which seemed to be not only outside her, but actually within her own soul.

How was it to end? Was there any end? Or was this the state to which her labors had brought her triumphantly, and in which she must remain? Impossible. This was not life; it was death. And was not her effort to attain to life in its essential vitality? Death surely could not be the final king!

Fleta, the powerful, the disciple, as she had imagined herself, with knowledge, thus doubted and despaired. Her confidence left her when she saw this blankness which lay before her.

So it must be always with the unknown.

Suddenly a new mood fell on her. She began to dread

lest she should see forms and shapes, or conjure up the voice or features of any one she knew or loved. Most of all, she dreaded to see again the image of Ivan at her side.

"If I see this," she said to herself, "then indeed I shall be fallen back into the world of forms. I must not look for anything but darkness."

At this moment a hand was very gently laid on her hair. Fleta was not so completely unnerved as to tremble or cry out; yet the shock of the sudden contact shook her so that she could not speak or move. Then came a voice:

"My child," said a very gentle voice, which sounded like a woman's, "do you not know that out of chaos must come order, out of darkness light, out of nothingness something? Neither state is permanent. Do not make the mistake of dreading or welcoming the return to the world of forms after having become one with the formless."

Fleta made no answer. She was aware that there was some deep familiarity about this voice which as yet she could not understand. She was at home, like a child with its mother. All fear, all anxiety, all doubt, had dropped from her.

"You must not die under this ordeal," said the voice, "and you have been here many hours. Come with me, and I will take you to a quiet place where you can rest."

Fleta rose; a hand was put into hers. When she attempted to move she realized that she must, indeed, have been here a long time, for she was entirely numbed and helpless, and found it almost impossible to use her limbs. She put out her right hand mechanically, as if to balance herself, and was much startled by being unable to stretch her arm. Immediately she touched a wall close to her. In a moment she understood that she was in no large hall, but in a small, narrow cell, scarcely wide enough for two steps to be taken in it. This seemed to her very strange, for she had so positively believed herself to be in some very spacious place.

"How wide my fancy is!" she thought, almost smiling to herself. For now she was at peace, without any anxiety, though she knew not where she was or who was with her.

CHAPTER XXXI.

A DOOR opened and shut. Fleta found herself in a soft, warm atmosphere, lit by a pale rosy light. At first it seemed as if she could not see or distinguish between the objects before her. But after a moment her ordinary sight came suddenly to her.

She was in a very strangely furnished room. Like the room Ivan used at the Dower House, it was hung with tapestry on which were life-size figures so cunningly worked that they looked real at first sight, and always produced the appearance rather of statues than of a flat presentment. The floor was uncarpeted and entirely covered with dried ferns and withered leaves. A quantity of these were gathered into a heap and on them was spread a tiger skin and a great rug of sheep's wool. This was very near the wide hearth, on which burned a wood fire. It was not a very large fire, but to Fleta's chilled form the warmth from it seemed delicious. The light came from a shaded lamp which stood on a bracket fastened above the chimney. In front of the hearth was a three-legged wooden stool on which was a large and most beautifully chased silver salver, holding bread, and milk, and fruit on silver dishes and in Venetian glass of the most delicate sort.

Fleta looked about her with a faint and almost pleased amusement at the quaint incongruity of these furnishings. They gave her the same sense of homeliness which the unknown voice had given her. After her first glance round she went straight to the fire, and began to eat the cakes and drink the milk prepared for her. She sat on the leaf-strewn ground; for there was neither chair nor table nor anything to be called furniture in the whole room, except this wooden stool.

This was the dead chatelaine's own room. Beyond it stretched a suite of rooms opening one into another, which had all been hers during her life, and were quaintly and barbarously furnished; these were shown to visitors. But this room was never entered. It was said that as during her life so after her death, the lamp burned in the room at night, and the fire on the hearth night and day, and none knew who tended them.

It was thoroughly the home of a gypsy, a nomad, a creature of the woods and fields. She had slept on that tigerskin as she might have slept on it beneath the skies. The rich salver and the rich service on it showed out oddly amid these surroundings; but they were characteristic too, belonging as they did to the rich family which she had helped to destroy.

An extraordinary sense of peace and quiet was in this room. It penetrated to Fleta's heart and soothed her more than any living touch could have done.

Presently she rose and laid herself down on the bed of skins and leaves. She did not know that Ivan's mother had lain on this same bed. Doubtless she might have discovered it had she tried it, but she was careless. She was content, and that was enough. In a little while she was fast asleep.

When she awoke the lamp was out, the curtains were drawn back from the great windows of the room, and the sunlight streamed in through them. The fire on the hearth burned steadily, and the moment Fleta looked at it she saw that it had been fed and tended. The stool stood by it, and on it the salver with all manner of provisions for her to breakfast. She found herself very hungry.

for, as a matter of fact, her physical body was busy recovering from the severe hardships of the recent weeks. There was a fount of natural youth within Fleta, apart from that which depended on the exercise of her will. It was a right of her condition, a permanent fee which she had earned.

After she had breakfasted she went to the window and looked out. A wide pale sea bathed in keen spring sunshine. She longed to go out and feel the air that came from it. Immediately she turned and approached the door of the room, although she dreaded a little passing through the place she had entered by. But there was no sign of this place; and she found at last another door hidden by the tapestry of the room. It opened upon a beautiful bath-room, the floor and bath of marble and the walls painted with dancing figures—a number of guests from a ball, or some other gayety, dressed in fantastic costumes, appeared to be careering round the room.

She bathed herself in the refreshing water, and then, wrapping herself again in her large cloak, went through the farther door. This admitted her to a large sitting-room with a magnificent view of the sea. It was very strangely and beautifully furnished, but it did not interest her; and it had the peculiarly dreary feeling which belongs to an uninhabited place. She walked quickly through it and came on to a landing from which a great oak staircase led both up and down. There were other rooms of the same character farther on; but she did not care to pursue the study of them; she longed to be out in the open and feel the breath of the sea. She went down the wide stairway quickly; but suddenly she was brought to a standstill by meeting with a great iron door which was closed, and which absolutely shut the way. Below it, in the steps, were gun holes; and Fleta shivered a little as she stood here, wondering what ugly tragedy in the past this barricade referred to. She never dreamed of its really being closed on her, and tried it again and again. But closed it was, and very safely locked.

She returned and went on through the other rooms. There was no way out from them. She went up the staircase to the rooms above. These were a similar suite, also without any other exit. Then in some wonder she returned to the room she had slept in and began to search for the door by which she had entered. She could not discover it. Evidently it was a secret door, and search was useless. Throwing aside her cloak, she went and sat down by the fire and began to think earnestly over her position.

It was very clear that she was a prisoner. Her mind turned to Ivan. It was he who had ushered her into that place of darkness. Doubtless, then, he had also sent her her mysterious deliverer.

For a little while this thought brought her comfort. But a moment later she saw her folly. Had she not forfeited Ivan's guardianship by her very longing for it?

She was facing the great problem which man still finds before him, even after innumerable incarnations and ceaseless efforts.

Was it indeed impossible for her to sever her link with humanity? Must she always cling to her master and look to his personal self for protection and strength?

It seemed as if for the first time she was able to ask herself this dispassionately. She had freed herself from every other link, from all else that held her back. And now she stood confronted by the rebellion of her own nature.

She sat by the hearth and fell into deep, active thought, in which it seemed as though she held a very serious conversation with herself.

She, the supreme, the powerful, the priestess and heroine in many lives, who in past incarnations had been the accomplished magician and intelligent pupil of the divine teachers, she was brought close now, after ages of development, to the kernel of difficulty in her own heart.

It is the same in every one who is capable of love, of sympathy, of any tenderness or deep emotion; this kernel exists within. In the selfish man it is given a powerful vitality, and grows so large that it absorbs his whole being. In the man with divine possibilities it grows hourly less and less as he develops, till at last he comes to the terrible moment which Fleta was now suffering. He finds then that there is some one being—perhaps a dependent creature, an invalid, or a little child, who affords him a purpose for which to live.

Fleta knew herself to be on the great white sea of impersonal life. It was as though she floated on this vast water and saw no horizon nor desired to see any, nor yet to find any resting-place. But there was one tiny fertile island, or one little peopled boat, to which her eyes wandered always. She did not wish to go to it, to reach it, to touch it—only she could not conceive enduring the blank which would be left, if that one speck vanished from the universe and was not. This that she gazed on and that her sight clung to, was Ivan, his life, his purpose, his knowledge. She realized now that it was the consciousness that this point was there for her thought to rest on, which had carried her through the ordeal of blankness to which she had been exposed. Therefore, she knew she had not succeeded; she had failed, and the deliverer who had come to her had only come to save her body from exhaustion and illness. That gentle voice had not brought to her the reward of success; only the pity given to the unsuccessful.

Realizing this, Fleta set herself to deal with the problem *by thought.*

This is the hardest way to deal with it. But Fleta was

courageous, and having failed in the easier effort, was determined to be successful in this heavier one.

The sun was high in the heavens, and the sea was like shining silver. But Fleta had forgotten sun and sea and the sweet air she had but just now been longing for. The sun fell to the edge of the waters, and still she sat motionless. Darkness came and found her too absorbed in thought to be aware of any change. The fire on the hearth burned out, the lamp remained unlit.

As the time passed on, the suffering within her grew more intense, more bitter, more biting. She, the powerful, began to realize her powerlessness.

This spot within her was ineradicable. As in the past night she had been physically conscious, through all her phantasies, of that door against which she leaned, and which formed a link between her and the physical world; so now her deep veneration for Ivan's personal character remained as an immovable bond between her and humanity, however she might otherwise raise her whole consciousness.

It appeared plain to her at last that if she succeeded in destroying this she would destroy her own life with it.

As she recognized this, and acknowledged the uselessness of her effort, the soft touch came on her again, and the gentle voice fell on her ears:

"My child, be warned. Long not too ardently for success, or you will overbalance yourself on the high place you have reached, and find yourself in the bottomless abyss, a magician and no more, one of the evil ones of the earth. There is yet a third way open to you. Will you serve Ivan like a slave, obeying him as you would obey some one to whom you had sold your very soul, surrendering all judgment to him?"

"No!" cried Fleta, throwing back her head. Her eyes

opened on the black darkness of the room. Whom had she spoken to? Her strength was gone, and with this cry of defiance and pride, exhaustion overpowered her and she fell back unconscious.

CHAPTER XXXII.

THE whole nobility of her nature had risen up to resist that fierce and awful temptation placed before her in the moment of her greatest weakness. To be his slave! She knew it now, as she had never known it before; she knew that she loved him. She, who had interpreted the highest mysteries to Otto and to Hilary! She, who had burned her soul on the altar! Yes, it was so. Purified utterly, deprived of every gross quality—yet it remained, it was love.

What a temptation was this, so suddenly offered her, when she had almost maddened herself by her despairing efforts! What a revulsion of feeling rushed over her! It was unendurable. She had the courage and the power to refuse it before she succumbed to the emotion it produced.

When she awoke again it was to realize all this in a flash. And as she awoke she suffered a sensation never yet known to her while she had been Fleta, the strong. It was the sharp sting of a tortured heart.

Oh, that moment of waking! How dreadful it is.

But Fleta had gathered some strength from her sleep. She had no idea how long it had lasted.

She awoke to such a turmoil of feeling as she had not experienced in the whole of her strange life. Hitherto, she had been able to hold herself above emotion; conscious of it, yet apart from it. But now it seemed as though she were paying a long debt all at once.

"I am a woman still, after all," she said wearily to herself. Then she sat up and looked round her.

While she slept, the room had been made like a home again. The light burned softly, the fire was lit, and the silver tray stood ready for her. A sense of fierce exhaustion took possession of her at the sight of it. She sprang up and ate some food, but while she ate and drank she moved restlessly about. This was not the quiet, powerful Fleta who had conquered and won in so many strange battles. But in those former battles she had fought against the passions of others; now she was fighting herself.

She set down the cup of milk, and clasping her hands behind her began to pace to and fro, to and fro, all the length of the great room, from end to end. Her trailing dress swept the withered leaves hither and thither, till a long bare pathway was made where she moved.

As she was turning back from the curtained window she saw the door open, and Ivan entered the room. He stood still and regarded her very earnestly.

"The tiger within you is strong," he said. "I need not tempt it. Know this, that I think it needless to practise such tests on you as you yourself have had power to use with Hilary Estanol, else I would have sent my shadow to mock and tempt you. It is unnecessary. Your imagination is powerful enough to bring before you every temptation from which it would be possible for you to suffer. Why then should I tease you with images?"

Fleta made no answer, though he paused. She stood silently gazing before her, as though something was visible to her which held all her attention.

"Do you see your own image?" he said, with a faint smile, noticing this look in her face. "Yes, it has accompanied me always since you entered this place. Be careful; you are creating a creature with which you will have to wrestle. Do not let it grow too strong, or there will come a day when you must test your strength against it— and perhaps you may succumb in the battle. Are you pleased with it? Do you like it? It does but reflect your thoughts. You have refused to listen to those thoughts, but they were strong enough to create this image of a passionate woman which follows and annoys me wheresoever I go. Come, be strong, and banish it as you banished Adine."

Fleta drew herself up, and seemed to rise far above her usual height, and raised her hands with a commanding gesture. A moment later she fell back a step, she seemed to dwarf suddenly, to stoop as if old age had fallen upon her.

"It is well," he said, "you have destroyed that creature. Now it is easier for you to work on. Rouse yourself, listen to me. Do you know who has waited on you here, and guarded you?"

"No," she answered dully.

"You have been haunted—visited by a gentle shape of airy elements, once my mother's servant—nothing else. It knew you must have a friend, and so it came to you in this shape. More than that—it has kept this place for you and for your work here."

"Was it foreseen then?" inquired Fleta.

"Certainly, this spot is full of the elements you want, and they have been preserved for you. But the service is over. The poor ghost, as ignorant people supposed it to be, has dwelled in this abnormal shape long enough for your use. Wake yourself, rouse yourself, for you have to be sole guardian of your own fate henceforward. Otherwise you must surrender this effort."

"I shall not surrender it," replied Fleta. "I am ready to go on, at any cost."

"Be it so," he said. "Then I have a history to tell you. Listen."

He went to the hearth and stood by it, leaning against the mantel-shelf. Fleta remained standing, as she had

stood since his entrance, but now instead of looking vaguely
before her she fixed her gaze on him.

"My ancestors came to this country with an army of
conquerors, but they came to save the land and implant a
growth upon it which should redeem it in its unhappy
future. The conflicting forces on this island are terrific;
it is eaten up by a giant growth of materialism springing
from the blackness of its psychic nature. Listen, Fleta;
you must remember these things. There is a wind that
comes across England, bringing with it a whole mass of
invisible beings which settle on it and spread over it and
darken the psychic and moral atmosphere. It is they who
make it so great although it is so small; it is they who
bring it power and wealth. But they obscure the sky
above. They are like the thoughts of men, which, when
centred on matters of one form of life too steadily, make
a mental veil which conceals from them the conception of
larger and wider forms of life. In fact, these beings are
little else than such thoughts individualized and grown
powerful. There is a great belt of the globe in which they
live most powerfully, being led always by the races of men
who dwell in that belt and who continue through century
after century, and æon after æon, in living within the
horizon of materialism. But there is another power, a
counteracting one, also on this island. Through all history and before it there has been a profound life dwelling
side by side with this dark one, and the knowledge of the
obscure and great facts of existence have found a narrow
but permanent home here. There are points in England
which, when an occultist looks at the country, shine out
like flames. They are the ancient and hereditary centres
of this inner life. London, Birmingham, Manchester,
show on the maps, and stand out in most men's minds;
and the railways lead to these places. But there is a shining track right across and through the island visible to a

seer; and the points on this track have always the astral flame alight. This castle is one of them. This room has been preserved absolutely, darkness never having been allowed to reign in it, until last night, when you, in your struggle with yourself, permitted it to enter. Here is a perfected atmosphere, but it is quiescent. I have come to this country to fulfil one of the duties of my life. I have to wake this atmosphere, to make it again a living thing. When it has been done here it has to be done at other points on the track. This must be done now, or the track would grow faint and the power would pale, and in the next generation it would be harder to find. This task I want your aid in."

Fleta made no answer. It did not appear to her that any answer was possible or necessary.

She had experienced a dull and bitter shock while he was speaking. She had recognized at once that it was part of her training, and although she scarcely understood its character immediately, she accepted it without complaint, even in her heart.

But now in the silence that followed, and which Ivan did not break for some time, the knowledge came to her of what this pain was which hurt her so keenly.

She, who had lived so long for others, who had sacrificed herself so utterly for their salvation, was hungry for some help for herself, some personal guidance, some stray word of help or encouragement. Instead, she was given a more impersonal task than any she had yet undertaken. A bitter sense of the uselessness and hopelessness of life overcame her. Of what use was aid given to the crowd of men if, after all, the persons who made up that crowd were indeed to have no greater sum of happiness? This question took shape in her mind, and at last seemed to fill it. She was standing moodily, her eyes now fixed on the ground. Suddenly some impulse made her look up, and she saw close beside her a creature, neither man nor woman, yet human in shape, with fierce eyes burning with passion, which were fixed on her and appeared to express by their gaze the thought in her mind. A moment, and the shape was gone—a dim cloud which had been in the room was gone also; and Ivan was standing quietly before her, regarding her very seriously.

"That is one of the beings from whom I desire to deliver this race of men," he said.

So saying he turned and left the room.

Wearied out, and very sad, Fleta lay down on the rugs which made her couch, and closing her eyes, tried to rest. But immediately this creature which she had seen returned to her, and appeared more vivid and real than before.

But its shape was altered; or rather it changed by degrees before her eyes. It was like a horrible nightmare to watch the change, for Fleta had enough knowledge to be perfectly aware that she herself, by her suppressed thought and emotion, was actually forming this thing into a human shape. It was Ivan who stood before her after a few seconds; Ivan, with the sternness gone from his face, and a gentle light upon it instead.

He approached her, and Fleta watched him with a fascination which seemed to hold her like fetters of iron.

"Because you work for humanity there is no reason to sacrifice your own happiness," he said, in a softer voice than she had ever heard from his lips. "I shall claim your absolute devotion to the work, it is true; but, remember, you will be associated with me through it all. We shall be together. The very nature of the work will bring us together. Will not that give you a little pleasure? We need not be apart any more, Fleta, now that you are with me in my work. Be it so; the order and law of life have decreed this. We have not looked for the pleasure for ourselves. It has come to us. Why not take it without question, as the flowers take the sunshine?"

He drew a step nearer to her, and this one step seemed to break the spell that held Fleta; it was more than she could endure. With a wild shriek she sprang to her feet.

"Go, devil!" she cried out. "I am stronger than you, subtle though you are!"

CHAPTER XXXIII.

HOW dark—how dull, and quiet, and still! Fleta woke to this consciousness and to nothing more. All life, and fire, and hope, seemed to have left the world. And why? That was what she asked herself the moment she awoke. But before she could attempt to answer the question she wondered from what she had awakened. It had not been sleep. What sort of unconsciousness had it been?

A moment later and a full knowledge of it all came to her.

She was like a person who has seen death suddenly, and been deprived by death of the one beloved creature in all the world. Yes, that was the meaning of this unutterable pain.

She looked back and saw herself—how long ago she could not tell—banishing from her the being she had so dearly loved; banishing him so utterly in that form, that he was, in fact, dead.

She desired him as her master, not as a lover, not even as a friend.

She had talked and thought of this act of renunciation before now many a time; but, as happens always with any great event in life, she had had no conception of the reality and agony of the thing until it was upon her. It was like tearing out her heart-strings. And the pain went on, or rather grew in intensity.

Through ages she had suffered alone and stood alone and acted alone. But she had never before faced that last and final and most awful isolation of the occultist; she had never been without love for any human being. Her heart had always clung to some one, perhaps often to someone weaker than herself. But now there was nothing for its tendrils to cling to. She had destroyed the last image left her, the last idol which had not already been destroyed by the development and circumstances of life. She had struck a death blow to the power of her imagination in connection with Ivan, and now that it was done she knew, looking back, how for years of her life that figure, created by her imagination, had been beside her. Never had she consciously recognized it till now, when her stronger and finer nature had instantly taken the initiative and killed it out; but she had been consoled and comforted, and indeed supported by it through her severest struggles in the past.

Well, it was gone; and she was utterly alone even in thought.

The pain which was caused by this state arose from the sense of dulness, darkness, void. With an effort she thought of Ivan; and the thought was weariness. His image no longer brought her enthusiasm, faith, longing, as it used to do.

What then was there to live for? Nothing. That was what she said to herself as she lay listlessly on her strange couch of withered leaves and furs and looked wearily at the strange bare room. Her eyes closed from mere want of purpose. But they had hardly shut before they were opened wide again, and she was staring before her with a gaze of horror. Slowly she raised herself up and sat there like one petrified. No horrid sight, no ordeal, had ever stricken her soul like this! Was it possible to go on living, without interest, without affection, objectless, heartless? No! For no ghost or devil could vie with this unutterable void within for horror,

She crouched—yes, Fleta, the powerful, the confident—she crouched before this vision of her own emptiness.

It was impossible to go on living in this manner. Yet to Fleta there was no alternative as there is to ordinary men and women. Suicide offered no opportunity to her. She knew that she had advanced too far to find oblivion anywhere. Death would bring no respite; she would carry memory with her, and wake to it afresh, as people wake to the pain of some new grief after sleep. She saw herself going on through æons of existence, blank, hopeless, heartless, for what was there to fill her horizon? What was there to hope for? Who was there to love? None! Nothing! These were all her answers. And she needed none but herself to answer them; she questioned her own soul and found her replies within it. She desired no speech of any one, not even of Ivan, for she could not imagine that any comfort could come to her from it. Poor Fleta! she tasted now the complete bitterness of failure and the despair it brings.

And comfort was what she wanted! Yes, her whole being was hungry for it. But there was none for her. She found herself back, far back, ranged beside the stoic philosopher. What an arid, intolerable waste was life thus viewed!

The moments were so weary and so full of pain that it appeared as if each were an eternity in itself. She rose at last, goaded by disgust of her endurance, and began to pace the room to and fro, to and fro, in a kind of madness. How long was it since she had suffered like this? Not since that flowery long ago, that age of bloom and pain beneath the wild apricot trees. She was as blind, as full of longing, of a wild and useless desire for action now as then. Was it then wasted, all this long and terrible novitiate of hers? Wasted? As the thought came to her, she *stood*, passion-struck, her hands clasped rigidly together.

If so, then indeed there was no choice. Madness must be king, and hell the kingdom.

We all know, as the span of human life wears itself out, the agony of anxiety and the despair of loss, which personal love brings with it. To us all, sooner or later, must come the overpowering pain, the one consummate moment of distress, when a personal love is forever torn away from the soul. Fleta was not ignorant—she was blind, for the wall she faced had no way through it, no window in it. But she was not ignorant. She knew the ordeal she was enduring, she knew its nature. This knowledge seemed to add the keenest sting, the final torture. For she knew that if she could not endure she must sink back into the blank darkness of ordinary human life. She was at the door of initiation; she knew it—and none may linger there —he must enter or turn back.

And it seemed to her—to Fleta the strong—that entrance was impossible. She could not endure this pain—she had not the strength.

She turned back in her thoughts to Hilary Estanol— could she have lived for him, even in this one life? Impossible! She would have wearied of the bondage of love in an hour. She could not even have given him any happiness, so immeasurable was the distance between them. What use was it to look back, knowing this? Otto—no! still less. And then her mind swung back to the thought of Ivan; and Etrenella's words flashed into her memory:

"You must go to the door of hell to find him."

Well, she was there now! But what folly had Etrenella spoken! It was absurd to suppose she had any power to save Ivan—it was absurd to suppose that he could love her even for an instant—except as his pupil. And yet what was that figure which had sickened her so utterly by its temptings? Was not that the figure of Ivan? No—she answered herself—it was a phantom, born of her own passion. In that sense, then, all Etrenellá said might be true—she prophesied this hideous moment. And this hell, now yawning before Fleta, might be as much of a phantom as Ivan's image!

"Bid it go," said a gentle voice, "and it will vanish as Ivan's image vanished."

Fleta recognized the voice of the tender presence which had twice come to her before in her bitterest moments. Without moving or looking round she replied:

"But how am I to save my master's soul? Surely that must have been a lie?"

"Draw on your cloak and follow where I lead," was the answer.

Fleta obeyed. Her cloak lay where she had thrown it when she had come back to this room disgusted at finding herself a prisoner. She put it on and turned to follow her guide, but no one was visible; and for a moment she stood confused and bewildered. A moment later and she had recalled her knowledge. She knew that she must simply obey her instinct.

She left the room and went through the next and out on to the stairway. The great gate stood open; she passed down and found herself in the great hall of the castle. The door stood ajar, and she went out into the air.

Now came a certain perplexity again—which way was she to turn? But she had will enough to control her vague desire for guidance, and to compel herself to follow her own spiritual instinct. It was late in the evening, and the stars shone; she looked at them and at the dark sea—what desolation there is in the beauty of nature only those know who have really suffered.

She hurried away over the grass, determined to let her feet find their own way and use her will to silence her mind. This was how she had found Ivan in this, to her, unknown country. She had to find him again in the same manner; it seemed a little more difficult to compel herself to the task now, because her soul was so full of fierce rebellion.

In a few moments she was at the door of Ivan's cottage. She went in without hesitation, for the door stood open. She paused on the threshold of a lighted room, looking in wonder at the scene before her. It seemed to be full of people, so real did the figures on the tapestry appear. Ivan sat at a large table which had nothing on it but a great map outspread. Fleta's occult knowledge, not utterly lost to her, awakened fully in the rapt atmosphere she found herself in. Ivan sat a long while studying the map, and then looked round at the figures on the wall. These changed in appearance sometimes, and Fleta knew at once that they were to him what the lay figure in her laboratory had been to her. But she had never had the power to control more than this one, though she could impose upon it a series of personalities, while here she saw Ivan influencing a great number of persons by the same magical process; and after a few moments' observation her heart began to beat high, for she saw with what great stakes he was playing. The figures had taken on the characters of kings, princes, emperors, diplomats, politicians. The fate of Europe, and, later on, the fate of the whole civilized surface of the globe, appeared to lie in this man's hand, or rather in his thoughts. Fleta, looking from the walls to the map, saw that the central point in the whole drama which was being enacted was that monastery in her father's forests. This was protected, made powerful, kept hidden; and in order that this might be so, war devastated whole countries. The sight, made so plainly visible to her, filled her soul with compassion, and she uttered a cry of dismay. Ivan turned and looked at her.

"Oh, have pity!" she said. "What does the fate of our

Order matter compared to that of these poor wretches, these masses of humanity who have no life but in humanity?"

There came on Ivan's face a faint smile of extraordinary sweetness.

"My child," he said, "understand that the Order exists upon earth and in human form simply for the benefit of these masses of humanity, to save them from a darkness and helplessness worse than hell. It is right, then, that they should give their lives to preserve it in existence from one generation to another. Is it not so?"

"Yes," she answered reluctantly, "but it is terrible to see these sufferings! these dead men, these broken hearts, these desolate homes! O master, have pity!"

"Is your heart empty now?" said Ivan.

"No!" she cried out, absorbed by her thought. "It cannot be till I have helped these people. O master, let me help them! Show me the way."

"Follow in my path," answered Ivan. "It is the only one. Help their souls, not their bodies. Put aside the illusion now before you, the imagination which makes me seem to you heartless, cruel, because my sight and knowledge reach farther than yours, and calculate for greater distances of time. Put this illusion aside as you have put the others—for your hell is banished already from you by the great love for man which has burst out in your heart—put this one aside also, and try to stand beside me. Work for the spirit of humanity, not for the pleasure of its individual members, and you will find yourself a part of it, and, therefore, never alone or loveless again. Is it not so?"

"Yes," she said slowly. As she spoke she became aware that there were others besides herself and Ivan in the room. Looking round at them she started and trembled; for here were the pale, passionless faces of the

Brothers of the White Star. How beautiful they were! how tender!

"To-morrow night," said Ivan, "you shall enter the Hall of Learning. You have earned the right and obtained the power. Go back now to your resting-place and reflect. Go in peace."

Fleta turned and left the room immediately, and slowly retraced her steps.

How near the stars seemed now! How soft the sea!

CHAPTER XXXIV.

THAT was a night of peace for Fleta, such as she had not had for a long time. She lay down on the tiger-skin in the corner of the haunted room—a place no man in the county would have entered alone after dark, even for a king's ransom—and slept like a tired child.

When she awoke it was dawn, and a dim, soft light came into the room through the wide windows. A profound sense of tenderness, of companionship, filled her heart. What a wonderful and beautiful thing was life when full of love like this. She was amazed at her own content, and set herself to understand the cause of it. Immediately she saw innumerable human faces, just touched faintly by the light of the dawn and stirring slowly toward the life of the day. Processions of men and women passed through her consciousness—working people, beggars, toilers of all sorts; kings, queens, and counsellors, passed by also, but more faintly, for they had not the same power of number, of duplication and reduplication, of types repeated and reproduced with endless and scarcely perceptible variation. It was this, the likeness, the similarity among the ant-like multitudes, that attracted and fascinated her, and warmed her heart with a new and hitherto unknown feeling. Before her inner vision passed all sorts of pictures—homes with sleeping children, seamstresses rising early with faded eyes to begin another day, as like the last as each of the women was like the one next her! Men roused from deep sleep at the first sign of daylight to go out in gangs and *engage* on hard work, fit only for beasts; yet, perfectly natural and satisfying to their unaroused natures. Men working underground in mines, among the gnomes and salamanders, knowing as little of the gladness of sunshine as of the inspiration of the spirit. The unnumbered great race of men engaged in offices all over the world, busy with produce and money, clerks, ambitionless, alike, shrewd and yet without knowledge, their souls asleep. Women living in the streets of the cities, and in the countless houses that trade in vice, women even more alike than the men of the cities, women that are of only three or four types, and numbering millions under each of these types, as similar as the peas in one pod are to each other. Men and women with money, with wealth, not working, but looking always for pleasure and amusement—what thousands of these, too, and how little difference among them, and how little and narrow the field in which they looked for pleasure! Oh, this great surging sea of human life, what a grand, giant force would it be if once awakened, if once intelligent, impersonal, united, aware of its own spiritual dignity and meaning. "I see it! I see it!" cried out Fleta. "I see your power, your possibilities, you, the human race that I am such a small fragment of. Oh let me speak to you, rouse you, help you, work for you!"

She sprang to her feet, full of a new energy. The dawn had come fully now, the day had begun, and her work must begin too. She did not know yet what her work was to be; but, nevertheless, she knew that she must be ready for it. All weariness had fallen from her, had left her forever, as it seemed. She went into the next room and stepped into the great bath which stood there, filling it full of keenly cold water. With its freshness came a lightness as though her youth had come back. She laughed to herself at the fancy. She could never lose her youth again, for the human race is young always as well as old! This was the thought that made her glad. For, indeed, what could it any longer concern her whether she had youth or age, beauty or ugliness, seeing that all these alike are parts of human life, forces in human nature. And with this indifference—or perhaps it would be better to say, with this wider possibility of content—came a new look on her face—a look neither of youth nor beauty, age nor illness—something indefinable, but more permanent than any of these.

"It is well," she said to herself. "I need not be a magician any longer, or take the trouble to work miracles on myself or on others. For if I am weak, what does it matter? I shall be in the great stream of life still, and weakness can be ennobled as well as strength."

As she moved to leave the room she came unexpectedly opposite to a great mirror. She stood for some moments, her brows knitted in perplexity. She scarcely recognized herself at first, her face was so changed. Its brilliance had gone, and in the place of it was an expression of quiet like that on the Egyptian statues. Her eyes wandered down, after a long, intense look at herself, to the dress she wore. And now for the first time did she realize how great an ordeal she had passed through, how far within herself she had retreated in these last hours. For she could not recollect for whom she wore this black dress. Hazy memories of different lives passed before her, when she had lost lover, husband, child, and worn this hateful color. Who was it now? What grief was that which had unseated her reason and destroyed her memory? As she looked and wondered, at last her eyes fell on her helpless and disfigured arm. The memory of the battle in which that injury was received came suddenly back to her.

"I am Fleta!" she exclaimed. "I remember myself now, and the dark tragedies through which I have lived."

CHAPTER XXXV.

SHE went out of the castle and walked over the lawn to the Lady's Walk, where she had met Ivan on her arrival. It was quite deserted now; but the sun made it pleasant, and she walked to and fro the whole length of it, with slow deliberate steps, thinking.

"Of what use is it to think?" she cried out suddenly, stopping in her walk. "Have I ever learned or done anything by thought? No—I must look to some higher place for guidance."

She left the Walk and went down a long flight of steps cut in the cliff, which took her to the edge of the sea.

Oh, the magical charm of that morning, with its freshness and sweetness and clear light! Like a child's, Fleta's heart beat higher with the excitement of the morning sea. She walked at the edge of the waves, playing with their movements, and forgot all anxiety, all concern for herself or others, in the pleasure of the moment. Presently, looking up, she saw that some one was walking on the cliff. It was a black, gaunt figure, looking strangely out of place in the sunshine. In another moment she recognized Amyot, wearing his monk's dress. It was very natural he should be here, since Ivan was.

"My poor servant," she said to herself. "I had forgotten him."

She went to the steps in the cliff and climbed them. When she reached the top, she looked down the sunlit path and could not at first see Amyot, but soon she found that he had seated himself on the bench that faced the sea.

She went quickly and sat down beside him; but Amyot took no notice of her.

"Speak to me, Amyot," she said gently.

He raised his head and turned his haggard face and sunken eyes toward her.

"What shall I say?" he replied.

"Have you no word of greeting?"

"None. I know you no longer, you have passed in, while I am still outside."

"I have not yet passed in," replied Fleta. "I have to demand entrance. I was told that I had to bring two souls with me, one in either hand. I have learned that this cannot be, that such a delusion was only a trick by which chains might be bound on me and on others. Yet, must I indeed go in utterly alone? You should take your place at my right hand, a child of the Brotherhood, saved by your own knowledge, your own sense of truth."

"No," answered Amyot, "it cannot be. I am weary. I do not want to go in. I have served the Brotherhood well, but I cannot give them that last thing, the kernel of my soul, the self that is me. No, I cannot, Fleta; you are a child in the world's ways beside me. Yet I have been your servant and am no more than that now. I am too strong for success in this effort."

"Too strong! Impossible!" said Fleta.

"And yet true," answered Amyot, gloomily. "I am so knit up with this world, so strongly compounded of its elements, that I cannot be separated from it without an unendurable agony worse than any sort of death. I have done all that man could do. When I found that by no other aid could I force myself to follow the necessary laws of life, nor acquire the necessary concentration, I offered myself for the service of religion. I have served truly. I, that am lost, have saved souls without number, I have done the work of the Brotherhood in the world. I, that have done that am now devoured by the world. Yes, it is useless. This life in which I have endeavored expiation, in which I have worn this dress, has been blameless, has brought to me only suffering. But the darkness of the past is on me still. I cannot escape from it. Do you know why you are to enter to-night?"

"No," answered Fleta, a little surprised by the abrupt question.

"It is the dawn of the year; the full moon of that dawn. It is the seventh year of seven years, the twenty-seventh of twenty-seven years. Do you know how old you are?"

Fleta rose suddenly and walked away down the path without answering him.

And there, straight before her, stood Ivan. He immediately began to speak to her. There was something in his face which overawed and silenced her, something so strong and powerful that she stood trembling to await the exercise of this force which she recognized in him.

"Amyot speaks well," said Ivan; "but it is not for you to listen to him. It is not you who can help him to enter among the initiates. You! How have you carried out your mission? After ages of degradation, in which you have sold your soul for magical powers, you are no stronger to help others than when first you came upon this earth, a savage and untaught creature. You are strong, Fleta; but, like Amyot, you are too strong. But he is a chosen one, and will remain guarded and cared for, because he desires no power for his own use, only power with which to help others. And you, who have had touch of the lofty order of the White Star, that brotherhood which lives for humanity, you have carried yourself so imperiously that you have not chosen to do good except by doing evil. Is it not so? Have you not, through innumerable lives, valued your power over Hilary Estanol so highly that you could not surrender it? Did you not give yourself beauty

and charm in order that you might read love in his eyes?
Weary as you were of him and of his weakness, did you
not still enchant him in order to feel the pleasure of his
love for you? And that, too, long after it was possible for
you to love any creature, when I had purified your soul
utterly from passion. O Fleta, this hunger for the exercise of power is indeed your destruction. Why did you
not call on the White Brotherhood to save Otto, instead
of endeavoring the task alone? You were driven back
upon your old magical rites that you practised in the dark
days when you and Etrenella worked together. Sorceress!
Witch! Do you think you helped Otto to his salvation?
Do you think that in using such destructive and gross
forms of power you could aid his divine spirit, or help to
free it? Not so. Awake from these delusions. You are
a woman still, and cannot escape from the love of power
and the love of pleasure, those laws which govern the life
of sex. You no longer love; but are you any better because you no longer love like other women? Not so; you
have transferred the emotions of sex on to a higher plane,
and have, therefore, sinned more deeply than if you had
left them on the simple plane of ordinary human nature.
Because you are freed from the ordinary passions which
affect men and women, is it any better to desire to dominate, to charm, to fascinate, to control? You, that have
the divine possibility in you, the vigor and strength necessary for the occultist, is it possible that you are not yet
aware of the mire in which you are still wandering? Rouse
yourself; look at the divine consciousness; fix your attention on that vision of humanity which I have given to you;
think of no person and of no persons, but of all; forget
that you are a woman, with power to charm; forget that
you are a magician with power to control. You know
that sorcery is of the same order as the passion of sex; it
is selfish, it desires to acquire, to intensify all that is per-

sonal. You know this, for you have learned it from me;
you have known it for ages. Yet you have madly let
yourself follow this passion, in its nobler form, and refused
to see that by merely elevating it you did not change its
character. Hilary Estanol, from the cruel wound you in-
flicted on him when you flung him from you, will be able
to learn the lesson you have failed yet to learn. He will
not love again; he will no longer desire to have or to hold.
He is free. He has lived through the experiences of sex;
the blossom has fallen. There is no more delusion for
him, for you killed the possibility of it in his soul by your
heartless acts. It is over. But he has found the fruit.
His soul has dissolved within him; it is soft, utterly tender, capable of all unselfishness. When you least knew it
you gave him his salvation. Now he can no longer suffer
at your hands. The thraldom he fell under ages ago in
that wild apricot orchard, when he first loved you, and
you showed him the fierce power that you possessed—it is
at an end. He has been your slave, tormented and maddened; but now he has escaped. He suffers like one in
physical torture, so great is his despair; but he is opening
his soul to the divine power, and he will when he is born
again to renew his efforts, find himself strong, calm, no
longer passionate, no longer a man; a divine being, im-
partial, indifferent, unselfish, all-loving, ready for my
service. And you? Amyot has told you that this is a
day which is a date in your life. To-day you must learn
the truth, and cast the glamour from your eyes."

Fleta trembled, shuddered, and drew back a step. What
glamour was there left to take from her? Had she anything left to lose? She uttered no word, for Ivan con-
tinued to speak:

"Did I not tell you that to-night you should enter the
Hall of Learning? It is true; but only after you have
fulfilled certain conditions. You will fulfil them, I know;

for had you not contained the power to do this within you, you would long since have lost my aid and the protection of the White Star. At sundown this day, you have your chance; the dial there will show you the moment when you must seize it. When the moment of sundown comes you can enter the hall if you choose, and become a true pupil of the divine teachers. But your spirit must be freed. I shall not help you to enter the hall; for you will never again see me, in the flesh or in the spirit. You must of your own free will give up my help and my guidance. You are a magician, and have the power, if you choose, to make a semblance of me which will supply my place. You must give up all delusions; you must root out your adoration for me from your heart and free me from it. I have to go on into another life, and you must willingly separate yourself from me utterly. You must give up forever your love of power, and swear solemnly within yourself that you will never use the powers you possess for your own ends again. You must do this willingly. Go over in your mind the many delusions to which you have allowed yourself to succumb. Consider this last and subtlest of all, in which you fancied yourself about to become my ally and servant in keeping these astral pathways ready for later humanity. The experience helped you toward the idea of impersonal work; and therefore I put you through it. But though your spirit was pure enough to resist that counterfeit presentment of myself which bade you remember that in doing this work you would be doing this with *me*—though you resisted that, were you strong enough to drain every drop of the delicious poison from out of the chalice of your heart? Was there not the faint, fond feeling there that you would not be utterly alone? That even if you might not adore me yet you might serve me? Root out these delusions utterly, Fleta. You have to forget you are a woman; more, you have to forget you are a person. Was not that dream that you must save two other souls, and take them with you into the hall, only another form of your passion for power? Who was it gave you that order? Was it not your own imperious soul? Did you not hope to pay for your entrance by giving earnest at the doorway of your power over others? O Fleta, be honest with yourself. When I came to you, now, were you not on the threshold of another folly? Had not Amyot's sad words tempted you to believe that in him you might find one of these souls you had to save? Fond madness! Did it not thrill you with a sense of new glory, the fancy that you might carry to the hall one so great as Amyot? Be courageous, and face the fact that you are nothing in yourself, that you are only a fragment tossed on the tide of the great powers that sweep over the world. You are a part of these; yes, in your inner self, you are, and cannot be entirely separated or cast off from them. But you have kept yourself a fragment instead of a part of the whole. Become that, dissolve your being in the infinite love, and it will be to you as death; but the re-awakening will be a new birth such as you have never known. For in it you will not be the strength of one poor human being, poor indeed, magician though you are, but the strength of the ageless consciousness that makes the worlds. Come, Fleta, to that divine estate! The dark power that made you a sorceress will make more keen and vivid, when translated and transmuted, the divine power which will make you divine. Come! But forget yourself, forget your power. Be courageous. Are you ready? Are you willing to surrender me, your master and friend, and let me go free, without any longing or lingering thought, from you? Are you ready to be utterly alone, without human face or voice, either near you in the world, or present in the world of thought within you? Are you ready to put me out of your memory?"

Fleta stood, as she had stood ever since he began speaking, motionless, save for that one shudder of pain; gazing on him as if she were turned to stone. For a moment she remained thus, statue-like, and as if all her senses were paralyzed, and she could neither speak nor move. But suddenly she seemed to regain power over herself; she flung out her hands with an imperative gesture. "I am ready," she said, "and your greater life is ready for you. I see it shining gloriously. From those splendid heights of thought and feeling, from that noble place of self-sacrifice, it would be hard indeed for you to touch one so mistaken, so deeply stained as I am. Your pupil shall not fail, my master, mine no longer. I will forget you. I will detach every thought and memory from you. I am ready. Go!"

He turned and walked away down the path. Fleta watched him till he was out of sight. Then she turned and looked for Amyot; but he, too, was gone. She was alone, before the sea and sky. Then she remembered the sundial and went to look for it. It was a long search, for an old rose-bush had clambered all over it and she had to tear the branches away with her hands. She fell on her knees beside it and there remained through the silent hours of the sunny afternoon.

Alone. At first that one word filled the whole horizon of her thought. She could not escape from it; she could not remove the ghastly consciousness from her vision.

When intense physical pain continues without intermission, the sufferer begins to battle against it; and succeeds at last, when no other remedy is possible, in retreating to another place of consciousness where the pain becomes tolerable, and then to a place where it suddenly transforms itself into pleasure. This is the whole secret of that mystery spoken of by occultists, that pleasure and pain are the same. It is so, for both are sensation, and there *is no* true means of discriminating between the kinds of sensations. What is pleasure to one person is pain to another. Had Fleta been a magician at heart and nothing more, this solitude, this utter loneliness, would have wrapped her round with comfort, as a garment might. It would have given her opportunity for personal thought, for plotting and scheming. But she was not that; she was only a magician, because of her innate power and the blindness of her ignorance. Her heart was tender now, full of love; but she knew not how, with this love in her, to forget her utter loneliness.

Yet it must be forgotten. She succeeded in changing her attitude toward it, in retreating from the agony and making it only sensation, which it was possible to regard as pleasure. At last it became pleasure. But she knew it had to be more than this. It had to be nothing!

It came at last, suddenly, this *un*consciousness. The fact that she was alone—that every thing and every one had fallen away from her, was nothing. And why—because *she* was nothing.

And then a new vigor flashed into her being. Something so strong it was, as though light ran through her veins instead of blood. Something so pure, it blotted out all memory of self. She rose to her feet.

"For all that lives, I live!"

Her voice rang out on the air and startled herself. It seemed unrecognizable, it was so bell-like. She looked down, and her glance fell on the dial. It was sun-down.

For a second, which seemed like a superb eternity, she stood quite still, her mind, her soul, her being, bathed in an unconsciousness which was more vivid than any consciousness. And then she fell forward, her face upon the earth, beside the rose-bush, among the flowers.

EPILOGUE.

TWO months later the agent visited the now-deserted Dower House, and then the castle. He found the door of the haunted room standing open for the first time in his experience. He looked in timidly, and saw nothing but a few autumn leaves, seemingly blown by the wind about the bare floor. Shuddering, he closed the door and went away.

Some wayward impulse prompted him, before leaving the castle grounds, to go down to the Lady's Walk and look at the sea. But he did not look at it, for the moment he entered the Walk he saw a figure lying among the flowers, and his whole attention was given to that. A woman—motionless, richly dressed, and with beautiful hair, which had fallen loose and lay beside her on the earth. What could it mean? Nerving himself he approached and touched her. Instantly he knew she was dead, and with a shudder of dread, turned the face upward. Ah, what a sight! None could tell this had been a human face save by the bones.

Where was Fleta's beauty now? Where was Fleta?

THE END.

NOTE.—The books of the Occult Series are called forth by the increasing demand for enlightenment upon occult themes. Those desiring to associate themselves with students of Theosophy and Occultism, can communicate with the General Secretary of the Theosophical Society in America. Wm. Q. Judge. P. O. Box 2659, New York City.

www.ingramcontent.com/pod-product-compliance
Ingram Content Group UK Ltd.
Pitfield, Milton Keynes, MK11 3LW, UK
UKHW041951230426
12048UKWH00008B/271